S0-CPD-255

Freedom of Speech

DOCUMENTS DECODED

The ABC-CLIO series *Documents Decoded* guides readers on a hunt for new secrets through an expertly curated selection of primary sources. Each book pairs key documents with in-depth analysis, all in an original and visually engaging side-by-side format. But *Documents Decoded* authors do more than just explain each source's context and significance—they give readers a front-row seat to their own investigation and interpretation of each essential document, line by line.

TITLES IN ABC-CLIO'S DOCUMENTS DECODED SERIES

Presidential Campaigns: Documents Decoded
Daniel M. Shea and Brian M. Harward

Women's Rights: Documents Decoded
Aimee D. Shouse

The Death Penalty: Documents Decoded
Joseph A. Melusky and Keith A. Pesto

The Abolitionist Movement: Documents Decoded
Christopher Cameron

The Great Depression and New Deal: Documents Decoded
Mario R. DiNunzio

The Democratic Party: Documents Decoded
Douglas B. Harris and Lonce H. Bailey

The Republican Party: Documents Decoded
Douglas B. Harris and Lonce H. Bailey

1960s Counterculture: Documents Decoded
Jim Willis

Founding Documents of America: Documents Decoded
John R. Vile

Presidential Power: Documents Decoded
Brian M. Harward

The Early Republic: Documents Decoded
John R. Vile

The Jacksonian and Antebellum Eras: Documents Decoded
John R. Vile

Freedom of Speech

DOCUMENTS DECODED

David L. Hudson Jr.

ABC-CLIO™

An Imprint of ABC-CLIO, LLC
Santa Barbara, California • Denver, Colorado

Copyright © 2017 by ABC-CLIO, LLC

All rights reserved. No part of this publication may be reproduced, stored in a retrieval system, or transmitted, in any form or by any means, electronic, mechanical, photocopying, recording, or otherwise, except for the inclusion of brief quotations in a review, without prior permission in writing from the publisher.

Library of Congress Cataloging-in-Publication Data

Names: Hudson, David L., 1969- compiler.
Title: Freedom of speech : documents decoded / [compiled by] David L. Hudson, Jr.
Other titles: Freedom of speech (ABC-CLIO)
Description: Santa Barbara, California : ABC-CLIO, an Imprint of ABC-CLIO, LLC, [2017] | Includes bibliographical references and index.
Identifiers: LCCN 2016051906| ISBN 9781440842504 (acid-free paper) | ISBN 9781440842511 (ebook)
Subjects: LCSH: Freedom of speech—United States—History—Sources.
Classification: LCC KF4770 .F765 2017 | DDC 342.7308/53—dc23
LC record available at https://lccn.loc.gov/2016051906

ISBN: 978-1-4408-4250-4
EISBN: 978-1-4408-4251-1

21 20 19 18 17 1 2 3 4 5

This book is also available as an eBook.

ABC-CLIO
An Imprint of ABC-CLIO, LLC

ABC-CLIO, LLC
130 Cremona Drive, P.O. Box 1911
Santa Barbara, California 93116-1911
www.abc-clio.com

This book is printed on acid-free paper ∞

Manufactured in the United States of America

R0452561250

Contents

Introduction

The first 45 words of the Bill of Rights comprise the First Amendment: "Congress shall make no law respecting an establishment of religion or prohibiting the free exercise thereof; or abridge the freedom of speech, or of the press, or the right of the people peaceably to assemble and to petition the government for a redress of grievances." The First Amendment serves as our blueprint for personal liberty, the freedom that gives "we the people" a chance to voice our opinions, criticize government officials, and take interesting and unorthodox stances.

The First Amendment contains five textually based freedoms: religion, speech, press, assembly, and petition. The amendment also protects the right of people to associate together with each other for expressive purposes. This is called the freedom of association.

James Madison introduced the Bill of Rights, including what became the First Amendment, in a June 8, 1789, speech before the U.S. House of Representatives. Madison told his colleagues that these were the "Great Rights of Mankind" that would ensure public support for the newly ratified Constitution. The ratification of the Constitution had been a difficult battle in certain states, and many politicians had promised that if the people supported the Constitution, the politicians would ensure that a Bill of Rights would be added to the body of the Constitution.

In this Documents Decoded volume, we examine the freedom of speech. An initial question in some situations is, "What is speech?" Obviously, verbal and printed communications are speech. But there are many other forms of symbolic speech and expressive conduct that deserve free-speech protection. For example, people often display flags, wear T-shirts with symbols, and engage in various forms of expressive conduct. In *United States v. O'Brien* (1968), the Supreme Court developed a test for when speech and non-speech elements are combined together.

As readers will see when examining *Texas v. Johnson* (1989), the Court references a two-part test: (1) Was there intent to convey a particularized message? (2) Is it a message that would be reasonably understood?

Categorization

The First Amendment contains absolutist language: "Congress shall make no law . . . abridging the freedom of speech." However, the Court declared in *Chaplinsky v. New Hampshire* (1942) that not all speech is protected—that there are certain limited unprotected categories of speech. These include obscenity, true threats, defamation, and fighting words. This book examines the seminal decisions on those unprotected categories in *Miller v. California* (1973), *Watts v. United States* (1969), *New York Times Co. v. Sullivan* (1964), and *Chaplinsky*.

The history of free speech shows that these unprotected categories have narrowed over time. For example, obscenity prosecutions used to occur for racy literature, like D. H. Lawrence novels. Now obscenity prosecutions are reserved for the most violent and vile hardcore pornography. "Fighting words" used to mean any profane word uttered at a government official. Now it takes much more, often threatening behavior or conduct, to cross the line into fighting words.

In recent years, government officials have tried to expand the number of unprotected categories for violent video games, images of animal cruelty, and protests at funerals. In several decisions, including *Brown v. Entertainment Merchants Association* (2011) and *Snyder v. Phelps* (2011), the Court has resisted the effort to create new unprotected categories in the First Amendment.

Content

Content matters in First Amendment law. The chief methodological tool used by the Court in areas of protected speech is the content discrimination principle. There are content-based laws and content-neutral laws. A content-based law is one that discriminates against speech based on content. A content-neutral law is one that applies across the board to all speech regardless of content.

Justice Thurgood Marshall expressed the concept memorably in *Police Department of Chicago v. Mosley* (1972): "But, above all else, the First Amendment means that government has no power to restrict expression because of its message, its ideas, its subject matter, or its content."

Readers will see in the recent decision of *Reed v. Town of Gilbert* (2015) that the U.S. Supreme Court considers the content discrimination principle paramount when examining the First Amendment.

Context

Context also matters in First Amendment cases. A contextual aspect of this jurisprudence revolves around the status of the speaker. In other words, when the speaker is a public school student, a public employee, a member of the military, or an inmate, his or her rights are limited. This means that the rights of a public school student, public employee, military member, or inmate are fewer than those of an adult outside of those specialized contexts.

That doesn't mean that the First Amendment does not protect public school students. The U.S. Supreme Court famously ruled in *West Virginia Board of Education v. Barnette* (1943) that students could not be compelled to salute the flag and recite the Pledge of Allegiance. Many years later, the Court ruled in *Tinker v. Des Moines Independent Community School District* (1969) that several public school students had the right to wear black armbands to protest the Vietnam War. The Court proclaimed, "It can hardly be argued that either students or teachers shed their constitutional rights to freedom of speech or expression at the schoolhouse gate."

Public employees used to have no free-speech rights. Justice Oliver Wendell Holmes Jr., when he sat on the Supreme Judicial Court of Massachusetts, famously proclaimed that a police officer "may have a constitutional right to talk politics, but he doesn't have a constitutional right to be a policeman." This rule meant that public employees relinquished their free-speech rights upon accepting public employment.

The Court changed that equation in *Pickering v. Board of Education* (1968) by proclaiming that a public school teacher had a free-speech right to write a letter to the editor complaining about how the school board allocated funds. The school board fired the teacher, claiming that the letter was disruptive. The Supreme Court ruled for the teacher and established a test: "The problem in any case is to arrive at a balance between the interests of the teacher, as a citizen, in commenting upon matters of public concern and the interest of the State, as an employer, in promoting the efficiency of the public services it performs through its employees."

However, readers will see that the U.S. Supreme Court has curtailed the free-speech rights of public employees in *Garcetti v. Ceballos* (2006) by creating a new categorical rule. Under this new rule, public employees do not have free-speech rights when they engage in official job-duty speech. This decision is very controversial, because it means that many employees who blow the whistle on government corruption have no First Amendment claim.

Principles

The First Amendment often gets judged by some of those persons it protects. The amendment has protected flag burners, political dissidents, tobacco merchants, and even hatemongers. It protects offensive, obnoxious, and even repugnant speech in some circumstances. Justice William J. Brennan expressed it well in *Texas v. Johnson* (1989): "If there is a bedrock principle underlying the First Amendment, it is that the government may not prohibit the expression of an idea simply because it finds the idea offensive or disagreeable."

Chief Justice John G. Roberts, Jr., the 17th chief justice in U.S. history, perhaps expressed it better than anyone when writing an opinion, *Snyder v. Phelps* (2011), defending the free-speech rights of those who protested at the funeral of a slain Marine. Chief Justice Roberts wrote,

> Speech is powerful. It can stir people to action, move them to tears of both joy and sorrow, and—as it did here—inflict great pain. On the facts before us, we cannot react to that pain by punishing the speaker. As a Nation we have chosen a different course—to protect even hurtful speech on public issues to ensure that we do not stifle public debate.

This Documents Decoded volume on free speech aims to strengthen public debate and provide a greater awareness and appreciation of First Amendment controversies and cases.

Freedom of Speech

Sedition Act

July 14, 1798

INTRODUCTION

On December 15, 1791, Congress ratified the U.S. Bill of Rights, including the First Amendment. This First Amendment provided that "Congress shall make no law . . . abridging the freedom of speech." Only seven years later, many of those same members of Congress approved of a law that imposed severe abridgment on free speech.

That law was the Sedition Act of 1798. It prohibited individuals from making "false, scandalous, or malicious" statements about the president and the government of the United States. The Federalist Party controlled the presidency and the Congress. They wanted to maintain their control and power over their opponents, the Democratic-Republicans.

At this time, there were hostilities between England and France, the two chief world powers. The Federalists tended to support England, and the Democratic-Republicans favored France. The United States feared a conflict with France. The Federalists also wanted to suppress those Democratic-Republicans who aroused public opposition to the Federalist Party and John Adams.

The result was prosecutions under the Sedition Act of 1798 or the common-law crime of sedition. Many of these early prosecutions were brought against Democratic-Republican newspaper editors, like Benjamin Bache (the grandson of Benjamin Franklin), William Duane, and Matthew Lyon.

President John Adams, a Federalist, supported the Sedition Act. His vice president and political opponent was Thomas Jefferson, a Democratic-Republican. Jefferson vigorously opposed the Sedition Act.

SECTION 1. Be it enacted by the Senate and House of Representatives of the United States of America, in Congress assembled, That if any persons shall unlawfully combine or conspire together, with intent to oppose any measure or measures of the government of the United States, which are or shall be directed by proper authority, or to impede the operation of any law of the United States, or to intimidate or prevent any person holding a place or office in or under the government of the United States, from undertaking, performing or executing his trust or duty, and if any person or persons, with intent as aforesaid, shall counsel, advise or attempt to procure any insurrection, riot, unlawful assembly, or combination, whether such conspiracy, threatening, counsel, advice, or attempt shall have the proposed effect or not, he or they shall be deemed guilty of a high misdemeanor, and on conviction, before any court of the United States having jurisdiction thereof, shall be punished by a fine not exceeding five thousand dollars, and by imprisonment during a term not less than six months nor exceeding five years; and further, at the discretion of the court may be holden to find sureties for his good behaviour in such sum, and for such time, as the said court may direct.

SEC. 2. And be it further enacted, That if any person shall write, print, utter or publish, or shall cause or procure to be written, printed, uttered or published, or shall knowingly and willingly assist or aid in writing, printing, uttering or publishing any false, scandalous and malicious writing or writings against the government of the United States,[1] or either house of the Congress of the United States, or the President of the United States, with intent to defame the said government, or either house of the said Congress, or the said President, or to bring them, or either of them, into contempt or disrepute; or to excite against them, or either or any of them, the hatred of the good people of the United States, or to stir up sedition within the United States, or to excite any unlawful combinations therein, for opposing or resisting any law of the United States, or any act of the President of the United States, done in pursuance of any such law, or of the powers in him vested by the constitution of the United States, or to resist, oppose, or defeat any such law or act, or to aid, encourage or abet any hostile designs of any foreign nation against United States, their people or government, then such person, being thereof convicted before any court of the United States having jurisdiction thereof, shall be punished by a fine not exceeding two thousand dollars, and by imprisonment not exceeding two years.

SEC. 3. And be it further enacted and declared, That if any person shall be prosecuted under this act, for the writing or publishing any libel aforesaid, it shall be lawful for the defendant, upon the trial of the cause, to give in evidence in his defence, the truth of the matter contained in publication charged as a libel.[2] And the jury who shall try the cause shall have a right to determine the law and the fact, under the direction of the court, as in other cases.

[1] This law targeted speech that was critical of Federalist government officials. While the language of the law may seem like it targeted false speech, the law applied to those who uttered opinion highly critical of Federalist officials. Remember that the core type of speech the First Amendment is supposed to protect is political speech. But the Sedition Act of 1798 imposes stiff penalties on those who engage in political speech critical of the government.

[2] Defamation or libel refers to a false statement of fact that harms another's reputation. Truth is a defense to a libel action. Today, a person suing for libel has the burden of proof to show that a defendant uttered a false statement. Back in 1798, the law required the defendant to prove that his or her statement was true. This made it very difficult for those charged with libel to defend themselves.

SEC. 4. And be it further enacted, That this act shall continue and be in force until the third day of March, one thousand eight hundred and one, and no longer:[3] Provided, that the expiration of the act shall not prevent or defeat a prosecution and punishment of any offence against the law, during the time it shall be in force.

[3] This law had a sunset provision, meaning that it would end in March 1801. Democratic-Republican Thomas Jefferson defeated Federalist John Adams in the presidential election of 1800. When Jefferson became president, he pardoned those convicted of violating the Sedition Act. Jefferson realized that the Sedition Act of 1798 was a political tool used by the Federalists to silence some of their more vociferous Democratic-Republican critics.

Source: An Act in Addition to the Act, Entitled "An Act for the Punishment of Certain Crimes Against the United States." *U.S. Statutes at Large*, 5th Congress, 2nd Session (Boston: Charles C. Little and James Brown, 1845), 596–597.

John Quincy Adams's Letter on the "Gag Rule"

May 25, 1836

INTRODUCTION

John Quincy Adams, the nation's sixth president, served as the country's chief executive from 1825 to 1829. He lost in his reelection bid to Andrew Jackson. Most presidents do not return to political life after leaving office; John Quincy Adams remains the only president to return and serve in the U.S. House of Representatives. He began serving as a congressman in 1830 and remained there until his death in 1848.

Adams fervently opposed the so-called "gag rule" in the House that prevented the introduction of anti-slavery petitions. He allegedly yelled on the House floor, "Am I gagged?" This letter to his constituents details his experience.

I presented twenty petitions, all of which were laid on the table[1] without being read, though in every instance I moved for the reading, which the Speaker[2] refused to permit—from his decision I took in every case an appeal, and the appeal was in every case laid on the table. . . .

But the petition, avowedly coming from slaves, though praying for my expulsion from the House if I should persevere in presenting abolition petitions, opened to my examination and enquiry a new question, or at least a question which had never occurred to me before, and which I never should have thought of starting upon speculation, namely, Whether the right to petition Congress, could in any case be exercised by slaves? And after giving to the subject all the reflection of which I was capable, I came to the conclusion, that however doubtful it might be whether slaves could petition Congress for anything incompatible with their condition as slaves, and with their subjection to servitude, yet that for all other wants, distresses and grievances incident to their nature as men and to their relations as members, degraded members as they may be, of this community, they do enjoy the right of petition;[3] and that if they enjoyed the right in any case whatsoever, there could be none in which they were more certainly entitled to it, than that of deprecating the attempts of

[1] This wording comes from the rule itself: "Resolved, That all petitions, memorials, resolutions, propositions, or papers, relating in any way or to any extent whatever to the subject of slavery, or the abolition of slavery, shall, without being either printed or referred, be laid upon the table, and that no further action whatever shall be had thereon."

[2] The Speaker of the House was James K. Polk from Tennessee, who himself would become the 11th President of the United States, winning the election of 1844.

[3] Adams believed that slaves, while not citizens, should have the right to petition Congress about their abominable condition.

deluded friends to release them from bondage; a case in which they alone could in the nature of things speak for themselves, and their masters could not possibly speak for them. . . .

But after getting these two questions to the satisfaction of my own mind, there remained another. With what temper they would be received in a house, the large majority of which consisted of slave-holders, and of their political Northern associates, whose mouth-pieces had already put forth their feelers to familiarize the freeman of the North with the fight of a representative expelled from his seat for the single offence of persisting to present abolition petitions. I foresaw that the very conception of a petition from slaves, would dismount all the slave-holding philosophy of the House, and expected it would produce an explosion, which would spent itself in wind. Without therefore presenting or offering to present the petition, I stated to the Speaker that I had such a paper in my possession, which I had been requested to present, and enquired whether it came within the Resolution of the 18th of January. Now the Speaker decided that under that order, no such paper should be read. . . . The Speaker . . . horrified at the idea of receiving and laying on the table a petition from slaves, said that in a case so novel and extraordinary he felt himself incompetent to decide and must take the advice and direction of the House. . . .

If I had stated that I had a petition from sundry persons in Fredericksburg, relating to slavery, without saying that the petitioners were, by their own avowal, slaves, the paper must have gone upon the table; but the discovery would soon have been made, that it came from slaves, and there the tempest of indignation would have burst upon me, with tenfold fury, and I should have been charged with having fraudulently introduced a petition from slaves, without letting the House know the condition of the petitioners.

To avoid the possibility of such a charge, I put the question to the Speaker, giving him notice that the petition purported to come from slaves, and that I had suspicions that it came from another, and a very different source. The Speaker after failing in the attempt to obtain possession of the paper, referred my question to the House for decision, and there ensued a scene of which I propose to give an account, in a subsequent address, entreating you only to remember, if what I have said, or may say to you hereafter on this subject [slavery] should tax your patience, that the stake in the question is your right to petition,[4] your freedom of thought[5] and of action, and the freedom in Congress of your Representative.

[4] Here, Rep. Adams emphasizes that the "gag rule" infringes on a core First Amendment freedom—freedom of petition. His relentless pursuit to end the notorious "gag rule" is itself one of the pristine examples of the use of the right to petition.

[5] Adams also felt that the "gag rule" impacted "freedom of thought"—the core beginning of freedom of expression.

CONCLUSION

Adams believed that the "gag rule" was fundamentally unfair, undemocratic, and against the traditions of a free and open government. He finally succeeded in persuading the House to end the rule in 1844.

Source: *Letters from John Quincy Adams to His Constituents* (Boston: Isaac Knapp, 1837), 5–9.

Robert LaFollette's "Free Speech during Wartime" Speech

October 6, 1917

INTRODUCTION

Senator Robert M. LaFollette Sr. (1855–1925) was a politician from Wisconsin who served as a member of the U.S. House of Representatives, as a member of the U.S. Senate, and as governor of Wisconsin. He is best known for battling for Progressive causes and against the conglomeration of extreme wealth.

For First Amendment purposes, LaFollette's legacy was secured in October 1917, when he spoke in favor of the ability to dissent during times of war. LaFollette believed that politicians, as well as the public, had the right to oppose the war and to dissent from majoritarian viewpoints.

In this mass of newspaper clippings which I have here upon my desk, and which I shall not trouble the Senate to read unless it is desired, and which represent but a small part of the accumulation clipped from the daily press of the country in the last three months, I find other Senators, as well as myself, accused of the highest crimes of which any man can be guilty—treason and disloyalty—and, sir, accused not only with no evidence to support the accusation, but without the suggestion that such evidence anywhere exists. It is not claimed that Senators who opposed the declaration of war have since that time acted with any concerted purpose either regarding war measures or any others. They have voted according to their individual opinions, have often been opposed to each other on bills which have come before the Senate since the declaration of war, and, according to my recollection, have never all voted together since that time upon any single proposition upon which the Senate has been divided.

I am aware, Mr. President, that in pursuance of this general campaign of vilification and attempted intimidation, requests from various individuals and certain organizations have been submitted to

[1] Senator LaFollette refers to comments by some in the partisan press for LaFollette's "expulsion" from the U.S. Senate. The fever of patriotism at times turned into jingoism, or excess patriotism. A senator should not be removed from the Senate simply because he or she holds an opinion contrary to the majority of his or her colleagues.

the Senate for my expulsion[1] from this body, and that such requests have been referred to and considered by one of the committees of the Senate.

If I alone had been made the victim of these attacks, I should not take one moment of the Senate's time for their consideration, and I believe that other Senators who have been unjustly and unfairly assailed, as I have been, hold the same attitude upon this that I do. Neither the clamor of the mob nor the voice of power will ever turn me by the breadth of a hair from the course I mark out for myself, guided by such knowledge as I can obtain and controlled and directed by a solemn conviction of right and duty.

But, sir, it is not alone Members of Congress that the war party in this country has sought to intimidate. The mandate seems to have gone forth to the sovereign people of this country that they must be silent while those things are being done by their Government which most vitally concern their well-being, their happiness, and their lives. Today and for weeks past honest and law-abiding citizens of this country are being terrorized and outraged in their rights by those sworn to uphold the laws and protect the rights of the people. I have in my possession numerous affidavits establishing the fact that people are being unlawfully arrested,[2] thrown into jail, held incommunicado for days, only to be eventually discharged without ever having been taken into court, because they have committed no crime. Private residences are being invaded, loyal citizens of undoubted integrity and probity arrested, cross-examined, and the most sacred constitutional rights guaranteed to every American citizen are being violated.

[2] Senator LaFollette warns that many citizens have been subjected to harassment and even imprisonment for alleged disloyalty. He explains that many of these victims never committed a crime. The excess patriotism surrounding the war effort led to excesses and the suppression of civil liberties.

It appears to be the purpose of those conducting this campaign to throw the country into a state of terror, to coerce public opinion,[3] to stifle criticism, and suppress discussion of the great issues involved in this war.

[3] The World War I period featured a significant amount of intolerance toward any speech or conduct in the United States critical of the country's participation in World War I. Those who criticized the war effort or the draft were labeled as traitors and viewed with great suspicion.

I think all men recognize that in time of war the citizen must surrender some rights[4] for the common good which he is entitled to enjoy in time of peace. But sir, the right to control their own Government according to constitutional forms is not one of the rights that the citizens of this country are called upon to surrender in time of war.

[4] Senator LaFollette recognizes that in times of war, there can be some restrictions on rights for the "common good." However, the senator cautions that citizens still retain a significant level of rights, including the right to criticize political leaders.

Rather in time of war the citizen must be more alert to the preservation of his right to control his Government. He must be most watchful of the encroachment of the military upon the civil power. He must beware of those precedents in support of arbitrary action by administrative officials which, excused on the plea of necessity in war time, become the fixed rule when the necessity has passed and normal conditions have been restored.

. . .

Mr. President, our government, above all others, is founded on the right of the people freely to discuss all matters pertaining to their government, in war not less than in peace, for in this government the people are the rulers[5] in war no less than in peace.

[5] Senator LaFollette explains that people should have the right to speak about public issues during times of war, as well as in times of peace. After all, the words of the Constitution begin with the words "We the People." He explains to his colleagues that the people are ultimately in charge, not the elected officials. This is the essence of what he later calls a "representative democracy."

Source: *Congressional Record*, 65th Congress, 1st Session, pp. 223–236.

Eugene Debs's Speech in Canton, Ohio

June 16, 1918

INTRODUCTION

Eugene Debs was a five-time candidate for president of the United States, an American labor organizer, defender of the working class, and politician who consistently advocated for fair treatment of workers. He risked his personal safety and well-being for the causes he supported. He also faced punishment for his speech critical of World War I, the draft, and the capitalist system.

In his June 1918 speech in Canton, Ohio, Debs extolled the virtues of socialism, criticized the war, blasted the punishment of dissenters, and even talked about how he had to be careful about what he said. Debs proved prescient, as he was prosecuted for violating the Espionage Act of 1917, a federal law often used to silence wartime dissenters.

Comrades, friends and fellow-workers, for this very cordial greeting, this very hearty reception, I thank you all with the fullest appreciation of your interest in and your devotion to the cause for which I am to speak to you this afternoon.

To speak for labor;[1] to plead the cause of the men and women and children who toil; to serve the working class, has always been to me a high privilege; a duty of love.

I have just returned from a visit over yonder, where three of our most loyal comrades are paying the penalty for their devotion to the cause of the working class. They have come to realize, as many of us have, that it is extremely dangerous to exercise the constitutional right of free speech[2] in a country fighting to make democracy safe in the world.

I realize that, in speaking to you this afternoon, there are certain limitations placed upon the right of free speech. I must be exceedingly careful, prudent, as to what I say, and even more careful and prudent

[1] Eugene Debs was a union leader who consistently advocated for the workingman. He also became a political force, running for president five times as the candidate for the Socialist Party. He believed fervently that wealth should be redistributed to the working men and women rather than rest in the hands of the privileged few.

[2] Debs realized that it was "extremely dangerous" to speak against the government and the capitalist power structure. At this time, people who spoke against the government and the war effort were subject to punishment. Legal historian and author Paul Murphy explained this process brilliantly in his book *World War I and the Origin of Civil Liberties*.

as to how I say it.[3] I may not be able to say all I think; but I am not going to say anything that I do not think. I would rather a thousand times be a free soul in jail than to be a sycophant and coward in the streets. They may put those boys in jail—and some of the rest of us in jail—but they can not put the Socialist movement in jail. Those prison bars separate their bodies from ours, but their souls are here this afternoon. They are simply paying the penalty that all men have paid in all the ages of history for standing erect, and for seeking to pave the way to better conditions for mankind.

[3] Debs knew he had to tread carefully or face prosecution for criticizing the war effort. At this time, the federal government actively enforced the Espionage Act of 1917, which was interpreted to prohibit virtually any criticism of the war effort and the draft. Debs proved prescient in his speech, as he was charged with violating the Espionage Act for words he spoke during this speech.

. . .

The other day they sentenced Kate Richards O'Hare[4] to the penitentiary for five years. Think of sentencing a woman to the penitentiary simply for talking. The United States, under plutocratic rule, is the only country that would send a woman to prison for five years for exercising the right of free speech. If this be treason, let them make the most of it.

[4] Kate Richards O'Hare was a leading socialist who was imprisoned after giving an antiwar speech in North Dakota. She was pardoned a few years later in 1920.

Let me review a bit of history in connection with this case. I have known Kate Richards O'Hare intimately for twenty years. I am familiar with her public record. Personally I know her as if she were my own sister. All who know Mrs. O'Hare know her to be a woman of unquestioned integrity. And they also know that she is a woman of unimpeachable loyalty to the Socialist movement. When she went out into North Dakota to make her speech, followed by plain-clothes men in the service of the government intent upon effecting her arrest and securing her prosecution and conviction—when she went out there, it was with the full knowledge on her part that sooner or later these detectives would accomplish their purpose. She made her speech, and that speech was deliberately misrepresented for the purpose of securing her conviction. The only testimony against her was that of a hired witness. And when the farmers, the men and women who were in the audience she addressed—when they went to Bismarck where the trial was held to testify in her favor, to swear that she had not used the language she was charged with having used, the judge refused to allow them to go upon the stand. This would seem incredible to me if I had not had some experience of my own with federal courts.

. . .

Max Eastman[5] has been indicted and his paper suppressed, just as the papers with which I have been connected have all been suppressed. What a wonderful compliment they pay us![6] They are afraid that we may mislead and contaminate you. You are their wards; they are your guardians and they know what is best for you to read and hear and know. They are bound to see to it that our vicious doctrines do not reach your ears. And so in our great democracy, under our free institutions, they flatter our press by suppression; and they ignorantly imagine that they have silenced revolutionary propaganda in the United States. What an awful mistake they make for our benefit! As a matter of justice to them we should respond with resolutions of thanks and gratitude. Thousands of people who had never before heard of our papers are now inquiring for and insisting upon seeing them. They have succeeded only in arousing curiosity in our literature and propaganda. And woe to him who reads Socialist literature from curiosity! He is surely a goner. I have known of a thousand experiments but never one that failed.

[5] Max Eastman was a leading American political thinker and writer who espoused support for socialism and communism early in his life. He founded the newspaper *The Masses*, the leading paper for socialism. For his efforts, he twice faced indictments for violating the Espionage Act of 1917.

[6] Debs expresses support for Eastman and explains that the government's attack on Eastman only encourages more people to read his newspaper and learn more about the socialist cause. In later years, Eastman moved away from socialism and communism.

. . .

Rose Pastor Stokes![7] And when I mention her name I take off my hat. Here we have another heroic and inspiring comrade.[8] She had her millions of dollars at command. Did her wealth restrain her an instant?

[7] Rose Pastor Stokes was a well-known American socialist who also was active in the Communist Party. She was arrested in part for writing to a newspaper, "I am for the people and the government is for the profiteers."

[8] Debs expresses his support for Stokes and criticizes her conviction as a "farcical affair."

. . .

What a compliment it is to the Socialist movement to be thus persecuted for the sake of the truth! The truth alone will make the people free. And for this reason the truth must not be permitted to reach the people. The truth has always been dangerous to the rule of the rogue, the exploiter, the robber. So the truth must be ruthlessly suppressed. That is why they are trying to destroy the Socialist movement; and every time they strike a blow they add a thousand new voices to the hosts proclaiming that socialism is the hope of humanity and has come to emancipate the people from their final form of servitude.

. . .

It is the minorities who have made the history of this world.[9] It is the few who have had the courage to take their places at the front;

[9] Debs explains that it is often "minorities" who challenge the established order. The history of First Amendment jurisprudence confirms this statement, as free-speech law was developed by cases involving socialists, anarchists, communists, Jehovah's Witnesses, civil rights protesters, and others.

who have been true enough to themselves to speak the truth that was in them; who have dared oppose the established order of things; who have espoused the cause of the suffering, struggling poor; who have upheld without regard to personal consequences the cause of freedom and righteousness.

. . .

You need at this time especially to know that you are fit for something better than slavery and cannon fodder.[10] You need to know that you were not created to work and produce and impoverish yourself to enrich an idle exploiter. You need to know that you have a mind to improve, a soul to develop, and a manhood to sustain.

[10] This phrase by Debs founds it way into Justice Oliver Wendell Holmes's opinion in *Debs v. United States* (1919). This was Debs's provocative way of explaining that the people in the crowd were better than being slaves to the capitalist system who could be drafted and then killed in the war.

You need to know that it is your duty to rise above the animal plane of existence. You need to know that it is for you to know something about literature and science and art. You need to know that you are verging on the edge of a great new world. You need to get in touch with your comrades and fellow workers and to become conscious of your interests, your powers and your possibilities as a class. You need to know that you belong to the great majority of mankind. You need to know that as long as you are ignorant, as long as you are indifferent, as long as you are apathetic, unorganized and content, you will remain exactly where you are. You will be exploited; you will be degraded, and you will have to beg for a job. You will get just enough for your slavish toil to keep you in working order, and you will be looked down upon with scorn and contempt by the very parasites that live and luxuriate out of your sweat and unpaid labor.

. . .

They are continually talking about your patriotic duty. It is not their but your patriotic duty that they are concerned about.[11] There is a decided difference. Their patriotic duty never takes them to the firing line or chucks them into the trenches.

[11] Debs informs the crowd that many of their political leaders have some hypocrisy. These leaders urge patriotism and support for the war, but they don't actually fight on the front lines and face death from enemy fire. This passage resonated with many people.

. . .

In passing I suggest that we stop a moment to think about the term "landlord." "LANDLORD!" Lord of the Land! The lord of the land is indeed a superpatriot. This lord who practically owns the earth tells you that we are fighting this war to make the world safe for democracy—he who shuts out all humanity from his private domain; he who profiteers at the expense of the people who have been slain and mutilated by multiplied thousands, under pretense of being the great American patriot. It is he, this identical patriot who is in fact the archenemy of the people; it is he that you need to wipe from power. It is he who is a far greater menace to your liberty and your well-being than the Prussian Junkers on the other side of the Atlantic ocean.

. . .

We Socialists say: "Take possession of the mines in the name of the people." Set the miners at work and give every miner the equivalent of all the coal he produces. Reduce the work day in proportion to the development of productive machinery. That would at once settle the matter of a coal famine and of idle miners. But that is too simple a proposition and the people will have none of it. The time will come, however, when the people will be driven to take such action for there is no other efficient and permanent solution of the problem.

In the present system the miner, a wage slave,[12] gets down into a pit 300 or 400 feet deep. He works hard and produces a ton of coal. But he does not own an ounce of it. That coal belongs to some mine-owning plutocrat who may be in New York or sailing the high seas in his private yacht; or he may be hobnobbing with royalty in the capitals of Europe, and that is where most of them were before the war was declared. The industrial captain, so-called, who lives in Paris, London, Vienna or some other center of gaiety does not have to work to revel in luxury. He owns the mines and he might as well own the miners.

[12] Debs uses the term "wage slave" to refer to miners. Many working-class people labored long hours for minimal pay. The Progressive movement, which began in the late 19th century, sought to increase wages for the working class, but it was a constant uphill battle.

That is where you workers are and where you will remain as long as you give your support to the political parties of your masters and exploiters. You vote these miners out of a job and reduce them to corporation vassals and paupers.

We Socialists say: "Take possession of the mines; call the miner to work and return to him the equivalent of the value of his product." He can then build himself a comfortable home; live in it; enjoy it with his family. He can provide himself and his wife and children with clothes—good clothes—not shoddy; wholesome food in abundance, education for the children, and the chance to live the lives of civilized human beings, while at the same time the people will get coal at just what it costs to mine it.

Of course that would be socialism as far as it goes. But you are not in favor of that program. It is too visionary because it is so simple and practical. So you will have to continue to wait until winter is upon you before you get your coal and then pay three prices for it because you insist upon voting a capitalist ticket and giving your support to the present wage-slave system. The trouble with you is that you are still in a capitalist state of mind.

. . .

Get into the Socialist Party and take your place in its ranks; help to inspire the weak and strengthen the faltering, and do your share to speed the coming of the brighter and better day for us all.

. . .

Yes, in good time we are going to sweep into power in this nation and throughout the world. We are going to destroy all enslaving and degrading capitalist institutions and re-create them as free and humanizing institutions. The world is daily changing before our eyes. The sun of capitalism is setting; the sun of socialism is rising. It is our duty to build the new nation and the free republic. We need industrial and social builders. We Socialists are the builders of the beautiful world that is to be. We are all pledged to do our part. We are inviting—aye, challenging you this afternoon in the name of your own manhood and womanhood to join us and do your part.

In due time the hour will strike and this great cause triumphant—the greatest in history—will proclaim the emancipation of the working class and the brotherhood of all mankind.

Source: *The United States of America v. Eugene V. Debs*, Criminal Case Files, National Archives, Records of District Courts of the United States, Record Group 21 (National Archives Identifier 2641497).

Schenck v. United States

March 3, 1919

INTRODUCTION

Many view the starting point of modern First Amendment jurisprudence to be a series of opinions issued shortly after World War I. The nation was embroiled in a world war, and political dissenters were viewed with great suspicion. The U.S. Congress had passed the Espionage Act of 1917 and the Sedition Act of 1918 to silence and even imprison some of these dissenters.

One of the seminal decisions was *Schenck v. United States*. The case involved the prosecution of political dissidents Charles Schenck and Elizabeth Baer. The author of the opinion for the Court was the legendary Oliver Wendell Holmes Jr., one of the most famous justices to ever sit on the United States Supreme Court. He served for more than 20 years on the Supreme Judicial Court of Massachusetts before he was appointed to serve on the U.S. Supreme Court. He was known as one of the "Fathers of the First Amendment" for having written some of the Court's early opinions on free speech.

Mr. Justice HOLMES delivered the opinion of the Court.

This is an indictment in three counts. The first charges a conspiracy to violate the Espionage Act[1] of June 15, 1917 . . . by causing and attempting to cause insubordination, &c., in the military and naval forces of the United States, and to obstruct the recruiting and enlistment service of the United States, when the United States was at war with the German Empire, to-wit, that the defendant wilfully conspired to have printed and circulated to men who had been called and accepted for military service under the Act of May 18, 1917, a document set forth and alleged to be calculated to cause such insubordination and obstruction. The count alleges overt acts in pursuance of the conspiracy, ending in the distribution of the document set forth. The second count alleges a conspiracy to commit an offence against the United States, to-wit, to use the mails for the transmission of matter declared to be non-mailable by Title XII, § 2 of the Act of June 15, 1917, to-wit, the above mentioned document, with an averment of the same overt acts. The third count charges an unlawful

[1] The Espionage Act was a federal law passed in 1917 that sought to suppress antiwar activity and, in some cases, speech. Those who engaged in dissident political speech criticizing or questioning the draft were sometimes subject to prosecution under the law.

use of the mails for the transmission of the same matter and otherwise as above. The defendants were found guilty on all the counts. They set up the First Amendment to the Constitution forbidding Congress to make any law abridging the freedom of speech, or of the press, and bringing the case here on that ground have argued some other points also of which we must dispose.

It is argued that the evidence, if admissible, was not sufficient to prove that the defendant Schenck was concerned in sending the documents. According to the testimony Schenck[2] said he was general secretary of the Socialist party, and had charge of the Socialist headquarters from which the documents were sent. He identified a book found there as the minutes of the Executive Committee of the party. The book showed a resolution of August 13, 1917, that 15,000 leaflets should be printed on the other side of one of them in use, to be mailed to men who had passed exemption boards, and for distribution. Schenck personally attended to the printing. On August 20, the general secretary's report said "Obtained new leaflets from printer and started work addressing envelopes" &c.; and there was a resolve that Comrade Schenck be allowed $125 for sending leaflets through the mail. He said that he had about fifteen or sixteen thousand printed. There were files of the circular in question in the inner office which he said were printed on the other side of the one sided circular and were there for distribution. Other copies were proved to have been sent through the mails to drafted men. Without going into confirmatory details that were proved, no reasonable man could doubt that the defendant Schenck was largely instrumental in sending the circulars about. As to the defendant Baer,[3] there was evidence that she was a member of the Executive Board and that the minutes of its transactions were hers. The argument as to the sufficiency of the evidence that the defendants conspired to send the documents only impairs the seriousness of the real defence.

It is objected that the documentary evidence was not admissible because obtained upon a search warrant, valid so far as appears. The contrary is established. . . . The search warrant did not issue against the defendant, but against the Socialist headquarters at 1326 Arch Street, and it would seem that the documents technically were not even in the defendants' possession. . . . Notwithstanding some protest in argument, the notion that evidence even directly proceeding from

[2] Charles T. Schenck was the general secretary of the Socialist Party. He was involved in the process that led to the distribution of the leaflet in question.

[3] The other, often forgotten defendant, Elizabeth Baer, was a member of the party's executive board. She later unsuccessfully ran for mayor of Philadelphia.

the defendant in a criminal proceeding is excluded in all cases by the Fifth Amendment is plainly unsound.

The document in question,[4] upon its first printed side, recited the first section of the Thirteenth Amendment, said that the idea embodied in it was violated by the Conscription Act, and that a conscript is little better than a convict. In impassioned language it intimated that conscription was despotism in its worst form and a monstrous wrong against humanity in the interest of Wall Street's chosen few. It said, "Do not submit to intimidation," but in form at least confined itself to peaceful measures such as a petition for the repeal of the act. The other and later printed side of the sheet was headed "Assert Your Rights."[5] It stated reasons for alleging that any one violated the Constitution when he refused to recognize "your right to assert your opposition to the draft," and went on, "If you do not assert and support your rights, you are helping to deny or disparage rights which it is the solemn duty of all citizens and residents of the United States to retain." It described the arguments on the other side as coming from cunning politicians and a mercenary capitalist press, and even silent consent to the conscription law as helping to support an infamous conspiracy. It denied the power to send our citizens away to foreign shores to shoot up the people of other lands, and added that words could not express the condemnation such cold-blooded ruthlessness deserves, &c., &c., winding up, "You must do your share to maintain, support and uphold the rights of the people of this country." Of course the document would not have been sent unless it had been intended to have some effect, and we do not see what effect it could be expected to have upon persons subject to the draft except to influence them to obstruct the carrying of it out. The defendants do not deny that the jury might find against them on this point.

But it is said, suppose that that was the tendency of this circular, it is protected by the First Amendment to the Constitution. Two of the strongest expressions are said to be quoted respectively from well-known public men. It well may be that the prohibition of laws abridging the freedom of speech is not confined to previous restraints,[6] although to prevent them may have been the main purpose . . . We admit that, in many places and in ordinary times, the defendants, in saying all that was said in the circular, would have been within their constitutional rights. But the character of every

[4] The document in question was a double-sided leaflet. The first side quoted the text of the Thirteenth Amendment, which outlaws slavery and involuntary servitude. Ratified in 1865, it was the first of the three Reconstruction Amendments. The Socialist Party recited the Thirteenth Amendment and compared the person conscripted to U.S. military service as nothing more than a convict.

[5] The other side of the document urged those facing the draft to "assert their rights" and resist the U.S. military effort and the draft.

[6] The traditional conception of free speech was very limited at this time. Many believed that the First Amendment was limited only to "previous restraints" on speech—often called "prior restraints." In this passage, Justice Holmes acknowledges that the First Amendment applies to much more than simply when the government prevents speech from occurring (a prior restraint). The First Amendment also applies when the government subsequently punishes an individual for unpopular, intemperate, or controversial speech.

act depends upon the circumstances in which it is done. . . . The most stringent protection of free speech would not protect a man in falsely shouting fire in a theatre and causing a panic.[7] It does not even protect a man from an injunction against uttering words that may have all the effect of force. . . . The question in every case is whether the words used are used in such circumstances and are of such a nature as to create a clear and present danger[8] that they will bring about the substantive evils that Congress has a right to prevent. It is a question of proximity and degree. When a nation is at war, many things that might be said in time of peace are such a hindrance to its effort that their utterance will not be endured[9] so long as men fight, and that no Court could regard them as protected by any constitutional right. It seems to be admitted that if an actual obstruction of the recruiting service were proved, liability for words that produced that effect might be enforced. The statute of 1917, in § 4, punishes conspiracies to obstruct as well as actual obstruction. If the act, (speaking, or circulating a paper), its tendency, and the intent with which it is done are the same, we perceive no ground for saying that success alone warrants making the act a crime. . . .

It was not argued that a conspiracy to obstruct the draft was not within the words of the Act of 1917. The words are "obstruct the recruiting or enlistment service," and it might be suggested that they refer only to making it hard to get volunteers. Recruiting heretofore usually having been accomplished by getting volunteers, the word is apt to call up that method only in our minds. But recruiting is gaining fresh supplies for the forces, as well by draft as otherwise. It is put as an alternative to enlistment or voluntary enrollment in this act. . . .

Judgments affirmed.

Source: *Schenck v. United States*, 219 U.S. 47 (1919).

[7] Justice Holmes explains that the First Amendment does not protect all forms of speech. He does this with a colorful example of "shouting fire in a theatre." This phrase has entered our cultural lexicon.

[8] Justice Holmes creates a test or rule that provides guidance to lower courts, prosecutors, and others as to when speech is protected and when it is unprotected. Speech is not protected when it creates a "clear and present danger" to social order. This term, "clear and present danger," had not been used before in Supreme Court history. Later in the fall of 1919, Justice Holmes used more speech-protective language in describing the "clear and present danger" test.

[9] Justice Holmes explains that free-speech protections vary with context. He explains that a person has more free-speech protection in times of peace than in times of war. This point of law from the *Schenck* case has never been overruled.

Abrams v. United States

November 10, 1919

INTRODUCTION

In the fall of 1919, Justice Oliver Wendell Holmes introduced the phrase "clear and present danger" into First Amendment jurisprudence. He did so in a unanimous opinion for the Supreme Court in *Schenck v. United States*.

The *Schenck* opinion was met with heavy criticism from some leading judges and scholars of the day—thinkers such as Judge Learned Hand, Harvard law professor Zechariah Chafee, political scientist Ernst Freund, and others.

In his book *The Great Dissent: How Oliver Wendell Holmes Changed His Mind—and Changed the History of Free Speech in America*, law professor and author Thomas Healy contends that Justice Holmes changed his position on freedom of speech during the months after the *Schenck* decision. Holmes reflected his new thinking on freedom of speech in another case involving critical speech by political dissidents, this time five Russian émigrés: Jacob Abrams, Mollie Steiner, Hyman Lachowsky, Samuel Lipman, and Hyman Rosansky. The defendants circulated petitions supportive of a workers' revolt against capitalism and against U.S. military efforts.

While the majority of the U.S. Supreme Court affirmed the convictions, Justice Holmes authored a dissenting opinion joined by Justice Brandeis. It has been called "the Great Dissent." In his opinion, Justice Holmes strengthened the "clear and present danger" test and introduced the "marketplace of ideas" theory for free speech.

Mr. Justice HOLMES, dissenting.

This indictment is founded wholly upon the publication of two leaflets[1] which I shall describe in a moment. The first count charges a conspiracy pending the war with Germany to publish abusive language about the form of government of the United States, laying the preparation and publishing of the first leaflet as overt acts. The second count charges a conspiracy pending the war to publish language intended to bring the form of government into contempt, laying the preparation and publishing of the two leaflets as overt acts. The third count alleges a conspiracy to encourage resistance to the United States in the same war and to attempt to effectuate the purpose by

[1] Jacob Abrams and his four colleagues distributed leaflets critical of the United States and the U.S. war effort, and urged support for the Russian Revolution. The leaflets urged resistance to the United States and its war efforts. The leaflets also blasted capitalism as the great evil in the world.

publishing the same leaflets. The fourth count lays a conspiracy to incite curtailment of production of things necessary to the prosecution of the war and to attempt to accomplish it by publishing the second leaflet to which I have referred.

The first of these leaflets says that the President's cowardly silence about the intervention in Russia reveals the hypocrisy of the plutocratic gang in Washington. It intimates that "German militarism combined with allied capitalism to crush the Russian revolution"—goes on that the tyrants of the world fight each other until they see a common enemy—working class enlightenment, when they combine to crush it; and that now militarism and capitalism combined, though not openly, to crush the Russian revolution. It says that there is only one enemy of the workers of the world[2] and that is capitalism; that it is a crime for workers of America, etc., to fight the workers' republic of Russia, and ends "Awake! Awake, you workers of the world! Revolutionists." A note adds, "It is absurd to call us pro-German. We hate and despise German militarism more than do you hypocritical tyrants. We have more reason for denouncing German militarism than has the coward of the White House."

. . .

I never have seen any reason to doubt that the questions of law that alone were before this Court in the Cases of Schenck, Frohwerk, and Debs[3] were rightly decided. I do not doubt for a moment that by the same reasoning that would justify punishing persuasion to murder, the United States constitutionally may punish speech that produces or is intended to produce a clear and imminent danger that it will bring about forthwith certain substantive evils that the United States constitutionally may seek to prevent. The power undoubtedly is greater in time of war than in time of peace, because war opens dangers that do not exist at other times.

But, as against dangers peculiar to war, as against others, the principle of the right to free speech is always the same. It is only the present danger of immediate evil[4] or an intent to bring it about that warrants Congress in setting a limit to the expression of opinion where private rights are not concerned. Congress certainly cannot forbid all effort to change the mind of the country. Now nobody

[2] The leaflets sound in the typical language advocating against capitalism and its excesses. Abrams and his colleagues supported the average working person rather than the world governments that supported World War I. Abrams hoped for a workers' revolution.

[3] Justice Holmes explains that the trilogy of decisions in *Schenck*, *Frohwerk*, and *Debs* were decided correctly. Holmes wrote the Court's opinion upholding the convictions of Charles Schenck and Elizabeth Baer in the *Schenck v. United States* decision. He also agreed with the convictions in the *Frohwerk* and *Debs* decisions.

Recall that it was Justice Holmes who introduced the concept of "clear and present danger" into First Amendment law in *Schenck*. Holmes received criticism of his decision in *Schenck* from several scholars that he respected, including federal judge Learned Hand, law professor Zechariah Chafee, and political scientist Ernst Freund.

Most scholars believe that Justice Holmes thought about freedom of speech significantly over the summer of 1919. The *Abrams* decision was released in the fall of 1919.

[4] Holmes strengthens the "clear and present danger" test that he introduced in *Schenck* by noting the immediacy required to form a "clear and present danger." It is the concept of "immediacy" that changed the "clear and present danger" test from *Schenck* to *Abrams*.

can suppose that the surreptitious publishing of a silly leaflet by an unknown man, without more, would present any immediate danger that its opinions would hinder the success of the government arms or have any appreciable tendency to do so. Publishing those opinions for the very purpose of obstructing, however, might indicate a greater danger, and, at any rate, would have the quality of an attempt. So I assume that the second leaflet, if published for the purposes alleged in the fourth count, might be punishable. But it seems pretty clear to me that nothing less than that would bring these papers within the scope of this law. . . .

I do not see how anyone can find the intent required by the statute in any of the defendants' words. The second leaflet is the only one that affords even a foundation for the charge, and there, without invoking the hatred of German militarism expressed in the former one, it is evident from the beginning to the end that the only object of the paper is to help Russia and stop American intervention there against the popular government—not to impede the United States in the war that it was carrying on. To say that two phrases, taken literally, might import a suggestion of conduct that would have interference with the war as an indirect and probably undesired effect seems to me by no means enough to show an attempt to produce that effect.

I return for a moment to the third count. That charges an intent to provoke resistance to the United States in its war with Germany. Taking the clause in the statute that deals with that in connection with the other elaborate provisions of the Act, I think that resistance to the United States means some forcible act of opposition[5] to some proceeding of the United States in pursuance of the war. I think the intent must be the specific intent that I have described, and, for the reasons that I have given, I think that no such intent was proved or existed in fact. I also think that there is no hint at resistance to the United States as I construe the phrase.

In this case sentences of twenty years' imprisonment have been imposed for the publishing of two leaflets that I believe the defendants had as much right to publish as the Government has to publish the Constitution[6] of the United States now vainly invoked by them. Even if I am technically wrong, and enough can be squeezed from these poor and puny anonymities to turn the color of legal

[5] Unlike the majority opinion, Justice Holmes believes that the leaflets in question were mere words that did not equate to a "forcible act of opposition." Holmes did not believe that the words on the leaflet equated to the intent necessary to convict under the Sedition Act of 1918.

[6] To Justice Holmes, this case involved the pure right of individuals to publish political dissent.

litmus paper, I will add, even if what I think the necessary intent were shown, the most nominal punishment seems to me all that possibly could be inflicted, unless the defendants are to be made to suffer not for what the indictment alleges, but for the creed that they avow—a creed that I believe to be the creed of ignorance and immaturity when honestly held, as I see no reason to doubt that it was held here, but which, although made the subject of examination at the trial, no one has a right even to consider in dealing with the charges before the Court.

Persecution for the expression of opinions seems to me perfectly logical. If you have no doubt of your premises or your power, and want a certain result with all your heart, you naturally express your wishes in law, and sweep away all opposition. To allow opposition by speech seems to indicate that you think the speech impotent, as when a man says that he has squared the circle, or that you do not care wholeheartedly for the result, or that you doubt either your power or your premises. But when men have realized that time has upset many fighting faiths, they may come to believe even more than they believe the very foundations of their own conduct that the ultimate good desired is better reached by free trade in ideas—that the best test of truth is the power of the thought to get itself accepted in the competition of the market,[7] and that truth is the only ground upon which their wishes safely can be carried out. That, at any rate, is the theory of our Constitution. It is an experiment, as all life is an experiment. Every year, if not every day, we have to wager our salvation upon some prophecy based upon imperfect knowledge. While that experiment is part of our system, I think that we should be eternally vigilant against attempts to check the expression of opinions that we loathe and believe to be fraught with death, unless they so imminently threaten immediate interference with the lawful and pressing purposes of the law that an immediate check is required to save the country. I wholly disagree with the argument of the Government that the First Amendment left the common law as to seditious libel in force. History seems to me against the notion. I had conceived that the United States, through many years, had shown its repentance for the Sedition Act of 1798 by repaying fines that it imposed. Only the emergency that makes it immediately dangerous to leave the correction of evil counsels to time warrants making any exception to the sweeping command, "Congress shall make no law abridging the freedom of speech." Of course, I am speaking only of

[7] This forms the basis of the "marketplace of ideas" metaphor for free speech. The idea is that the government should allow different ideas into the marketplace and let the people decide what the better ideas are. The "marketplace of ideas" fit nicely into Justice Holmes's support for laissez-faire economic policies by the government. Courts today still cite the "marketplace of ideas" metaphor when arguing against governmental censorship.

expressions of opinion and exhortations, which were all that were uttered here, but I regret that I cannot put into more impressive words my belief that, in their conviction upon this indictment, the defendants were deprived of their rights under the Constitution of the United States.

Source: *Abrams v. United States,* 250 U.S. 616 (1919).

Whitney v. California
May 16, 1927

INTRODUCTION

Most of the time in law, majority opinions dominate the discussion and stand as guiding precedent. Concurring and dissenting opinions often are interesting but do not become the law. A concurring opinion is an opinion where the judge or justice agrees with the result of the main opinion but applies a different form of reasoning.

Arguably, the most influential concurring opinion in First Amendment cases was Justice Louis Brandeis's concurring opinion in *Whitney v. California* (1927). The case involved the prosecution of Charlotte Anita Whitney, a niece of former U.S. Supreme Court justice Stephen Field, for allegedly helping the Communist Party. In reality, Ms. Whitney, a socialist, was not a danger to society. In fact, after her conviction was affirmed, the California governor granted her a pardon. The following is Justice Brandeis's concurring opinion.

Miss Whitney was convicted of the felony of assisting in organizing, in the year 1919, the Communist Labor Party[1] of California, of being a member of it, and of assembling with it. These acts are held to constitute a crime, because the party was formed to teach criminal syndicalism.[2] The statute which made these acts a crime restricted the right of free speech and of assembly theretofore existing. The claim is that the statute, as applied, denied to Miss Whitney the liberty guaranteed by the Fourteenth Amendment.

The felony which the statute created is a crime very unlike the old felony of conspiracy or the old misdemeanor of unlawful assembly. The mere act of assisting in forming a society for teaching syndicalism, of becoming a member of it, or of assembling with others for that purpose, is given the dynamic quality of crime. There is guilt although the society may not contemplate immediate promulgation of the doctrine. Thus, the accused is to be punished not for attempt, incitement, or conspiracy, but for a step in preparation, which, if it threatens the public order at all, does so only remotely. The novelty in the prohibition introduced is that the statute aims not at the practice of criminal syndicalism, nor

[1] The Communist Party was viewed as a threat and a world danger to democracies and capitalist government. The Bolshevik Revolution of 1919 in Russia only exacerbated fears of a worldwide communist threat. Note that Whitney was charged with violating a California state criminal syndicalism law.

[2] "Criminal syndicalism" was a term used to describe sabotage and other unlawful actions by radical leftist activists, who sought to undermine the capitalistic system in the United States. About 20 states, including California, enacted so-called criminal syndicalism laws.

[3] Justice Brandeis points out that under this California state law, a person could be charged merely with associating with Communists, not with actually organizing or preaching the doctrine of Communism.

[4] Justice Brandeis explains that speech can be criminalized only if it presents a "clear and imminent danger" of evil. He emphasizes the word "imminent" in his opinion. The introduction of "imminent" means that much hateful and even harmful speech cannot be criminalized, because that speech does not cause immediate harm. This is a significant level of protection for speech.

even directly at the preaching of it, but at association[3] with those who propose to preach it.

Despite arguments to the contrary which had seemed to me persuasive, it is settled that the due process clause of the Fourteenth Amendment applies to matters of substantive law as well as to matters of procedure. Thus, all fundamental rights comprised within the term liberty are protected by the Federal Constitution from invasion by the States. The right of free speech, the right to teach, and the right of assembly are, of course, fundamental rights. These may not be denied or abridged. But, although the rights of free speech and assembly are fundamental, they are not in their nature absolute. . . . That the necessity which is essential to a valid restriction does not exist unless speech would produce, or is intended to produce, a clear and imminent danger[4] of some substantive evil which the state constitutionally may seek to prevent has been settled. It is said to be the function of the legislature to determine whether, at a particular time and under the particular circumstances, the formation of, or assembly with, a society organized to advocate criminal syndicalism constitutes a clear and present danger of substantive evil, and that, by enacting the law here in question, the legislature of California determined that question in the affirmative. The legislature must obviously decide, in the first instance, whether a danger exists which calls for a particular protective measure. But where a statute is valid only in case certain conditions exist, the enactment of the statute cannot alone establish the facts which are essential to its validity. Prohibitory legislation has repeatedly been held invalid, because unnecessary, where the denial of liberty involved was that of engaging in a particular business. The power of the courts to strike down an offending law is no less when the interests involved are not property rights, but the fundamental personal rights of free speech and assembly.

. . .

They valued liberty both as an end, and as a means. They believed liberty to be the secret of happiness, and courage to be the secret of liberty. They believed that freedom to think as you will and to speak as you think are means indispensable to the discovery and spread of political truth; that, without free speech and assembly, discussion would be futile; that, with them, discussion affords ordinarily adequate protection against the dissemination of noxious doctrine;

that the greatest menace to freedom is an inert people;[5] that public discussion is a political duty, and that this should be a fundamental principle of the American government. They recognized the risks to which all human institutions are subject. But they knew that order cannot be secured merely through fear of punishment for its infraction; that it is hazardous to discourage thought, hope and imagination; that fear breeds repression; that repression breeds hate; that hate menaces stable government; that the path of safety lies in the opportunity to discuss[6] freely supposed grievances and proposed remedies, and that the fitting remedy for evil counsels is good ones. Believing in the power of reason as applied through public discussion, they eschewed silence coerced by law—the argument of force in its worst form. Recognizing the occasional tyrannies of governing majorities, they amended the Constitution so that free speech and assembly should be guaranteed.

[5] In this paragraph, Justice Brandeis emphasizes the importance of debate and discussion in a free society. He explains that public apathy is the "greatest menace to freedom." Many critics of modern America maintain that this remains the greatest danger.

[6] Justice Brandeis also articulates the basis for what is called the "safety valve" theory of speech. This theory posits that people let off steam by expressing their grievances. Stated another way, we need to let people vent their frustrations, lest they resort to bad conduct rather than just intemperate speech.

Fear of serious injury cannot alone justify suppression of free speech and assembly. Men feared witches and burnt women. It is the function of speech to free men from the bondage of irrational fears. To justify suppression of free speech, there must be reasonable ground to fear that serious evil will result if free speech is practiced. There must be reasonable ground to believe that the danger apprehended is imminent. There must be reasonable ground to believe that the evil to be prevented is a serious one. Every denunciation of existing law tends in some measure to increase the probability that there will be violation of it. Condonation of a breach enhances the probability. Expressions of approval add to the probability. Propagation of the criminal state of mind by teaching syndicalism increases it. Advocacy of law-breaking heightens it still further. But even advocacy of violation, however reprehensible morally, is not a justification for denying free speech where the advocacy falls short of incitement and there is nothing to indicate that the advocacy would be immediately acted on. The wide difference between advocacy and incitement,[7] between preparation and attempt, between assembling and conspiracy, must be borne in mind. In order to support a finding of clear and present danger, it must be shown either that immediate serious violence was to be expected or was advocated, or that the past conduct furnished reason to believe that such advocacy was then contemplated.

[7] The above paragraph is one of the most important in Supreme Court history. Justice Brandeis reasons that there is a great difference between advocacy and incitement. Only when someone engages in speech intending to cause imminent harm should he or she be punished.

Those who won our independence by revolution were not cowards. They did not fear political change. They did not exalt order at the cost of liberty. To courageous, self-reliant men, with confidence in the power of free and fearless reasoning applied through the processes of popular government, no danger flowing from speech can be deemed clear and present unless the incidence of the evil apprehended is so imminent that it may befall before there is opportunity for full discussion. If there be time to expose through discussion the falsehood and fallacies, to avert the evil by the processes of education, the remedy to be applied is more speech, not enforced silence.[8] Only an emergency can justify repression. Such must be the rule if authority is to be reconciled with freedom. Such, in my opinion, is the command of the Constitution. It is therefore always open to Americans to challenge a law abridging free speech and assembly by showing that there was no emergency justifying it.

[8] Justice Brandeis also articulates the basis for what is known as the "counter-speech doctrine." This means that the government should not try to silence a speaker; rather, it should counter the speaker's noxious speech with good speech.

. . .

Whether in 1919, when Miss Whitney did the things complained of, there was in California such clear and present danger of serious evil might have been made the important issue in the case. She might have required that the issue be determined either by the court or the jury. She claimed below that the statute, as applied to her, violated the Federal Constitution; but she did not claim that it was void because there was no clear and present danger of serious evil,[9] nor did she request that the existence of these conditions of a valid measure thus restricting the rights of free speech and assembly be passed upon by the court or a jury. On the other hand, there was evidence on which the court or jury might have found that such danger existed. I am unable to assent to the suggestion in the opinion of the court that assembling with a political party, formed to advocate the desirability of a proletarian revolution by mass action at some date necessarily far in the future, is not a right within the protection of the Fourteenth Amendment. In the present case, however, there was other testimony which tended to establish the existence of a conspiracy, on the part of members of the International Workers of the World, to commit present serious crimes, and likewise to show that such a conspiracy would be furthered by the activity of the society of which Miss Whitney was a member. Under these circumstances, the judgment of the State court cannot be disturbed. . . . Because we may not enquire into the errors now alleged, I concur in affirming the judgment of the state court.

[9] Justice Brandeis's opinion reads like a dissenting opinion, but he does write to affirm the conviction. Thus, his opinion is classified as a concurring opinion. He points out that Miss Whitney's legal counsel could have advanced more forcefully the argument that her speech-related activities did not pose a "clear and present danger of serious evil." However, her legal counsel did not preserve this challenge at the trial court level, and thus it was not properly preserved.

CONCLUSION

While Justice Brandeis wrote a concurring opinion in Whitney's case, it reads more like a dissent. In his *Whitney* opinion, one can see many of the foundational principles of modern First Amendment law. Many scholars refer to this opinion as the most important in all of First Amendment jurisprudence.

Source: *Whitney v. California*, 274 U.S. 357 (1927).

President Franklin D. Roosevelt's "Four Freedoms" Speech

January 6, 1941

INTRODUCTION

Every year the president of the United States delivers a State of the Union address. One of the more significant ones in American history was delivered by President Franklin D. Roosevelt, the only person ever elected president of the United States more than twice—an unprecedented four times. In fact, it was due to his domination and long tenure that Congress enacted the Twenty-Second Amendment, which limits the president to two terms.

In his speech, President Roosevelt identified the unique threat by Nazi Germany to American democracy and the American way of life. He also articulated "four essential freedoms": (1) freedom of speech and expression, (2) freedom of religion, (3) freedom from want, and (4) freedom from fear.

Two of these four freedoms are found in the text of the First Amendment.

Mr. President, Mr. Speaker, members of the 77th Congress:

I address you, the members of this new Congress, at a moment unprecedented in the history of the union. I use the word "unprecedented" because at no previous time has American security been as seriously threatened[1] from without as it is today.

Since the permanent formation of our government under the Constitution in 1789, most of the periods of crisis in our history have related to our domestic affairs.[2] And, fortunately, only one of these—the four-year war between the States—ever threatened our national unity. Today, thank God, 130,000,000 Americans in 48 States have forgotten points of the compass in our national unity.

It is true that prior to 1914 the United States often has been disturbed by events in other continents. We have even engaged in two wars with European nations and in a number of undeclared wars in the West Indies, in the Mediterranean and in the Pacific, for the

[1] President Roosevelt delivered this speech while World War II was raging elsewhere in the world. While the United States did not enter the war until December 1941, President Roosevelt warned that the war presented a threat to American democracy and the American way of life. America traditionally had a policy of nonintervention in such affairs, but President Roosevelt said that support for U.S. allies was necessary to preserve American values.

[2] The great exception to this was World War I, from 1914 through 1917.

maintenance of American rights and for the principles of peaceful commerce. But in no case had a serious threat been raised against our national safety or our continued independence.

What I seek to convey is the historic truth that the United States as a nation has at all times maintained opposition—clear, definite opposition—to any attempt to lock us in behind an ancient Chinese wall while the procession of civilization went past. Today, thinking of our children and of their children, we oppose enforced isolation for ourselves or for any other part of the Americas.

That determination of ours, extending over all these years, was proved, for example, in the early days during the quarter century of wars following the French Revolution. While the Napoleonic struggles did threaten interests of the United States because of the French foothold in the West Indies and in Louisiana, and while we engaged in the War of 1812 to vindicate our right to peaceful trade, it is nevertheless clear that neither France nor Great Britain nor any other nation was aiming at domination of the whole world.[3]

And in like fashion, from 1815 to 1914—ninety-nine years—no single war in Europe or in Asia constituted a real threat against our future or against the future of any other American nation.

. . .

In times like these it is immature—and, incidentally, untrue—for anybody to brag that an unprepared America, single-handed and with one hand tied behind its back, can hold off the whole world.

No realistic American can expect from a dictator's peace international generosity, or return of true independence, or world disarmament, or freedom of expression, or freedom of religion—or even good business. Such a peace would bring no security for us or for our neighbors. Those who would give up essential liberty to purchase a little temporary safety[4] deserve neither liberty nor safety.

. . .

And that is why the future of all the American Republics is today in serious danger. That is why this annual message to the Congress[5]

[3] Adolf Hitler, the führer of Nazi Germany, had a goal of world domination. President Roosevelt recognized that Hitler and Nazi Germany represented a threat not seen before in the world. Roosevelt pointed to examples of world powers like France and Great Britain, which waged war on foreign soils but—unlike Hitler—were not "aiming at domination of the whole world." In other words, Roosevelt was warning of the unprecedented threat presented by Hitler's German empire.

[4] This famous phrase is borrowed from the great Benjamin Franklin, who allegedly said, "They who can give up essential liberty to obtain a little temporary safety deserve neither liberty nor safety."

[5] An annual message to Congress is required by Article II, Section 3 of the Constitution. It began as a written report, but since Woodrow Wilson, every president except Herbert Hoover has delivered a speech in front of a joint session of Congress.

is unique in our history. That is why every member of the executive branch of the government and every member of the Congress face great responsibility, great accountability. The need of the moment is that our actions and our policy should be devoted primarily—almost exclusively—to meeting this foreign peril. For all our domestic problems are now a part of the great emergency.

. . .

Our national policy is this:

First, by an impressive expression of the public will and without regard to partisanship, we are committed to all-inclusive national defense.

Secondly, by an impressive expression of the public will and without regard to partisanship, we are committed to full support of all those resolute people everywhere who are resisting aggression and are thereby keeping war away from our hemisphere. By this support we express our determination that the democratic cause shall prevail, and we strengthen the defense and the security of our own nation.

. . .

Let us say to the democracies: "We Americans are vitally concerned in your defense of freedom. We are putting forth our energies, our resources, and our organizing powers to give you the strength to regain and maintain a free world. We shall send you, in ever-increasing numbers, ships, planes, tanks, guns. That is our purpose and our pledge."

In fulfillment of this purpose we will not be intimidated by the threats of dictators that they will regard as a breach of international law or as an act of war our aid to the democracies which dare to resist their aggression. Such aid—such aid is not an act of war, even if a dictator should unilaterally proclaim it so to be.

And when the dictators—if the dictators—are ready to make war upon us, they will not wait for an act of war on our part.

. . .

Yes, and we must prepare, all of us prepare, to make the sacrifices that the emergency—almost as serious as war itself—demands. Whatever stands in the way of speed and efficiency in defense, in defense preparations of any kind, must give way to the national need.

. . .

As men do not live by bread alone, they do not fight by armaments alone. Those who man our defenses and those behind them who build our defenses must have the stamina and the courage which come from unshakable belief in the manner of life which they are defending. The mighty action that we are calling for cannot be based on a disregard of all the things worth fighting for.

. . .

The basic things expected by our people of their political and economic systems are simple. They are:

> Equality of opportunity for youth and for others.
>
> Jobs for those who can work.
>
> Security for those who need it.
>
> The ending of special privilege for the few.
>
> The preservation of civil liberties for all.
>
> The enjoyment of the fruits of scientific progress in a wider and constantly rising standard of living.

These are the simple, the basic things that must never be lost sight of in the turmoil and unbelievable complexity of our modern world. The inner and abiding strength of our economic and political systems is dependent upon the degree to which they fulfill these expectations.

Many subjects connected with our social economy call for immediate improvement. As examples:

> We should bring more citizens under the coverage of old-age pensions and unemployment insurance.

We should widen the opportunities for adequate medical care.

We should plan a better system by which persons deserving or needing gainful employment may obtain it.

. . .

In the future days, which we seek to make secure, we look forward to a world founded upon four essential human freedoms.

The first is freedom of speech and expression[6]—everywhere in the world.

The second is freedom of every person to worship[7] God in his own way—everywhere in the world.

The third is freedom from want, which, translated into world terms, means economic understandings which will secure to every nation a healthy peacetime life for its inhabitants—everywhere in the world.

The fourth is freedom from fear, which, translated into world terms, means a world-wide reduction of armaments to such a point and in such a thorough fashion that no nation will be in a position to commit an act of physical aggression against any neighbor—anywhere in the world.

. . .

To that new order we oppose the greater conception—the moral order. A good society is able to face schemes of world domination and foreign revolutions alike without fear.

Since the beginning of our American history we have been engaged in change, in a perpetual, peaceful revolution, a revolution which goes on steadily, quietly, adjusting itself to changing conditions without the concentration camp or the quicklime in the ditch. The world order which we seek is the cooperation of free countries, working together in a friendly, civilized society.

This nation has placed its destiny in the hands and heads and hearts of its millions of free men and women, and its faith in freedom under

[6] The first of President Roosevelt's "four essential freedoms" was "freedom of speech and expression." Freedom of speech is a textually based freedom in the First Amendment. "Freedom of expression" is a term that often encompasses not only freedom of speech but also the freedoms of press, assembly, and petition. Collectively, these four freedoms are often called "freedom of expression."

[7] The first 16 words of the First Amendment—"Congress shall make no law respecting an establishment of religion or prohibiting the free exercise thereof"—represent the two religious liberty clauses of the amendment. President Roosevelt is speaking to the Free Exercise Clause of the First Amendment, which gives persons the ability to believe in whatever religion or non-religion they want. The Free Exercise Clause protects both the religious devotee and the fierce atheist.

the guidance of God. Freedom means the supremacy of human rights[8] everywhere. Our support goes to those who struggle to gain those rights and keep them. Our strength is our unity of purpose.

[8] Human rights are a high priority for leaders and countries that care about freedom. Freedom of speech and expression is a key aspect of human rights and something that should be lauded everywhere in the world.

To that high concept there can be no end save victory.

Source: *Congressional Record*, 77th Congress, 1st Session, pp. 44–47.

Chaplinsky v. New Hampshire

March 9, 1942

INTRODUCTION

In *Chaplinsky v. New Hampshire* (1942), the U.S. Supreme Court created the "fighting words" exception to the First Amendment. Fighting words are direct, face-to-face personal insults that cause an immediate breach of the peace. The Supreme Court reasoned that such fighting words don't contribute to the development of ideas and have very slight social value.

The Court also created the blueprint for the categorical method of interpreting the First Amendment. The Court explained that there are certain categories of speech that don't deserve free-speech protection. In later decisions, most notably *Cohen v. California* (1971), the Court limited the fighting-words doctrine, but the doctrine remains alive and well, particularly in the lower courts.

Justice Frank Murphy delivered the opinion of the Court.

Appellant, a member of the sect known as Jehovah's Witnesses, was convicted in the municipal court of Rochester, New Hampshire, for violation of Chapter 378, § 2, of the Public Laws of New Hampshire: "No person shall address any offensive, derisive or annoying word[1] to any other person who is lawfully in any street or other public place, nor call him by any offensive or derisive name, nor make any noise or exclamation in his presence and hearing with intent to deride, offend or annoy him, or to prevent him from pursuing his lawful business or occupation."

[1] The New Hampshire law under which Walter Chaplinsky was convicted prohibits any person from saying "any offensive, derisive, or annoying word" to another. This law on its face is too broad. It is "overbroad," in First Amendment language. However, the New Hampshire Supreme Court had interpreted the law narrowly, employing what is called a "limiting construction." This means that the law on its face was valid.

The complaint charged that appellant, "with force and arms, in a certain public place in said city of Rochester, to wit, on the public sidewalk on the easterly side of Wakefield Street, near unto the entrance of the City Hall, did unlawfully repeat the words following, addressed to the complainant, that is to say, 'You are a God damned racketeer' and 'a damned Fascist and the whole government of Rochester are Fascists or agents of Fascists,' the same being offensive, derisive and annoying words and names."

. . .

There is no substantial dispute over the facts. Chaplinsky was distributing the literature of his sect on the streets of Rochester on a busy Saturday afternoon. Members of the local citizenry complained to the City Marshal, Bowering, that Chaplinsky was denouncing all religion[2] as a "racket." Bowering told them that Chaplinsky was lawfully engaged, and then warned Chaplinsky that the crowd was getting restless. Some time later, a disturbance occurred and the traffic officer on duty at the busy intersection started with Chaplinsky for the police station, but did not inform him that he was under arrest or that he was going to be arrested. On the way, they encountered Marshal Bowering, who had been advised that a riot was under way and was therefore hurrying to the scene. Bowering repeated his earlier warning to Chaplinsky, who then addressed to Bowering the words set forth in the complaint.

[2] Allegedly, Chaplinsky got into a dispute with others and began denouncing their religion. Marshal Bowering attempted to broker a peace but seemed to take the side of the others. When Chaplinsky cursed Bowering, the marshal arrested him for violating the New Hampshire law.

Chaplinsky's version of the affair[3] was slightly different. He testified that when he met Bowering, he asked him to arrest the ones responsible for the disturbance. In reply, Bowering cursed him and told him to come along. Appellant admitted that he said the words charged in the complaint, with the exception of the name of the Deity.

[3] Chaplinsky contended that the authorities should have arrested the others, not him. He also contended that Marshal Bowering cursed him. However, the lower courts believed Marshal Bowering, not Walter Chaplinsky. The U.S. Supreme Court seemingly deferred to the factual determinations of the New Hampshire courts.

. . .

Appellant assails the statute as a violation of all three freedoms, speech, press and worship, but only an attack on the basis of free speech is warranted. The spoken, not the written, word is involved. And we cannot conceive that cursing a public officer is the exercise of religion in any sense of the term. But even if the activities of the appellant which preceded the incident could be viewed as religious in character, and therefore entitled to the protection of the Fourteenth Amendment, they would not cloak him with immunity[4] from the legal consequences for concomitant acts committed in violation of a valid criminal statute. We turn, therefore, to an examination of the statute itself.

[4] The Court explains that Chaplinsky's profane words toward a law enforcement official cannot be defended as a free exercise of religion. A few years earlier, in *Cantwell v. Connecticut* (1940), the Court had protected several Jehovah's Witnesses who also had a dispute with others. The Court viewed the *Cantwell* case as a freedom of religion case, but it viewed the *Chaplinsky* case as a freedom of speech case.

Allowing the broadest scope to the language and purpose of the Fourteenth Amendment, it is well understood that the right of free speech is not absolute[5] at all times and under all circumstances. There are certain well-defined and narrowly limited classes of speech,[6] the prevention and punishment of which has never been thought to raise any Constitutional problem. These include the lewd and obscene, the profane, the libelous, and the insulting or

[5] The Supreme Court explains that the First Amendment does not protect all forms of speech. The Court also explains that there are several categories of speech that do not deserve First Amendment protection.

[6] This passage forms the basis for the categorical model of First Amendment jurisprudence—that there are certain unprotected categories of speech.

"fighting" words[7]—those which, by their very utterance, inflict injury or tend to incite an immediate breach of the peace. It has been well observed that such utterances are no essential part of any exposition of ideas, and are of such slight social value as a step to truth that any benefit that may be derived from them is clearly outweighed by the social interest in order and morality. "Resort to epithets or personal abuse is not in any proper sense communication of information or opinion safeguarded by the Constitution, and its punishment as a criminal act would raise no question under that instrument."

[7] The Court in *Chaplinsky* introduced the concept of "fighting words" into free-speech jurisprudence. Fighting words are those that, by their very utterance, cause injury or an immediate breach of the peace. The Court explains that such words have little to no social value and don't contribute to the explanation of ideas.

The state statute here challenged comes to us authoritatively construed[8] by the highest court of New Hampshire. It has two provisions—the first relates to words or names addressed to another in a public place; the second refers to noises and exclamations.... On the authority of its earlier decisions, the state court declared that the statute's purpose was to preserve the public peace, no words being "forbidden except such as have a direct tendency to cause acts of violence by the person to whom, individually, the remark is addressed." It was further said: "... The statute, as construed, does no more than prohibit the face-to-face words plainly likely to cause a breach of the peace by the addressee, words whose speaking constitute a breach of the peace by the speaker—including 'classical fighting words,' words in current use less 'classical' but equally likely to cause violence, and other disorderly words, including profanity, obscenity and threats."...

[8] The Supreme Court explained that the New Hampshire high court had imposed a limiting or narrowing construction on this statute. This means that the New Hampshire law only applies to fighting words, which do not deserve free-speech protection.

Nor can we say that the application of the statute to the facts disclosed by the record substantially or unreasonably impinges upon the privilege of free speech.[9] Argument is unnecessary to demonstrate that the appellations "damn racketeer" and "damn Fascist" are epithets likely to provoke the average person to retaliation, and thereby cause a breach of the peace.

[9] The Supreme Court explains that Walter Chaplinsky does not have a valid free-speech defense for violating the New Hampshire law. The words spoken by Chaplinsky are epithets easily classified as fighting words.

The refusal of the state court to admit evidence of provocation and evidence bearing on the truth or falsity of the utterances is open to no Constitutional objection. Whether the facts sought to be proved by such evidence constitute a defense to the charge, or may be shown in mitigation, are questions for the state court to determine. Our function is fulfilled by a determination that the challenged statute, on its face and as applied, does not contravene the Fourteenth Amendment.

Source: *Chaplinsky v. New Hampshire*, 315 U.S. 568 (1942).

West Virginia State Board of Education v. Barnette

June 14, 1943

INTRODUCTION

The U.S. Supreme Court first applied the First Amendment to limit public school officials in *West Virginia State Board of Education v. Barnette*, a case decided on June 14th, Flag Day. The case involved a West Virginia policy that required all public school students to salute the flag and recite the Pledge of Allegiance.

Three years earlier, the Supreme Court had upheld a similar Pennsylvania law in *Minersville School District v. Gobitis* (1940). In that decision, the Court reasoned that religious liberty must give way to political authority and nationalism. Remember that the decision was rendered as the United States was battling Nazi Germany and Imperial Japan in World War II.

The decision led to much discrimination and harassment of Jehovah's Witnesses, who had taken a religious stand against saluting the flag. This caused several members of the Supreme Court—including William O. Douglas, Hugo Black, and Frank Murphy—to acknowledge publicly their mistake in *Gobitis*.

Thus, at least several justices were eager for another flag salute case. They found one in West Virginia, where Marie and Gathie Barnette were suspended from their elementary school for failing to salute the flag. Their case afforded the Court a chance to overrule *Gobitis*.

The case is important for two primary reasons: (1) it establishes that the First Amendment applies in public schools and protects public school students; and (2) it creates the compelled-speech doctrine. The compelled-speech doctrine means that government officials can violate the First Amendment by compelling individuals to engage in certain speech.

Mr. Justice JACKSON delivered the opinion of the Court.

Following the decision by this Court on June 3, 1940, in *Minersville School District v. Gobitis*,[1] the West Virginia legislature amended its statutes to require all schools therein to conduct courses of instruction in history, civics, and in the Constitutions of the United States and of the State "for the purpose of teaching, fostering and perpetuating

[1] The Supreme Court immediately addresses its decision in *Minersville School District v. Gobitis* (1940), in which the Court, by an 8–1 vote upheld a Pennsylvania flag salute law. The Court ruled that religious liberty must give way to political authority and national unity. In *Barnette*, the Court is reexamining the question.

the ideals, principles and spirit of Americanism, and increasing the knowledge of the organization and machinery of the government." Appellant Board of Education was directed, with advice of the State Superintendent of Schools, to "prescribe the courses of study covering these subjects" for public schools. The Act made it the duty of private, parochial and denominational schools to prescribe courses of study "similar to those required for the public schools."

The Board of Education on January 9, 1942, adopted a resolution containing recitals taken largely from the Court's *Gobitis* opinion and ordering that the salute to the flag become "a regular part of the program of activities in the public schools," that all teachers and pupils "shall be required to participate[2] in the salute honoring the Nation represented by the Flag; provided, however, that refusal to salute the Flag be regarded as an act of insubordination, and shall be dealt with accordingly." . . . What is now required is the "stiff-arm" salute, the saluter to keep the right hand raised with palm turned up while the following is repeated: "I pledge allegiance to the Flag of the United States of America and to the Republic for which it stands; one Nation, indivisible, with liberty and justice for all."

[2] Under the resolution, students had no choice but to participate in saluting the flag and reciting the Pledge of Allegiance. The Pledge of Allegiance was created in 1892, but the words "under God" were not added to the Pledge until 1954, 11 years after the Court's decision in *Barnette*.

Failure to conform is "insubordination," dealt with by expulsion.[3] Readmission is denied by statute until compliance. Meanwhile, the expelled child is "unlawfully absent," and may be proceeded against as a delinquent. His parents or guardians are liable to prosecution, and, if convicted, are subject to fine not exceeding $50 and jail term not exceeding thirty days.

[3] The punishment for violating the flag-salute requirement was severe. As the text of the decision indicates, a student failing to conform was expelled from school. Parents of those students were subject to 30 days in jail. These heavy punishments are hard to understand from a current perspective.

Appellees, citizens of the United States and of West Virginia, brought suit in the United States District Court for themselves and others similarly situated asking its injunction to restrain enforcement of these laws and regulations against Jehovah's Witnesses. The Witnesses are an unincorporated body teaching that the obligation imposed by law of God is superior to that of laws enacted by temporal government. Their religious beliefs include a literal version of Exodus, Chapter 20, verses 4 and 5, which says: "Thou shalt not make unto thee any graven image,[4] or any likeness of anything that is in heaven above, or that is in the earth beneath, or that is in the water under the earth; thou shalt not bow down thyself to them nor serve them." They consider that the flag is an "image" within this command. For this reason, they refuse to salute it. Children of this

[4] Jehovah's Witnesses believe that the flag is a "graven image" within the meaning of the biblical book of Exodus. The religious group believed that saluting the flag was bowing down to an earthly object in violation of their faith.

faith have been expelled from school and are threatened with exclusion for no other cause. Officials threaten to send them to reformatories maintained for criminally inclined juveniles. Parents of such children have been prosecuted and are threatened with prosecutions for causing delinquency.

This case calls upon us to reconsider a precedent[5] decision, as the Court throughout its history often has been required to do. Before turning to the *Gobitis* case, however, it is desirable to notice certain characteristics by which this controversy is distinguished.

. . .

As the present Chief Justice[6] said in dissent in the *Gobitis* case, the State may "require teaching by instruction and study of all in our history and in the structure and organization of our government, including the guaranties of civil liberty which tend to inspire patriotism and love of country." Here, however, we are dealing with a compulsion of students to declare a belief. They are not merely made acquainted with the flag salute so that they may be informed as to what it is or even what it means. . . .

There is no doubt that, in connection with the pledges, the flag salute is a form of utterance.[7] Symbolism is a primitive but effective way of communicating ideas. The use of an emblem or flag to symbolize some system, idea, institution, or personality is a short-cut from mind to mind. Causes and nations, political parties, lodges and ecclesiastical groups seek to knit the loyalty of their followings to a flag or banner, a color or design. The State announces rank, function, and authority through crowns and maces, uniforms and black robes; the church speaks through the Cross, the Crucifix, the altar and shrine, and clerical raiment. Symbols of State often convey political ideas, just as religious symbols come to convey theological ones. Associated with many of these symbols are appropriate gestures of acceptance or respect: a salute, a bowed or bared head, a bended knee. A person gets from a symbol the meaning he puts into it, and what is one man's comfort and inspiration is another's jest and scorn.

Over a decade ago, Chief Justice Hughes led this Court in holding that the display of a red flag[8] as a symbol of opposition by peaceful and legal means to organized government was protected by the free

[5] One of the foundational principles of American jurisprudence is *stare decisis*, a Latin phrase meaning "let the decision stand." *Stare decisis* means that courts generally respect precedent, or cases already on the books. However, adherence to *stare decisis* is not absolute; otherwise, the law would never evolve and change but instead would remain ossified in time.

[6] Justice Robert Jackson refers to Chief Justice Harlan Fiske Stone when he writes "the present Chief Justice." Justice Stone was appointed as an associate justice in 1925. In 1940 he was the lone dissenter in the *Gobitis* case. The next year, in 1941, President Franklin D. Roosevelt nominated him to be chief justice of the Supreme Court. He served as the chief justice until his death in 1946.

[7] The Supreme Court explains that saluting the flag is a form of utterance, or speech, protected by the First Amendment. This paragraph elaborates on the importance of symbolic speech.

[8] The Supreme Court ruled in *Stromberg v. California* (1931) that the display of the red flag, associated with communism, was a form of speech protected by the First Amendment. The Court reversed the conviction of Yetta Stromberg, a woman who was a counselor at a communist youth camp.

speech guaranties of the Constitution. *Stromberg v. California*, 283 U.S. 359. Here it is the State that employs a flag as a symbol of adherence to government as presently organized. It requires the individual to communicate by word and sign his acceptance of the political ideas it thus bespeaks. Objection to this form of communication when coerced is an old one, well known to the framers of the Bill of Rights.

It is also to be noted that the compulsory flag salute and pledge requires affirmation of a belief and an attitude of mind. It is not clear whether the regulation contemplates that pupils forego any contrary convictions of their own and become unwilling converts to the prescribed ceremony, or whether it will be acceptable if they simulate assent by words without belief, and by a gesture barren of meaning. It is now a commonplace that censorship or suppression of expression of opinion is tolerated by our Constitution only when the expression presents a clear and present danger[9] of action of a kind the State is empowered to prevent and punish. It would seem that involuntary affirmation could be commanded only on even more immediate and urgent grounds than silence. But here, the power of compulsion is invoked without any allegation that remaining passive during a flag salute ritual creates a clear and present danger that would justify an effort even to muffle expression. To sustain the compulsory flag salute, we are required to say that a Bill of Rights which guards the individual's right to speak his own mind left it open to public authorities to compel him to utter what is not in his mind.

[9] The "clear and present danger" standard used to be advanced only in the dissenting opinions of justices Oliver Wendell Holmes and Louis Brandeis. By 1943, the majority of the Supreme Court had accepted the "clear and present danger" test as the proper guide for evaluating restrictions on speech.

. . .

Nor does the issue, as we see it, turn on one's possession of particular religious views or the sincerity with which they are held. While religion supplies appellees' motive for enduring the discomforts of making the issue in this case, many citizens who do not share these religious views hold such a compulsory rite to infringe constitutional liberty of the individual. It is not necessary to inquire whether nonconformist beliefs will exempt from the duty to salute unless we first find power to make the salute a legal duty.

. . .

Government of limited power need not be anemic government. Assurance that rights are secure tends to diminish fear and jealousy of strong government, and, by making us feel safe to live under it, makes for its better support. Without promise of a limiting Bill of Rights,[10] it is doubtful if our Constitution could have mustered enough strength to enable its ratification. To enforce those rights today is not to choose weak government over strong government. It is only to adhere as a means of strength to individual freedom of mind in preference to officially disciplined uniformity for which history indicates a disappointing and disastrous end.

[10] The Supreme Court speaks of a "limiting Bill of Rights." The Bill of Rights prevents the power of government officials from restricting individual freedoms. The Court explains that the Constitution was ratified only after a promise was made to add a Bill of Rights to the end of the Constitution.

. . .

The Fourteenth Amendment, as now applied to the States, protects the citizen against the State itself and all of its creatures—Boards of Education not excepted. These have, of course, important, delicate, and highly discretionary functions, but none that they may not perform within the limits of the Bill of Rights. That they are educating the young for citizenship is reason for scrupulous protection of Constitutional freedoms[11] of the individual, if we are not to strangle the free mind at its source and teach youth to discount important principles of our government as mere platitudes.

[11] The Fourteenth Amendment extends the freedoms of the First Amendment to state and local governments, including school boards. This means that local school boards can violate the First Amendment just as much as can the federal government. The Court explains that because school officials are educating the young, they should take affirmative steps to ensure that young people appreciate the freedoms in the Bill of Rights. The *Barnette* decision is important because it means that the First Amendment applies in public schools.

. . .

The very purpose of a Bill of Rights was to withdraw certain subjects from the vicissitudes of political controversy,[12] to place them beyond the reach of majorities and officials, and to establish them as legal principles to be applied by the courts. One's right to life, liberty, and property, to free speech, a free press, freedom of worship and assembly, and other fundamental rights may not be submitted to vote; they depend on the outcome of no elections.

[12] This passage explains that the Bill of Rights is a counter-majoritarian document. This means that the Bill of Rights protects certain rights or freedoms even if the expression is unpopular with the majority.

In weighing arguments of the parties, it is important to distinguish between the due process clause of the Fourteenth Amendment as an instrument for transmitting the principles of the First Amendment and those cases in which it is applied for its own sake. The test of legislation which collides with the Fourteenth Amendment, because it also collides with the principles of the First, is much more definite than the test when only the Fourteenth is involved. Much of the vagueness of the due process clause disappears when the specific prohibitions of the First become its standard. The right of a State to regulate, for example, a public utility may well include, so far as the due process test is concerned, power to impose all of the restrictions which a legislature may have a "rational basis" for adopting. But freedoms of speech and of press, of assembly, and of worship may not be infringed on such slender grounds. They are susceptible of restriction only to prevent grave and immediate danger to interests which the state may lawfully protect. It is important to note that, while it is the Fourteenth Amendment which bears directly upon the State, it is the more specific limiting principles of the First Amendment that finally govern this case.

. . .

Lastly, and this is the very heart of the *Gobitis* opinion, it reasons that "National unity is the basis of national security,"[13] that the authorities have "the right to select appropriate means for its attainment," and hence reaches the conclusion that such compulsory measures toward "national unity" are constitutional. Upon the verity of this assumption depends our answer in this case.

[13] The basis of the *Gobitis* decision was that the flag salute was a necessary form of patriotism. Recall that these decisions occurred while the United States was involved in World War II. Patriotism and nationalism were valued highly through much of the country.

National unity, as an end which officials may foster by persuasion and example, is not in question. The problem is whether, under our Constitution, compulsion as here employed is a permissible means for its achievement.

. . .

It seems trite but necessary to say that the First Amendment to our Constitution was designed to avoid these ends by avoiding these beginnings. There is no mysticism in the American concept of the State or of the nature or origin of its authority. We set up government by consent of the governed,[14] and the Bill of Rights denies those in power any legal opportunity to coerce that consent. Authority here is to be controlled by public opinion, not public opinion by authority.

[14] The Constitution begins with the words "We the People." The Constitution supposedly sets up a limited government, and the ultimate power resides with the people. When the opinion text speaks of "consent of the governed," it means that the government exists by the will of the people.

The case is made difficult not because the principles of its decision are obscure, but because the flag involved is our own. Nevertheless, we apply the limitations of the Constitution with no fear that freedom to be intellectually and spiritually diverse or even contrary will disintegrate the social organization. To believe that patriotism will not flourish if patriotic ceremonies are voluntary and spontaneous, instead of a compulsory routine, is to make an unflattering estimate of the appeal of our institutions to free minds. We can have intellectual individualism and the rich cultural diversities that we owe to exceptional minds only at the price of occasional eccentricity and abnormal attitudes. When they are so harmless to others or to the State as those we deal with here, the price is not too great. But freedom to differ is not limited to things that do not matter much.[15] That would be a mere shadow of freedom. The test of its substance is the right to differ as to things that touch the heart of the existing order.

[15] The "freedom to differ" means little if people do not have the freedom to differ on the most important issues in society. Justice Jackson writes that if such freedom to differ does not exist, then there is a "mere shadow of freedom."

If there is any fixed star in our constitutional constellation,[16] it is that no official, high or petty, can prescribe what shall be orthodox in politics, nationalism, religion, or other matters of opinion, or force citizens to confess by word or act their faith therein. If there are any circumstances which permit an exception, they do not now occur to us.

[16] The passage about the "fixed star in our constitutional constellation" is one of the most valued in all of constitutional law. It means that the government cannot force people what to believe; it cannot compel people to adopt certain religious beliefs or to engage in nationalism.

We think the action of the local authorities in compelling the flag salute and pledge transcends constitutional limitations on their power and invades the sphere of intellect[17] and spirit which it is the purpose of the First Amendment to our Constitution to reserve from all official control.

[17] The Court concluded in *Barnette* that forcing the Jehovah's Witness children to salute the flag and recite the Pledge invaded their private sphere of belief.

The decision of this Court in *Minersville School District v. Gobitis*, and the holdings of those few per curiam decisions which preceded and foreshadowed it, are overruled, and the judgment enjoining enforcement of the West Virginia Regulation is

AFFIRMED.

Source: *West Virginia State Board of Education v. Barnette*, 319 U.S. 624 (1943).

Margaret Chase Smith's "Declaration of Conscience" Speech

June 1, 1950

INTRODUCTION

Margaret Chase Smith (1897–1995) was the first woman to serve in both the U.S. House of Representatives and the U.S. Senate. She represented her home state of Maine in the Senate from 1949 until 1973.

One of her most famous moments occurred on June 1, 1950, when she delivered her memorable "Declaration of Conscience" speech criticizing the behavior of fellow Republican senator Joseph McCarthy. Senator McCarthy had embarked on a vigorous campaign of exposing people he believed were communists and communist sympathizers. He ushered in an age of blacklisting and paranoia known pejoratively as "McCarthyism."

Senator Smith objected to these practices with eloquence.

Mr. President: I would like to speak briefly and simply about a serious national condition. It is a national feeling of fear and frustration that could result in national suicide and the end of everything that we Americans hold dear. It is a condition that comes from the lack of effective leadership in either the Legislative Branch or the Executive Branch of our Government.

That leadership is so lacking that serious and responsible proposals are being made that national advisory commissions be appointed to provide such critically needed leadership.

I speak as briefly as possible because too much harm has already been done with irresponsible words of bitterness and selfish political opportunism. I speak as simply as possible because the issue is too great to be obscured by eloquence. I speak simply and briefly in the hope that my words will be taken to heart.

Mr. President, I speak as a Republican. I speak as a woman. I speak as a United States Senator. I speak as an American.

The United States Senate has long enjoyed worldwide respect as the greatest deliberative body in the world. But recently that deliberative character has too often been debased to the level of a forum of hate and character assassination sheltered by the shield of congressional immunity.

It is ironical that we senators can in debate in the Senate, directly or indirectly, by any form of words, impute to any American who is not a senator any conduct or motive unworthy or unbecoming an American—and without that non-senator American having any legal redress against us—yet if we say the same thing in the Senate about our colleagues we can be stopped on the grounds of being out of order.

It is strange that we can verbally attack anyone else without restraint and with full protection, and yet we hold ourselves above the same type of criticism here on the Senate floor. Surely the United States Senate is big enough to take self-criticism and self-appraisal. Surely we should be able to take the same kind of character attacks that we dish out to outsiders.

I think that it is high time for the United States Senate and its members to do some real soul searching and to weigh our consciences as to the manner in which we are performing our duty to the people of America and the manner in which we are using or abusing our individual powers and privileges.

I think that it is high time that we remembered that we have sworn to uphold and defend the Constitution. I think that it is high time that we remembered that the Constitution, as amended, speaks not only of the freedom of speech but also of trial by jury instead of trial by accusation.[1]

[1] Smith notes that the Constitution protects not only the freedom of speech in the First Amendment but also the right to trial by jury. People charged with crimes are entitled to the presumption of innocence. Senator McCarthy employed a tactic known as "guilt by association." He also routinely accused people of being communists without having any real proof.

Whether it be a criminal prosecution in court or a character prosecution in the Senate, there is little practical distinction when the life of a person has been ruined.

Those of us who shout the loudest about Americanism in making character assassinations are all too frequently those who, by our own words and acts, ignore some of the basic principles of Americanism—

The right to criticize.

The right to hold unpopular beliefs.

The right to protest.

The right of independent thought.[2]

[2] The First Amendment protects all of these rights. The First Amendment would be a most hollow document if it only protected thoughts or beliefs held by a majority of the citizens. It has been said that the Bill of Rights is a counter-majoritarian document, because it uniquely protects the rights of the minority from majority rule.

The exercise of these rights should not cost one single American citizen his reputation or his right to a livelihood nor should he be in danger of losing his reputation or livelihood merely because he happens to know someone who holds unpopular beliefs. Who of us does not? Otherwise none of us could call our souls our own. Otherwise thought control would have set in.

The American people are sick and tired of being afraid to speak their minds lest they be politically smeared as "Communists" or "Fascists" by their opponents. Freedom of speech is not what it used to be in America.[3] It has been so abused by some that it is not exercised by others. The American people are sick and tired of seeing innocent people smeared and guilty people whitewashed. But there have been enough proved cases . . . to cause nationwide distrust and strong suspicion that there may be something to the unproved, sensational accusations.

[3] Smith and several other moderate Republicans believed that many people feared to exercise their free-speech rights in this type of political climate of fear and fearmongering.

As a Republican, I say to my colleagues on this side of the aisle that the Republican Party faces a challenge today that is not unlike the challenge that it faced back in Lincoln's day. The Republican Party so successfully met that challenge that it emerged from the Civil War as the champion of a united nation[4]—in addition to being a party that unrelentingly fought loose spending and loose programs.

[4] The Republican Party still today touts itself as "the Party of Lincoln" responsible for saving the nation, freeing the slaves, and uniting the country. Senator Smith asserts this legacy and contends that some in her own party are not acting according to this noble tradition.

. . .

Surely these are sufficient reasons to make it clear to the American people that it is time for a change and that a Republican victory is necessary to the security of this country. Surely it is clear that this nation will continue to suffer as long as it is governed by the present ineffective Democratic administration.

Yet to displace it with a Republican regime embracing a philosophy that lacks political integrity or intellectual honesty would prove equally disastrous to this nation. The nation sorely needs a Republican victory. But I do not want to see the Republican Party ride to political victory on the Four Horsemen of Calumny—Fear, Ignorance, Bigotry and Smear.

I doubt if the Republican Party could do so, simply because I don't believe the American people will uphold any political party that puts political exploitation above national interest. Surely we Republicans are not that desperate for victory.

I do not want to see the Republican Party win that way. While it might be a fleeting victory for the Republican Party, it would be a more lasting defeat for the American people. Surely it would ultimately be suicide for the Republican Party and the two-party system that has protected our American liberties from the dictatorship of a one-party system.

As members of the minority party, we do not have the primary authority to formulate the policy of our government. But we do have the responsibility of rendering constructive criticism, of clarifying issues, of allaying fears by acting as responsible citizens.

As a woman, I wonder how the mothers, wives, sisters and daughters feel about the way in which members of their families have been politically mangled in Senate debate—and I use the word "debate" advisedly.

As a United States senator, I am not proud of the way in which the Senate has been made a publicity platform for irresponsible sensationalism. I am not proud of the reckless abandon in which unproved charges have been hurled from this side of the aisle.[5] I am not proud of the obviously staged, undignified countercharges that have been attempted in retaliation from the other side of the aisle.

[5] Smith never named her fellow senator Joseph McCarthy by name in her speech but everyone knew who she was referring to when she spoke about "unproved charges" and "reckless abandon." McCarthy was unbowed by the criticism and referred to Smith and the six other Republicans who signed on to her speech as "Snow White and the Six Dwarves."

I do not like the way the Senate has been made a rendezvous for vilification, for selfish political gain at the sacrifice of individual reputations and national unity. I am not proud of the way we smear outsiders from the floor of the Senate and hide behind the cloak of congressional immunity and still place ourselves beyond criticism on the floor of the Senate.

As an American, I am shocked at the way Republicans and Democrats alike are playing directly into the Communist design of "confuse, divide, and conquer." As an American, I do not want a Democratic administration "whitewash" or "coverup" any more than I want a Republican smear or witch hunt.

As an American, I condemn a Republican Fascist just as much as I condemn a Democrat Communist. I condemn a Democrat Fascist just as much as I condemn a Republican Communist. They are equally dangerous to you and me and to our country. As an American, I want to see our nation recapture the strength and unity it once had when we fought the enemy instead of ourselves.

It is with these thoughts that I have drafted what I call a Declaration of Conscience. I am gratified that Senator Tobey, Senator Aiken, Senator Morse, Senator Ives, Senator Thye and Senator Hendrickson[6] have concurred in that declaration and have authorized me to announce their concurrence.

[6] The six fellow Republican senators who signed on to her speech were Charles Tobey of New Hampshire, George Aiken of Vermont, Wayne Morse of Oregon, Irving Ives of New York, Edward Thye of Minnesota, and Robert C. Hendrickson of New Jersey.

CONCLUSION

By 1953, Republican leaders were growing wary of McCarthy and his investigations. After a disastrous investigation of the Army, McCarthy lost face and was censured by the Senate. Senator Margaret Chase Smith voted for the censure.

Source: *Congressional Record*, 81st Congress, 2nd Session, pp. 7894–7895.

Talley v. California

March 7, 1960

INTRODUCTION

One of the more underappreciated U.S. Supreme Court First Amendment decisions is *Talley v. California*. In this decision, the Court explained that anonymous speech is protected by the First Amendment.

The case concerned the distribution of anonymous handbills by Manuel Talley, the founder of the Los Angeles chapter of the Congress on Racial Equality (CORE), a significant civil rights organization. Talley organized a boycott of businesses that practiced racial discrimination. Talley's handbills stated, "I believe that every man should have an equal opportunity for employment no matter what his race, religion, or place of birth."

Officials charged him with violating a 1932 ordinance that prohibited anonymous handbills. Talley contended that the ordinance violated his First Amendment free-speech rights. The U.S. Supreme Court agreed in an opinion authored by Justice Hugo Black, who emphasized the importance of anonymous speech during the 18th century at the founding of the country and the Constitution.

MR. JUSTICE BLACK delivered the opinion of the Court.

The question presented here is whether the provisions of a Los Angeles City ordinance restricting the distribution of handbills[1] "abridge the freedom of speech and of the press secured against state invasion by the Fourteenth Amendment of the Constitution." The ordinance . . . provides:

"No person shall distribute any hand-bill in any place under any circumstances, which does not have printed on the cover, or the face thereof, the name and address of the following:

"(a) The person who printed, wrote, compiled or manufactured the same.

"(b) The person who caused the same to be distributed; provided, however, that in the case of a fictitious person or club, in addition to such fictitious name, the true names and addresses of the owners, managers or agents of the person sponsoring said hand-bill shall also appear thereon."

[1] Handbills—small, printed pamphlets or flyers—are a time-honored way of communication. The U.S. Supreme Court made several decisions protecting the right of Jehovah's Witnesses to distribute handbills on public streets. Here, Mr. Talley wanted to distribute handbills to protest businesses that practiced racial discrimination.

The petitioner was arrested and tried in a Los Angeles Municipal Court for violating this ordinance. It was stipulated that the petitioner had distributed handbills in Los Angeles, and two of them were presented in evidence. . . .

The handbills urged readers to help the organization carry on a boycott against certain merchants and businessmen, whose names were given, on the ground that, as one set of handbills said, they carried products of "manufacturers who will not offer equal employment opportunities to Negroes, Mexicans, and Orientals." . . .

The Municipal Court held that the information printed on the handbills did not meet the requirements of the ordinance, found the petitioner guilty as charged, and fined him $10. The Appellate Department of the Superior Court of the County of Los Angeles affirmed the conviction, rejecting petitioner's contention, timely made in both state courts, that the ordinance invaded his freedom of speech and press in violation of the Fourteenth and First Amendments to the Federal Constitution. Since this was the highest state court available to petitioner, we granted certiorari to consider this constitutional contention.

In Lovell v. Griffin,[2] we held void on its face an ordinance that comprehensively forbade any distribution of literature at any time or place in Griffin, Georgia, without a license. Pamphlets and leaflets, it was pointed out, "have been historic weapons in the defense of liberty" and enforcement of the Griffin ordinance "would restore the system of license and censorship in its baldest form." A year later we had before us four ordinances each forbidding distribution of leaflets—one in Irvington, New Jersey, one in Los Angeles, California, one in Milwaukee, Wisconsin, and one in Worcester, Massachusetts. Efforts were made to distinguish these four ordinances from the one held void in the Griffin case. The chief grounds urged for distinction were that the four ordinances had been passed to prevent either frauds, disorder, or littering, according to the records in these cases, and another ground urged was that two of the ordinances applied only to certain city areas. This Court refused to uphold the four ordinances on those grounds pointing out that there were other ways to accomplish these legitimate aims without abridging freedom of speech and press. Frauds, street littering and disorderly conduct could be denounced and punished as offenses, the Court said. . . .

[2] The cases Justice Black refers to in this paragraph are *Lovell v. Griffin* (1938) and *Schneider v. State* (1939). These cases involved Jehovah's Witnesses seeking to distribute religious handbills in towns or cities that restricted the distribution of such materials. In these decisions, the Court recognized the importance of the distribution of handbills.

This ordinance simply bars all handbills under all circumstances[3] anywhere that do not have the names and addresses printed on them in the place the ordinance requires.

There can be no doubt that such an identification requirement would tend to restrict freedom to distribute information and thereby freedom of expression. "Liberty of circulating is as essential to that freedom as liberty of publishing; indeed, without the circulation, the publication would be of little value."

Anonymous pamphlets, leaflets, brochures and even books have played an important role in the progress of mankind.[4] Persecuted groups and sects from time to time throughout history have been able to criticize oppressive practices and laws either anonymously or not at all. The obnoxious press licensing law of England, which was also enforced on the Colonies was due in part to the knowledge that exposure of the names of printers, writers and distributors would lessen the circulation of literature critical of the government. The old seditious libel cases in England show the lengths to which government had to go to find out who was responsible for books that were obnoxious to the rulers. . . . Even the Federalist Papers,[5] written in favor of the adoption of our Constitution, were published under fictitious names. It is plain that anonymity has sometimes been assumed for the most constructive purposes.

We have recently had occasion to hold in two cases that there are times and circumstances when States may not compel members of groups engaged in the dissemination of ideas to be publicly identified. The reason for those holdings was that identification and fear of reprisal might deter perfectly peaceful discussions of public matters of importance. This broad Los Angeles ordinance is subject to the same infirmity. We hold that it, like the Griffin, Georgia, ordinance, is void on its face.

The judgment of the Appellate Department of the Superior Court of the State of California is reversed and the cause is remanded to it for further proceedings not inconsistent with this opinion.

It is so ordered.

Source: *Talley v. California*, 362 U.S. 60 (1960).

[3] By barring all anonymous handbills, this ordinance differs in kind from the Jehovah's Witness cases in *Lovell* and *Schneider*. In First Amendment law, total bans on a medium of communication are reviewed with suspicion and often are invalidated.

[4] The chief importance of the *Talley* decision is its protection of anonymous speech. The Court explains that anonymous speech was important during the Revolutionary War era, as individuals often criticized the Crown anonymously.

[5] Perhaps the finest examples of anonymous speech were the Federalist Papers, the 85 essays written by John Jay, James Madison, and Alexander Hamilton. The papers were instrumental in leading to the ratification of the United States Constitution.

Edwards v. South Carolina

February 25, 1963

INTRODUCTION

A dynamic and courageous social campaign known as the civil rights movement fundamentally changed the United States of America. Individuals, even young people and children, took their cause to the streets in mass collective action. Nonviolent direct action became a common mode of expression. These committed activists exercised their First Amendment rights in their most pristine form. They protested, picketed, and petitioned. They assembled and marched on state capitals and the U.S. capital.

Many government officials, particularly southern city leaders and police chiefs, reacted with repression and even violence. They denied parade permits, arrested marchers, and even used fire hoses, dogs, and extrajudicial means of punishment to attempt to silence these voices. Many of these controversies led to legal battles that caused the courts to interpret the First Amendment.

An example of this occurred when 187 African American students, including James Edwards, marched to the statehouse in Columbia, South Carolina, to protest segregation laws. They were arrested for "breach of the peace." State courts affirmed their convictions.

But the U.S. Supreme Court reversed in *Edwards v. South Carolina* (1963), in an 8–1 opinion written by Justice Potter Stewart. The Court majority recognized that the protesters were engaging in a classic exercise of protected constitutional freedoms.

MR. JUSTICE STEWART delivered the opinion of the Court.

The petitioners, 187 in number, were convicted in a magistrate's court in Columbia, South Carolina, of the common-law crime of breach of the peace.[1] Their convictions were ultimately affirmed by the South Carolina Supreme Court. We granted certiorari to consider the claim that these convictions cannot be squared with the Fourteenth Amendment of the United States Constitution.

There was no substantial conflict in the trial evidence. Late in the morning of March 2, 1961, the petitioners, high school and college

[1] Breach of the peace, or disorderly conduct, was the common criminal charge imposed on civil rights protesters during the 1960s. The problem with many of these charges is that they were imposed selectively. The ordinances often called for law enforcement to exercise much discretion. For example, in the *Edwards* case, the protesters acted peacefully, yet they were charged with "breach of the peace."

students of the Negro race, met at the Zion Baptist Church[2] in Columbia. From there, at about noon, they walked in separate groups of about 15 to the South Carolina State House grounds, an area of two city blocks open to the general public. Their purpose was "to submit a protest to the citizens of South Carolina, along with the Legislative Bodies of South Carolina, our feelings and our dissatisfaction with the present condition of discriminatory actions against Negroes, in general, and to let them know that we were dissatisfied and that we would like for the laws which prohibited Negro privileges in this State to be removed."

[2] The church was intimately involved in the civil rights movement. Many of the movement's leaders were church leaders, such as the Rev. Martin Luther King Jr. and the Rev. Fred Shuttlesworth. The church also was instrumental in advocating the approach known as nonviolent direct action, explained by Dr. King in his influential "Letter from a Birmingham Jail."

Already on the State House grounds when the petitioners arrived were 30 or more law enforcement officers, who had advance knowledge that the petitioners were coming. Each group of petitioners entered the grounds through a driveway and parking area known in the record as the "horseshoe." As they entered, they were told by the law enforcement officials that "they had a right, as a citizen, to go through the State House grounds, as any other citizen has, as long as they were peaceful." During the next half hour or 45 minutes, the petitioners, in the same small groups, walked single file or two abreast in an orderly way through the grounds, each group carrying placards bearing such messages as "I am proud to be a Negro" and "Down with segregation."[3]

[3] The most odious aspect of the societal structure in America, particularly in the South, was segregation laws. These laws mandated that blacks had to use facilities separate from whites. Most of the time, the facilities used by blacks were significantly inferior to the facilities provided to whites.

During this time a crowd of some 200 to 300 onlookers had collected in the horseshoe area and on the adjacent sidewalks. There was no evidence to suggest that these onlookers were anything but curious, and no evidence at all of any threatening remarks, hostile gestures, or offensive language on the part of any member of the crowd. The City Manager testified that he recognized some of the onlookers, whom he did not identify, as "possible trouble makers," but his subsequent testimony made clear that nobody among the crowd actually caused or threatened any trouble. There was no obstruction of pedestrian or vehicular traffic within the State House grounds. No vehicle was prevented from entering or leaving the horseshoe area. Although vehicular traffic at a nearby street intersection was slowed down somewhat, an officer was dispatched to keep traffic moving. There were a number of bystanders on the public sidewalks adjacent to the State House grounds, but they all moved on when asked to do so, and there was no impediment of pedestrian traffic. Police protection at the scene was at all times sufficient to meet any foreseeable possibility of disorder.

In the situation and under the circumstances thus described, the police authorities advised the petitioners that they would be arrested if they did not disperse within 15 minutes. Instead of dispersing, the petitioners engaged in what the City Manager described as "boisterous," "loud," and "flamboyant" conduct, which, as his later testimony made clear, consisted of listening to a "religious harangue" by one of their leaders, and loudly singing "The Star Spangled Banner" and other patriotic and religious songs, while stamping their feet and clapping their hands. After 15 minutes had passed, the police arrested the petitioners and marched them off to jail.

Upon this evidence the state trial court convicted the petitioners of breach of the peace, and imposed sentences ranging from a $10 fine or five days in jail, to a $100 fine or 30 days in jail. In affirming the judgments, the Supreme Court of South Carolina said that under the law of that State the offense of breach of the peace "is not susceptible of exact definition," but that the "general definition of the offense" is as follows:

"In general terms, a breach of the peace is a violation of public order, a disturbance of the public tranquility, by any act or conduct inciting to violence . . . , it includes any violation of any law enacted to preserve peace and good order. It may consist of an act of violence or an act likely to produce violence. It is not necessary that the peace be actually broken to lay the foundation for a prosecution for this offense. If what is done is unjustifiable and unlawful, tending with sufficient directness to break the peace, no more is required. Nor is actual personal violence an essential element in the offense. . . .

"By 'peace,' as used in the law in this connection, is meant the tranquility enjoyed by citizens of a municipality or community where good order reigns among its members, which is the natural right of all persons in political society."

The petitioners contend that there was a complete absence of any evidence of the commission of this offense, and that they were thus denied one of the most basic elements of due process of law. Whatever the merits of this contention, we need not pass upon it in the present case. The state courts have held that the petitioners' conduct constituted breach of the peace under state law, and we may accept their decision as binding upon us to that extent. But it nevertheless remains our duty in a case such as this to make an independent examination of the whole record. And it is clear to us that in arresting, convicting, and punishing the petitioners under the circumstances disclosed by this record, South Carolina infringed the petitioners' constitutionally protected rights of free speech, free assembly, and freedom to petition[4] for redress of their grievances.

It has long been established that these First Amendment freedoms are protected by the Fourteenth Amendment from invasion by the States. The circumstances in this case reflect an exercise of these basic constitutional rights in their most pristine and classic form.[5] The petitioners felt aggrieved by laws of South Carolina which allegedly "prohibited Negro privileges in this State." They peaceably assembled at the site of the State Government and there peaceably expressed their grievances "to the citizens of South Carolina, along with the Legislative Bodies of South Carolina." Not until they were told by police officials that they must disperse on pain of arrest did they do more. Even then, they but sang patriotic and religious songs after one of their leaders had delivered a "religious harangue." There was no violence or threat of violence on their part, or on the part of any member of the crowd watching them. Police protection was "ample."

This, therefore, was a far cry from the situation in *Feiner v. New York* . . . where two policemen were faced with a crowd which was "pushing, shoving and milling around," where at least one member of the crowd "threatened violence if the police did not act," where "the crowd was pressing closer around petitioner and the officer," and where "the speaker passes the bounds of argument or persuasion and undertakes incitement to riot." And the record is barren of any evidence of "fighting words."[6]

We do not review in this case criminal convictions resulting from the evenhanded application of a precise and narrowly drawn regulatory statute evincing a legislative judgment that certain specific conduct be limited or proscribed. If, for example, the petitioners had been convicted upon evidence that they had violated a law regulating traffic, or had disobeyed a law reasonably limiting the periods during which the State House grounds were open to the public, this would be a different case. These petitioners were convicted of an offense so generalized as to be, in the words of the South Carolina Supreme Court, "not susceptible of exact definition." And they were

[4] The Court finds that South Carolina officials violated three different First Amendment freedoms of the protesters—freedom of speech, freedom of assembly, and freedom of petition. The rights of assembly and petition often go hand in hand, as those who gather together and march often have a message they wish to deliver to government officials. Furthermore, assembly and petition are often related to freedom of speech.

[5] Sometimes in First Amendment cases, the claimant asserting a violation of rights has to make the case that he or she was actually engaged in expressive conduct. That was not the case here. The petitioners were clearly exercising their First Amendment freedoms.

[6] The U.S. Supreme Court defined "fighting words" as words that inflict injury or incite an immediate breach of the peace. Fighting words normally involve direct, face-to-face, personal insults. Here, the civil rights protesters were merely singing religious hymns and carrying signs against segregation.

convicted upon evidence which showed no more than that the opinions which they were peaceably expressing were sufficiently opposed to the views of the majority of the community to attract a crowd and necessitate police protection.

The Fourteenth Amendment does not permit a State to make criminal the peaceful expression of unpopular views.[7] "[A] function of free speech under our system of government is to invite dispute. It may indeed best serve its high purpose when it induces a condition of unrest, creates dissatisfaction with conditions as they are, or even stirs people to anger. Speech is often provocative and challenging. It may strike at prejudices and preconceptions and have profound unsettling effects as it presses for acceptance of an idea. That is why freedom of speech . . . is . . . protected against censorship or punishment, unless shown likely to produce a clear and present danger of a serious substantive evil that rises far above public inconvenience, annoyance, or unrest. . . . There is no room under our Constitution for a more restrictive view. For the alternative would lead to standardization of ideas either by legislatures, courts, or dominant political or community groups." As in the *Terminiello* case, the courts of South Carolina have defined a criminal offense so as to permit conviction of the petitioners if their speech "stirred people to anger, invited public dispute, or brought about a condition of unrest. A conviction resting on any of those grounds may not stand."

[7] This may be the most oft-quoted language from the *Edwards* decision. It captures the plight of these protesters, who were arrested for their peaceful protest of segregation policies.

As Chief Justice Hughes wrote in *Stromberg v. California*, "The maintenance of the opportunity for free political discussion to the end that government may be responsive to the will of the people and that changes may be obtained by lawful means, an opportunity essential to the security of the Republic, is a fundamental principle of our constitutional system. A statute which upon its face, and as authoritatively construed, is so vague[8] and indefinite as to permit the punishment of the fair use of this opportunity is repugnant to the guaranty of liberty contained in the Fourteenth Amendment. . . ."

[8] Vagueness is an important concept in constitutional law. If a law is too vague, it does not give adequate notice to persons as to when their conduct is unlawful and when it is lawful. Vague laws pose a special threat to First Amendment freedoms, as people may refrain from exercising their free-speech rights for fear of being arrested. This is called a "chilling effect."

For these reasons we conclude that these criminal convictions cannot stand.

Reversed.

Source: *Edwards v. South Carolina,* 372 U.S. 229 (1963).

New York Times Co. v. Sullivan

March 9, 1964

INTRODUCTION

One of the most important decisions in American history is *New York Times Co. v. Sullivan*. The Court's decision not only constitutionalized libel law, but it also saved the civil rights movement. The case began when the *New York Times* published an editorial advertisement titled "Heed Their Rising Voices." The advertisement featured descriptions of human rights abuses in Montgomery, Alabama.

L. B. Sullivan, a city commissioner in charge of the police department, sued the newspaper and four clergymen who signed the ad, for libel. Libel is a false statement of fact that harms someone's reputation. Sullivan contended that errors in the ad made false statements about the police department and him—even though he was not named in the article.

Sullivan sued in an Alabama state court; the jury awarded him $500,000. The Alabama appellate courts upheld the verdict. The *Times'* last chance was an appeal to the U.S. Supreme Court, which granted review.

The Court explained that newspapers and individuals need the ability to criticize public officials without fearing that every mistake could lead to crushing liability. Otherwise, people would steer far clear of making any controversial statements. The Court established a new standard that public officials would have to meet in order to recover damages for libel.

The case was also important because at the time of this lawsuit, there were many lawsuits against various media entities for coverage of civil rights abuses. If the *New York Times* lost its appeal, then many of those media entities probably would have quit reporting on these abuses to avoid lawsuits. That is why the case saved the civil rights movement.

MR. JUSTICE BRENNAN delivered the opinion of the Court.

We are required in this case to determine for the first time the extent to which the constitutional protections for speech and press limit a State's power to award damages in a libel action[1] brought by a public official against critics of his official conduct.

[1] The term "libel" refers to a false statement of fact that harms an individual's reputation. Libel and slander are forms of defamation. Libel generally means written defamation, while slander refers to oral defamation. Traditionally, libel law was governed purely by state law without any regard for the First Amendment. In this case, the Court examines whether state libel laws must comport with the First Amendment.

Respondent L. B. Sullivan[2] is one of the three elected Commissioners of the City of Montgomery, Alabama. He testified that he was "Commissioner of Public Affairs and the duties are supervision of the Police Department, Fire Department, Department of Cemetery and Department of Scales." He brought this civil libel action against the four individual petitioners, who are Negroes and Alabama clergymen, and against petitioner the New York Times Company, a New York corporation which publishes the New York Times, a daily newspaper. A jury in the Circuit Court of Montgomery County awarded him damages of $500,000, the full amount claimed, against all the petitioners, and the Supreme Court of Alabama affirmed.

[2] L. B. Sullivan was a Montgomery commissioner in charge of the police department. He sued the *New York Times* and four clergymen—Ralph Abernathy, S. S. Seay, Fred Shuttlesworth, and Joseph Lowry. Sullivan contended that certain statements in an editorial advertisement published in the *New York Times* defamed him. He sued in an Alabama state court, and a jury awarded him $500,000. The Alabama appeals courts affirmed the trial court's action. The *New York Times* then appealed to the U.S. Supreme Court.

Respondent's complaint alleged that he had been libeled by statements in a full-page advertisement that was carried in the New York Times on March 29, 1960. Entitled "Heed Their Rising Voices,"[3] the advertisement began by stating that "As the whole world knows by now, thousands of Southern Negro students are engaged in widespread non-violent demonstrations in positive affirmation of the right to live in human dignity as guaranteed by the U.S. Constitution and the Bill of Rights." It went on to charge that "in their efforts to uphold these guarantees, they are being met by an unprecedented wave of terror by those who would deny and negate that document which the whole world looks upon as setting the pattern for modern freedom. . . ." Succeeding paragraphs purported to illustrate the "wave of terror" by describing certain alleged events. The text concluded with an appeal for funds for three purposes: support of the student movement, "the struggle for the right-to-vote," and the legal defense of Dr. Martin Luther King, Jr., leader of the movement, against a perjury indictment then pending in Montgomery.

[3] The editorial advertisement in question was titled "Heed Their Rising Voices." It talked about "Southern violators" of human rights that took place on the Alabama State campus. It also spoke about a "wave of terror" against the student movement for civil rights. Unfortunately, there were several errors in the advertisement. The school campus was not "ringed with tear gas," cafeteria doors were not padlocked, and Dr. Martin Luther King Jr. was arrested four times, not seven times. In other words, L. B. Sullivan and his lawyers were correct—there were false statements of fact in the advertisement.

. . .

Although neither of these statements mentions respondent by name,[4] he contended that the word "police" in the third paragraph referred to him as the Montgomery Commissioner who supervised the Police Department, so that he was being accused of "ringing" the campus with police. He further claimed that the paragraph would be read as imputing to the police, and hence to him, the padlocking of the dining hall in order to starve the students into submission.

[4] A key question in the case is whether L. B. Sullivan could sue for libel even though he was not named in the advertisement. A key requirement in defamation cases is that the plaintiff—the person suing—must show that he or she was identified. Identification does not necessarily have to name the person, but there must be some means by which third parties would know that the allegedly false statements refer to a specific person or persons.

. . .

The trial judge submitted the case to the jury under instructions that the statements in the advertisement were "libelous per se" and were not privileged, so that petitioners might be held liable if the jury found that they had published the advertisement and that the statements were made "of and concerning"[5] respondent.

. . .

We may dispose at the outset of two grounds asserted to insulate the judgment of the Alabama courts from constitutional scrutiny. The first is the proposition relied on by the State Supreme Court—that "The Fourteenth Amendment is directed against State action[6] and not private action." That proposition has no application to this case. Although this is a civil lawsuit between private parties, the Alabama courts have applied a state rule of law which petitioners claim to impose invalid restrictions on their constitutional freedoms of speech and press. It matters not that that law has been applied in a civil action and that it is common law only, though supplemented by statute. The test is not the form in which state power has been applied but, whatever the form, whether such power has in fact been exercised.

The second contention is that the constitutional guarantees of freedom of speech and of the press are inapplicable here, at least so far as the Times is concerned, because the allegedly libelous statements were published as part of a paid, "commercial" advertisement.[7] The argument relies on *Valentine v. Chrestensen*, where the Court held that a city ordinance forbidding street distribution of commercial and business advertising matter did not abridge the First Amendment freedoms, even as applied to a handbill having a commercial message on one side but a protest against certain official action on the other. The reliance is wholly misplaced. The Court in *Chrestensen* reaffirmed the constitutional protection for "the freedom of communicating information and disseminating opinion"; its holding was based upon the factual conclusions that the handbill was "purely commercial advertising" and that the protest against official action had been added only to evade the ordinance.

. . .

Thus we consider this case against the background of a profound national commitment to the principle that debate on public issues

[5] The "of and concerning" requirement means that the allegedly defamatory statements must be about the plaintiff. This is another way of stating the identification requirement in this type of case.

[6] Sullivan's lawyers argued that the First Amendment did not apply in this case, because there was no state action. The state-action doctrine is a principle that limits the Bill of Rights (including the First Amendment) as protecting infringements by governmental, or state, actors instead of private actors. However, the Court explains that the state-action principle is satisfied because the Alabama state courts applied "a state rule of law." This state rule of law satisfies the state-action requirement.

[7] L. B. Sullivan argued that the *New York Times* had no First Amendment–based defense for this libel action, because the editorial advertisement was a form of commercial speech. This seemed like a decent argument, because at that time, purely commercial advertising did not receive any free-speech protection. It was not until 1976 that the U.S. Supreme Court first ruled that commercial advertising was entitled to some free-speech protection. In this case, the U.S. Supreme Court sidestepped the commercial speech rule by explaining that "Heed Their Rising Voices" was not a commercial advertisement but instead a form of political speech about a pressing issue in the United States—civil rights.

[8]The written statement by Justice Brennan explaining that "debate on public issues should be uninhibited, robust, and wide-open" is one of the most oft-quoted in all of First Amendment jurisprudence. Brennan explains that in a free society, individuals have a right to criticize government and public officials. In fact, this represents the core type of speech that the First Amendment was designed to protect.

[9] Justice Brennan explains that we often must protect erroneous statements in order to provide "breathing space" to speakers and free speech in general. The Court once again refers to "breathing space" years later in *Hustler Magazine v. Falwell* (1988).

[10] Notice that Justice Brennan refers to the Sedition Act of 1798. He explains that many Americans first thought deeply about the meaning of free speech and the First Amendment when there were prosecutions under the Sedition Act. Brennan later explains that the Sedition Act of 1798 did not comport with the First Amendment.

[11] Criminal libel laws are not the only way that people can be deterred from engaging in critical speech. Justice Brennan explains here that damage awards in a civil lawsuit (like the defamation lawsuit against the *New York Times*) can deter speech every bit as much as a criminal libel law.

[12] A rule mandating that every statement be true would cause individuals to avoid any controversial statements. This would lead to what Justice Brennan refers to here as "self-censorship." That would not protect political speech consistent with the First Amendment.

should be uninhibited, robust, and wide-open,[8] and that it may well include vehement, caustic, and sometimes unpleasantly sharp attacks on government and public officials. . . .

. . .

That erroneous statement is inevitable in free debate,[9] and that it must be protected if the freedoms of expression are to have the "breathing space" that they "need . . . to survive." . . .

. . .

If neither factual error nor defamatory content suffices to remove the constitutional shield from criticism of official conduct, the combination of the two elements is no less inadequate. This is the lesson to be drawn from the great controversy over the Sedition Act of 1798,[10] which first crystallized a national awareness of the central meaning of the First Amendment. . . .

. . .

Although the Sedition Act was never tested in this Court, the attack upon its validity has carried the day in the court of history. Fines levied in its prosecution were repaid by Act of Congress on the ground that it was unconstitutional.

. . .

What a State may not constitutionally bring about by means of a criminal statute is likewise beyond the reach of its civil law of libel. The fear of damage awards[11] under a rule such as that invoked by the Alabama courts here may be markedly more inhibiting than the fear of prosecution under a criminal statute.

. . .

A rule compelling the critic of official conduct to guarantee the truth of all his factual assertions—and to do so on pain of libel judgments virtually unlimited in amount—leads to a comparable "self-censorship."[12] Allowance of the defense of truth, with the burden of proving it on the defendant, does not mean that only false speech will be deterred. Even courts accepting this defense as an adequate safeguard have recognized the difficulties of adducing legal proofs that the alleged libel was true in all its factual particulars. . . . They tend to make only statements which "steer far wider of the unlawful zone." The rule thus dampens the vigor and limits the variety of public debate. It is inconsistent with the First and Fourteenth Amendments.

The constitutional guarantees require, we think, a federal rule that prohibits a public official from recovering damages for a defamatory falsehood relating to his official conduct unless he proves that the statement was made with "actual malice"[13]—that is, with knowledge that it was false or with reckless disregard of whether it was false or not.

[13] The main finding from *New York Times Co. v. Sullivan* is the actual malice rule. The rule means that a public official suing for libel may prevail only by showing that the speaker acted knowing that a statement was false or acted with "actual malice"—defined as reckless disregard as to the truth or falsity of a statement. This is a high hurdle for public official defamation plaintiffs. They must prove that the speaker knew that the statement was false or acted recklessly. A private person suing for defamation generally must show only negligence, or fault.

. . .

Applying these standards, we consider that the proof presented to show actual malice lacks the convincing clarity[14] which the constitutional standard demands, and hence that it would not constitutionally sustain the judgment for respondent under the proper rule of law. The case of the individual petitioners requires little discussion. Even assuming that they could constitutionally be found to have authorized the use of their names on the advertisement, there was no evidence whatever that they were aware of any erroneous statements or were in any way reckless in that regard. The judgment against them is thus without constitutional support.

[14] Courts have interpreted this phrase as the equivalent of "clear and convincing evidence." This evidentiary statement is more demanding than the typical evidentiary standard in civil cases—known as "preponderance of the evidence" or "more likely than not."

As to the Times, we similarly conclude that the facts do not support a finding of actual malice.[15] The statement by the Times' Secretary that, apart from the padlocking allegation, he thought the advertisement was "substantially correct," affords no constitutional warrant for the Alabama Supreme Court's conclusion that it was a "cavalier ignoring of the falsity of the advertisement [from which] the jury could not have but been impressed with the bad faith of The Times, and its maliciousness inferable therefrom." The statement does not indicate malice at the time of the publication; even if the advertisement was not "substantially correct"—although respondent's own proofs tend to show that it was—that opinion was at least a reasonable one, and there was no evidence to impeach the witness' good faith in holding it.

[15] The Court finds that the *New York Times* did not act with actual malice. The newspaper may have been negligent in not catching errors in the editorial advertisement, but these errors did not rise to the level of knowing falsity or recklessness.

. . .

We also think the evidence was constitutionally defective in another respect: it was incapable of supporting the jury's finding that the allegedly libelous statements were made "of and concerning" respondent.[16]

[16] The Court concludes that there was not a sufficient showing that the statements in the editorial advertisement referenced or referred to L. B. Sullivan, the plaintiff. The Court explains that the oblique reference to the police is not enough to be about Mr. Sullivan.

. . .

The judgment of the Supreme Court of Alabama is reversed and the case is remanded to that court for further proceedings not inconsistent with this opinion.

Reversed and remanded.

Source: *New York Times Co. v. Sullivan*, 376 U.S. 254 (1964).

Mario Savio's "Bodies upon the Gears" Speech

December 2, 1964

INTRODUCTION

In the 1960s, a group of students at the University of California, Berkeley, engaged in political activities and activism, challenging various policies at the university. Their efforts were known collectively as the Berkeley Free Speech Movement.

A highlight of the movement was in 1964, when student Mario Savio and about 500 fellow students marched on an administration building to protest the university's way of doing business. Savio delivered a rousing speech, which was seen as the intellectual and moral fiber of the movement.

You know, I just want to say one brief thing about something the previous speaker said. I didn't want to spend too much time on that because I don't think it's important enough. But one thing is worth considering.

. . .

I'd like to say . . . one other thing about a union problem. Upstairs, you may have noticed already on the second floor of Sproul Hall, Locals 40 and 127 of the Painters' Union are painting the inside of the second floor of Sproul Hall. Now, apparently that action had been planned sometime in the past. I've tried to contact those unions. Unfortunately, and it tears my heart out—they're as bureaucratized as the administration—it's difficult to get through to anyone in authority there. Very sad. We're still . . . making an attempt. Those people up there have no desire to interfere with what we're doing. I would ask that they be considered and that they not be heckled in any way. And I think that . . . while there's unfortunately no sense of solidarity at this point between unions and students, there at least need be no . . . excessively hard feelings between the two groups.

Now, there are at least two ways in which sit-ins, and civil disobedience,[1] and whatever, at least two major ways in which it can occur.

[1] The sit-in was a significant form of protest during this time in American history. The modern civil rights movement featured sit-ins at various restaurants, businesses, libraries, and other facilities that were segregated on the basis of race. Sit-ins were not the only form of civil disobedience by the civil rights movement and the Free Speech Movement at Berkeley, but they were a prominent and highly effective method of protest. Savio had participated in Freedom Summer in Mississippi and had received training in forms of nonviolent protest. He brought much of what he learned to his fellow students in California.

One, when a law exists, is promulgated, which is totally unacceptable to people and they violate it again and again and again until it's rescinded, repealed. All right, but there's another way.

Sometimes the form of the law is such as to render impossible its effective violation as a method to have it repealed. Sometimes the grievances of people are more, extend . . . to more than just the law, extend to a whole mode of arbitrary power,[2] a whole mode of arbitrary exercise of arbitrary power. And that's what we have here.

[2] Savio and other student protesters believed that the university leaders had created a system of arbitrary power and repression of students.

We have an autocracy which runs this university. It's managed! We were told the following: If President Kerr actually tried to get something more liberal out of the regents in his telephone conversation, why didn't he make some public statement to that effect? And the answer we received, from a well-meaning liberal, was the following. He said: "Would you ever imagine the manager of a firm making a statement publicly in opposition to his Board of Directors?" That's the answer! Now I ask you to consider: if this is a firm, and if the Board of Regents are the board of directors, and if President Kerr in fact is the manager, then I'll tell you something, the faculty are a bunch of employees, and we're the raw materials! But we're a bunch of raw materials that don't mean to . . . have any process upon us, don't mean to be made into any product, don't mean . . . to end up being bought by some clients of the University, be they the government, be they industry, be they organized labor, be they anyone! We're human beings!

And that . . . brings me to the second mode of civil disobedience. There's a time when the operation of the machine[3] becomes so odious, makes you so sick at heart that you can't take part; you can't even passively take part! And you've got to put your bodies upon the gears and upon the wheels,[4] upon the levers, upon all the apparatus, and you've got to make it stop! And you've got to indicate to the people who run it, to the people who own it, that unless you're free, the machine will be prevented from working at all!!

[3] Savio's speech is often called "Operation of the Machine."

[4] Savio believes that the only way to force positive change at the university is for students to put their bodies on the line. He doesn't mean violence.

That doesn't mean—and it will be interpreted to mean, unfortunately, by the bigots who run the *[San Francisco] Examiner*, for example— . . . that you have to break anything. One thousand people sitting down someplace, not letting anybody by, not letting anything happen, can stop any machine, including this machine! And it will stop!!

We're going to do the following, and the greater the number of people, the safer they'll be and the more effective it will be. We're going, once again, to march up to the second floor[5] of Sproul Hall. And we're going to conduct our lives for a while in the second floor of Sproul Hall.

We'll show movies, for example. We tried to get *Un Chant d'Amour*. Unfortunately, that's tied up in the courts because of a lot of squeamish moral mothers for a moral America and other people on the outside, the same people who get all their ideas out of the *San Francisco Examiner*. Sad, sad. But, Mr. Landau . . . has gotten us some other films.

Likewise, we'll do something . . . that hasn't occurred at this University in a good long time. We're going to have real classes up there. There are going to be Freedom Schools conducted up there. We're going to have classes on [the] First and Fourteenth amendments![6] We're going to spend our time learning about the things this University is afraid that we know! We're going to learn about freedom up there, and we're going to learn by doing!!

Now, we've had some good long rallies. We've had some good long rallies, and I think I'm sicker of rallies than anyone else here. It's not going to be long. I'd like to introduce one last person . . . before we enter Sproul Hall. And the person is Joan Baez.[7]

[5] Marches are a historic form of free expression in American history. Women suffragists marched for the right to vote in the 1910s, and civil rights protesters marched in the 1950s and 1960s. Gay rights activists marched for decades, and many marched for marriage equality in the 21st century. Savio's appeal to marches is a savvy choice—a form of nonviolent direct action common to successful social movements.

[6] Notice the explicit mention to students of learning about the First and Fourteenth amendments to the U.S. Constitution. It is the First Amendment that protects the right to dissent in a free society. But the First Amendment technically only limits the federal government. It is the Fourteenth Amendment's due process clause that extends the First Amendment right to free speech to the state and local government level.

[7] Joan Baez is a legendary folk singer who often sang songs of protest. Baez has been not only a talented musician but also a committed social activist. She often sang "We Shall Overcome" during major civil rights protests. She sang the great protest song at Sproul Hall after being introduced by Savio.

Source: Mario Savio, "Bodies Upon the Gears." Used by permission of Lynne Hollander Savio.

United States v. O'Brien

May 27, 1968

INTRODUCTION

In 1968, the U.S. Supreme Court created a test or rule for evaluating whether expressive conduct or symbolic speech merits free-speech protection. The Court recognized that often speech and non-speech elements are mixed together.

The case in which the Court developed this test arose from a draft-card burning. The burning of a draft card is a form of conduct. However, the individual burned the draft card as a means of political protest and as an expression of antiwar beliefs. The government claimed that it had the power to enforce laws that prohibited this type of conduct. The individual countered that the government really was trying to silence antiwar dissenters. The case is important for First Amendment jurisprudence because many courts still use the O'Brien test to evaluate the constitutionality of laws impacting expressive conduct.

MR. CHIEF JUSTICE WARREN delivered the opinion of the Court.

On the morning of March 31, 1966, David Paul O'Brien and three companions burned their Selective Service registration certificates[1] on the steps of the South Boston Courthouse. A sizable crowd, including several agents of the Federal Bureau of Investigation, witnessed the event. Immediately after the burning, members of the crowd began attacking O'Brien and his companions. An FBI agent ushered O'Brien to safety inside the courthouse. After he was advised of his right to counsel and to silence, O'Brien stated to FBI agents that he had burned his registration certificate because of his beliefs, knowing that he was violating federal law. He produced the charred remains of the certificate, which, with his consent, were photographed.

[1] David Paul O'Brien and three others burned their draft cards on the steps of a South Boston courthouse to protest the draft and the Vietnam War. O'Brien argued that his act of burning the draft card was a form of political speech protected by the First Amendment. The government contended that this act was unlawful conduct not meriting any free-speech protection.

For this act, O'Brien was indicted, tried, convicted, and sentenced in the United States District Court for the District of Massachusetts. He did not contest the fact that he had burned the certificate. He stated in argument to the jury that he burned the certificate publicly to influence others to adopt his antiwar beliefs,[2] as he put it, "so that other people would reevaluate their positions with Selective Service, with the armed forces, and reevaluate their place in the culture of today, to hopefully consider my position."

[2] O'Brien admitted burning the draft card. He contended, however, that this act was a form of protected expressive conduct because it was done to promote his antiwar beliefs.

. . .

In the District Court, O'Brien argued that the 1965 Amendment prohibiting the knowing destruction or mutilation of certificates[3] was unconstitutional because it was enacted to abridge free speech, and because it served no legitimate legislative purpose. The District Court rejected these arguments, holding that the statute on its face did not abridge First Amendment rights, that the court was not competent to inquire into the motives of Congress in enacting the 1965 Amendment, and that the Amendment was a reasonable exercise of the power of Congress to raise armies.

[3] In 1965, Congress amended the Selective Service Act to prohibit the knowing mutilation or destruction of draft cards. Many people had burned their draft cards in protest of the draft, and Congress wanted to stop this type of behavior. O'Brien argued that the specific addition of the 1965 amendment was designed to suppress political dissident speech.

On appeal, the Court of Appeals for the First Circuit[4] held the 1965 Amendment unconstitutional as a law abridging freedom of speech. . . .

[4] O'Brien was convicted in a federal district court. He appealed his conviction to the U.S. Court of Appeals for the First Circuit. The federal appeals court agreed with O'Brien in part. The appeals court agreed that the 1965 law was unconstitutional. However, the court upheld O'Brien's conviction under another law that required people to keep their draft cards on their person at all times.

The Government petitioned for certiorari in No. 232, arguing that the Court of Appeals erred in holding the statute unconstitutional, and that its decision conflicted with decisions[5] by the Courts of Appeals for the Second and Eighth Circuits upholding the 1965 Amendment against identical constitutional challenges. O'Brien cross-petitioned for certiorari in No. 233, arguing that the Court of Appeals erred in sustaining his conviction on the basis of a crime of which he was neither charged nor tried. We granted the Government's petition to resolve the conflict in the circuits, and we also granted O'Brien's cross-petition. We hold that the 1965 Amendment is constitutional both as enacted and as applied. We therefore vacate the judgment of the Court of Appeals and reinstate the judgment and sentence of the District Court without reaching the issue raised by O'Brien in No. 233.

[5] The U.S. Supreme Court has what is known as "discretionary jurisdiction." This means that the Court has the power or discretion to pick and choose which, of the cases appealed to it, it wishes to hear. A key predictor of when the Supreme Court might take a case is when there is a split in the circuits, or a "circuit split." The Supreme Court likes to take cases in order to provide uniformity on legal issues. In the *O'Brien* case, the First Circuit had invalidated the 1965 law, but two other circuits (the Seventh and Eighth circuits) had upheld the law. Thus there was a classic circuit split.

. . .

O'Brien first argues that the 1965 Amendment is unconstitutional as applied to him because his act of burning his registration certificate was protected "symbolic speech"[6] within the First Amendment. His argument is that the freedom of expression which the First Amendment guarantees includes all modes of "communication of ideas by conduct," and that his conduct is within this definition because he did it in "demonstration against the war and against the draft."

[6] "Symbolic speech" refers to forms of expression other than the printed or spoken word. Examples of symbolic speech include wearing armbands, displaying flags, or even burning a flag as a form of political protest. The government generally has more authority to regulate symbolic speech than it does pure speech, because symbolic speech often involves conduct or action.

We cannot accept the view that an apparently limitless variety of conduct can be labeled "speech" whenever the person engaging in the conduct intends thereby to express an idea. However, even on the assumption that the alleged communicative element in O'Brien's conduct is sufficient to bring into play the First Amendment, it does not necessarily follow that the destruction of a registration certificate is constitutionally protected activity. This Court has held that when "speech" and "nonspeech" elements are combined in the same course of conduct, a sufficiently important governmental interest in regulating the nonspeech element can justify incidental limitations on First Amendment freedoms. . . . Whatever imprecision inheres in these terms, we think it clear that a government regulation is sufficiently justified if it is within the constitutional power of the Government; if it furthers an important or substantial governmental interest; if the governmental interest is unrelated to the suppression of free expression; and if the incidental restriction on alleged First Amendment freedoms is no greater than is essential to the furtherance of that interest.[7] We find that the 1965 Amendment to 12 (b) (3) of the Universal Military Training and Service Act meets all of these requirements, and consequently that O'Brien can be constitutionally convicted for violating it.

[7] The Court created what is known as the "O'Brien test" when speech and non-speech elements are tied together. The O'Brien test has four parts: (1) whether the government has the power to enact the law; (2) whether the government has a substantial interest in passing the law; (3) whether the government's regulatory interest is related or unrelated to the suppression of free expression; and (4) whether the incidental restriction on speech is too great. The Supreme Court has used the O'Brien test many times through the years when evaluating restrictions on expressive conduct or symbolic speech.

The constitutional power of Congress to raise and support armies and to make all laws necessary and proper to that end is broad and sweeping. . . . Pursuant to this power, Congress may establish a system of registration for individuals liable for training and service, and may require such individuals within reason to cooperate in the registration system. The issuance of certificates indicating the registration and eligibility classification of individuals is a legitimate and substantial administrative aid in the functioning of this system.[8] And legislation to insure the continuing availability of issued certificates serves a legitimate and substantial purpose in the system's administration.

[8] The Supreme Court finds that Congress clearly has the power to require draft cards and to prohibit their destruction. The Court explains that this power flows from the express grant of power given to Congress in the United States Constitution through the power to raise and support armies.

. . .

The many functions performed by Selective Service certificates establish beyond doubt that Congress has a legitimate and substantial interest in preventing their wanton and unrestrained destruction and assuring their continuing availability[9] by punishing people who knowingly and wilfully destroy or mutilate them. And we are unpersuaded that the pre-existence of the nonpossession regulations in any way negates this interest.

[9] The Supreme Court accepts the government's argument that there are many legitimate and substantial interests in having draft cards and preventing their destruction. The Court explains that the draft cards serve many functions related to the efficient operation of the war effort and the draft system.

. . .

It is equally clear that the 1965 Amendment specifically protects this substantial governmental interest. We perceive no alternative means that would more precisely and narrowly assure the continuing availability of issued Selective Service certificates than a law which prohibits their wilful mutilation or destruction. The 1965 Amendment prohibits such conduct and does nothing more. In other words, both the governmental interest and the operation of the 1965 Amendment are limited to the noncommunicative aspect of O'Brien's conduct. The governmental interest and the scope of the 1965 Amendment are limited to preventing harm to the smooth and efficient functioning of the Selective Service System. When O'Brien deliberately rendered unavailable his registration certificate, he wilfully frustrated this governmental interest. For this noncommunicative impact of his conduct, and for nothing else, he was convicted.[10]

[10] The Court also accepts the government's argument that O'Brien was punished for the "noncommunicative impact of his conduct" and not for any antiwar beliefs. In other words, the Court says he was punished for burning the draft card, not for any specific viewpoint or motivation for that underlying conduct.

. . .

O'Brien finally argues that the 1965 Amendment is unconstitutional as enacted because what he calls the "purpose" of Congress was "to suppress freedom of speech."[11] We reject this argument because under settled principles the purpose of Congress, as O'Brien uses that term, is not a basis for declaring this legislation unconstitutional.

[11] The most important part of the O'Brien test is the third prong—whether the government's regulatory interest is related or unrelated to the suppression of free expression. This means that if the government's purpose is to silence political dissenters, there is a First Amendment violation. It also means that if the government's regulatory interest is not related to speech suppression, then the law is constitutional and there is no First Amendment violation.

It is a familiar principle of constitutional law that this Court will not strike down an otherwise constitutional statute on the basis of an alleged illicit legislative motive. . . .

Inquiries into congressional motives or purposes are a hazardous matter. When the issue is simply the interpretation of legislation, the Court will look to statements by legislators for guidance as to the purpose of the legislature, because the benefit to sound decision-making in this circumstance is thought sufficient to risk the possibility of misreading Congress' purpose. It is entirely a different matter when we are asked to void a statute that is, under well-settled criteria, constitutional on its face, on the basis of what fewer than a handful of Congressmen said about it. What motivates one legislator to make a speech about a statute is not necessarily what motivates scores of others to enact it, and the stakes are sufficiently high for us to eschew guesswork.[12] We decline to void essentially on the ground that it is unwise legislation which Congress had the undoubted power to enact and which could be reenacted in its exact form if the same or another legislator made a "wiser" speech about it.

[12] O'Brien claimed that the law was related to the suppression of free expression because some legislators voted for the 1965 law in order to silence antiwar protesters. The Court expresses skepticism of this type of inquiry, finding that there are many reasons why members of Congress may support or reject proposed legislation. In other words, the Court is saying that it is very difficult to determine legislative intent by looking at statements from individual legislators.

. . .

[The law] is constitutional as enacted and as applied, the Court of Appeals should have affirmed the judgment of conviction entered by the District Court. Accordingly, we vacate the judgment of the Court of Appeals, and reinstate the judgment and sentence of the District Court. This disposition makes unnecessary consideration of O'Brien's claim that the Court of Appeals erred in affirming his conviction on the basis of the nonpossession regulation.

It is so ordered.

Source: *United States v. O'Brien*, 391 U.S. 367 (1968).

Pickering v. Board of Education

June 3, 1968

INTRODUCTION

Public employees used to have zero free-speech protections when they took employment. The prevailing view was encapsulated by Justice Oliver Wendell Holmes's statement when he was sitting on the Supreme Judicial Court of Massachusetts. The case involved a police officer, John J. McAuliffe, who was canvassing for a political candidate. The problem was that a city ordinance prohibited such political activities by police officers. In *McAuliffe v. City of New Bedford* (1892), Justice Holmes wrote, "Petitioner may have a constitutional right to talk politics, but he does not have a constitutional right to be a policeman."

The U.S. Supreme Court did not rule explicitly that public employees retain free-speech protections until a case involving a public high school teacher named Marvin Pickering. Mr. Pickering wrote a letter to the editor of his local newspaper criticizing how the school board spent money on athletics instead of academics. He lost his job because of the letter. Pickering challenged his dismissal all the way to the U.S. Supreme Court.

MR. JUSTICE MARSHALL[1] delivered the opinion of the Court.

Appellant Marvin L. Pickering, a teacher in Township High School District 205, Will County, Illinois, was dismissed from his position by the appellee Board of Education for sending a letter to a local newspaper in connection with a recently proposed tax increase that was critical of the way in which the Board and the district superintendent of schools had handled past proposals to raise new revenue for the schools. Appellant's dismissal resulted from a determination by the Board, after a full hearing, that the publication of the letter was "detrimental to the efficient operation and administration of the schools of the district" and hence, under the relevant Illinois statute, Ill. Rev. Stat., c. 122, § 10-22.4 (1963), that "interests of the school require[d] [his dismissal]."

. . .

[1] When the name Thurgood Marshall is mentioned, most people focus on his advocacy for the NAACP in the fight to declare segregated schools unconstitutional. He was one of the country's most famous lawyers before President Lyndon Johnson nominated him to the federal judiciary—first to the 2nd U.S. Circuit Court of Appeals and then to the U.S. Supreme Court. Even on the Supreme Court, Marshall often was known for his forceful opinions on racial equality. But Justice Marshall was a consistent defender of the First Amendment too. His opinion in the Marvin Pickering case is a prime example.

I.

In February of 1961 the appellee Board of Education asked the voters of the school district to approve a bond issue to raise $4,875,000 to erect two new schools. The proposal was defeated. Then, in December of 1961, the Board submitted another bond proposal to the voters which called for the raising of $5,500,000 to build two new schools. This second proposal passed and the schools were built with the money raised by the bond sales. In May of 1964 a proposed increase in the tax rate to be used for educational purposes was submitted to the voters by the Board and was defeated. Finally, on September 19, 1964, a second proposal to increase the tax rate was submitted by the Board and was likewise defeated. It was in connection with this last proposal of the School Board that appellant wrote the letter to the editor (which we reproduce in an Appendix to this opinion) that resulted in his dismissal.

. . .

The letter constituted, basically, an attack on the School Board's handling of the 1961 bond issue proposals and its subsequent allocation of financial resources between the schools' educational and athletic programs. It also charged the superintendent of schools with attempting to prevent teachers in the district from opposing or criticizing the proposed bond issue.

The Board dismissed Pickering for writing and publishing the letter.[2] Pursuant to Illinois law, the Board was then required to hold a hearing on the dismissal. At the hearing the Board charged that numerous statements in the letter were false and that the publication of the statements unjustifiably impugned the "motives, honesty, integrity, truthfulness, responsibility and competence" of both the Board and the school administration. The Board also charged that the false statements damaged the professional reputations of its members and of the school administrators, would be disruptive of faculty discipline, and would tend to foment "controversy, conflict and dissension" among teachers, administrators, the Board of Education, and the residents of the district. Testimony was introduced from a variety of witnesses on the truth or falsity of the particular statements in the letter with which the Board took issue. The Board found the statements to be false as charged. No evidence was

[2] Marvin Pickering lost his job because of the letter he sent about the school board. When he lost his job, no other school system would hire him in the state of Illinois. While he appealed his case, he worked at a soup factory in Chicago to support his family.

introduced at any point in the proceedings as to the effect of the publication of the letter on the community as a whole or on the administration of the school system in particular, and no specific findings along these lines were made.

. . .

To the extent that the Illinois Supreme Court's opinion may be read to suggest that teachers may constitutionally be compelled to relinquish the First Amendment rights they would otherwise enjoy as citizens to comment on matters of public interest in connection with the operation of the public schools in which they work, it proceeds on a premise that has been unequivocally rejected in numerous prior decisions of this Court. . . . At the same time it cannot be gainsaid that the State has interests as an employer in regulating the speech of its employees that differ significantly from those it possesses in connection with regulation of the speech of the citizenry in general. The problem in any case is to arrive at a balance between the interests of the teacher, as a citizen, in commenting upon matters of public concern[3] and the interest of the State, as an employer, in promoting the efficiency of the public services it performs through its employees.

[3] The Supreme Court established a test known as the Pickering balancing test. It balances the right of public employees to speak on matters of public concern or importance against the employer's efficiency interests. Speech on a matter of public concern means speech that is important to the public.

. . .

An examination of the statements in appellant's letter objected to by the Board reveals that they, like the letter as a whole, consist essentially of criticism of the Board's allocation of school funds between educational and athletic programs, and of both the Board's and the superintendent's methods of informing, or preventing the informing of, the district's taxpayers of the real reasons why additional tax revenues were being sought for the schools. The statements are in no way directed towards any person with whom appellant would normally be in contact in the course of his daily work as a teacher. Thus no question of maintaining either discipline by immediate superiors or harmony among coworkers is presented here. Appellant's employment relationships with the Board and, to a somewhat lesser extent, with the superintendent are not the kind of close working relationships[4] for which it can persuasively be claimed that personal loyalty and confidence are necessary to their proper functioning. Accordingly, to the extent that the Board's position here can be taken to

[4] The Court explains that teacher Marvin Pickering's letter did not criticize coworkers or bosses with whom he worked with on a daily basis. Instead, his letter criticized the school board, and Pickering did not work with school board members. When a public employee engages in speech critical of fellow employees, the public employer has a stronger interest in preventing such disruption.

suggest that even comments on matters of public concern that are substantially correct, such as statements (1)–(4) of appellant's letter, see Appendix, infra, may furnish grounds for dismissal if they are sufficiently critical in tone, we unequivocally reject it.

. . .

More importantly, the question whether a school system requires additional funds is a matter of legitimate public concern on which the judgment of the school administration, including the School Board, cannot, in a society that leaves such questions to popular vote, be taken as conclusive. On such a question free and open debate is vital to informed decision-making by the electorate. Teachers are, as a class, the members of a community most likely to have informed and definite opinions[5] as to how funds allotted to the operation of the schools should be spent. Accordingly, it is essential that they be able to speak out freely on such questions without fear of retaliatory dismissal.

[5] Public employees are often in the best position to provide information to the public about their governmental institutions. In this case, the Court reasoned that Marvin Pickering, as a teacher, could inform members of the community about school issues.

. . .

What we do have before us is a case in which a teacher has made erroneous public statements upon issues then currently the subject of public attention, which are critical of his ultimate employer but which are neither shown nor can be presumed to have in any way either impeded the teacher's proper performance of his daily duties in the classroom or to have interfered with the regular operation of the schools[6] generally. In these circumstances we conclude that the interest of the school administration in limiting teachers' opportunities to contribute to public debate is not significantly greater than its interest in limiting a similar contribution by any member of the general public.

[6] When a public employee's speech interferes with the ability of the employer to carry out its mission or business, the employee usually loses his First Amendment claim. The theory is that the employee's right to speak out on matters of public importance is trumped by the employer's vital interest in the ability to perform its functions. Here, the Court reasoned that Marvin Pickering's letter did not interfere with the daily functioning of the school.

. . .

In sum, we hold that, in a case such as this, absent proof of false statements knowingly or recklessly made by him, a teacher's exercise of his right to speak on issues of public importance may not furnish the basis for his dismissal from public employment. Since no such showing has been made in this case regarding appellant's letter, see Appendix, infra, his dismissal for writing it cannot be upheld and the judgment of the Illinois Supreme Court must, accordingly, be reversed and the case remanded for further proceedings not inconsistent with this opinion.

It is so ordered.

Source: *Pickering v. Board of Education*, 391 U.S. 563 (1968).

Tinker v. Des Moines Independent Community School District

February 24, 1969

INTRODUCTION

In 1943, the U.S. Supreme Court implicitly recognized in *West Virginia Board of Education v. Barnette* that public school students possessed some level of First Amendment rights. In that case, the Court invalidated a state law mandating that all students salute the flag and recite the Pledge of Allegiance.

But the Court in *Barnette* failed to articulate a test for determining the level and extent of public school students' free-speech rights. The Court developed a framework in *Tinker v. Des Moines Independent Community School District* (1969). The *Tinker* case involved several students wearing black peace armbands to their schools to protest the Vietnam War, to support Robert Kennedy's Christmas truce, and to mourn those who had perished in the conflict.

School officials learned of the impending armband protest and passed a rule that prohibited students from wearing the armbands. The school district's rule singled out the black armbands for prohibition. Students were allowed to wear other symbols on their clothing.

Tinker remains the seminal Supreme Court case addressing the First Amendment free-speech rights of public school students. In later decisions, the Court carved out exceptions to the *Tinker* ruling for lewd or vulgar speech, for school-sponsored speech, and for speech that promotes the illegal use of drugs. But *Tinker* remains a vital precedent in First Amendment jurisprudence.

Justice Abe Fortas delivered the opinion of the Court.

Petitioner John F. Tinker, 15 years old, and petitioner Christopher Eckhardt, 16 years old, attended high schools in Des Moines, Iowa. Petitioner Mary Beth Tinker, John's sister, was a 13-year-old student in junior high school.[1]

[1] John and Mary Beth Tinker were siblings. Both siblings are still involved in First Amendment activity. They recently conducted a "Tinker Tour," traveling the country to speak about the case and the First Amendment rights of students. Christopher Eckhardt also cared deeply about First Amendment freedoms. He died in 2011.

In December 1965, a group of adults and students in Des Moines held a meeting at the Eckhardt home. The group determined to publicize their objections to the hostilities in Vietnam and their support for a truce by wearing black armbands during the holiday season and by fasting on December 16 and New Year's Eve. Petitioners and their parents had previously engaged in similar activities, and they decided to participate in the program.

The principals of the Des Moines schools became aware of the plan to wear armbands. On December 14, 1965, they met and adopted a policy that any student wearing an armband to school would be asked to remove it, and, if he refused, he would be suspended until he returned without the armband. Petitioners were aware of the regulation that the school authorities adopted.

On December 16, Mary Beth and Christopher wore black armbands to their schools. John Tinker wore his armband the next day. They were all sent home and suspended from school until they would come back without their armbands.

. . .

I.

As we shall discuss, the wearing of armbands in the circumstances of this case was entirely divorced from actually or potentially disruptive conduct by those participating in it. It was closely akin to "pure speech"[2] which, we have repeatedly held, is entitled to comprehensive protection under the First Amendment.

First Amendment rights, applied in light of the special characteristics of the school environment, are available to teachers and students. It can hardly be argued that either students or teachers shed their constitutional rights to freedom of speech or expression at the schoolhouse gate.[3] This has been the unmistakable holding of this Court for almost 50 years.

. . .

On the other hand, the Court has repeatedly emphasized the need for affirming the comprehensive authority of the States and of school officials, consistent with fundamental constitutional safeguards, to prescribe and control conduct in the schools. Our problem lies in the area where students in the exercise of First Amendment rights collide with the rules of the school authorities.

[2] Justice Fortas describes the act of wearing the black armband as "akin to pure speech." The school officials argued that wearing armbands was not a form of pure speech. But clearly the black armbands conveyed a political message.

[3] This passage is cited in countless student First Amendment cases. While it is true that students possessed some level of First Amendment rights, the Court in *Tinker* established the first real test for student speech cases.

II.

The problem posed by the present case does not relate to regulation of the length of skirts or the type of clothing, to hair style, or deportment.[4] It does not concern aggressive, disruptive action or even group demonstrations. Our problem involves direct, primary First Amendment rights akin to "pure speech."

[4] Dress code proponents often point to this passage that says the case does not relate to the type of clothing. They argue that school officials should be able to impose dress codes or even uniforms to create an environment more conducive to learning.

The school officials banned and sought to punish petitioners for a silent, passive expression of opinion, unaccompanied by any disorder or disturbance on the part of petitioners. There is here no evidence whatever of petitioners' interference, actual or nascent, with the schools' work[5] or of collision with the rights of other students to be secure and to be let alone. Accordingly, this case does not concern speech or action that intrudes upon the work of the schools or the rights of other students.

[5] The Court suggests that if student speech intrudes upon the rights of other students, it can be limited or prohibited. Those who support cyberbullying laws cite this passage from *Tinker*. The idea is that a person who bullies another person online has invaded the rights of others and is not entitled to First Amendment protection. The Supreme Court has never clarified when student speech invades the rights of other students.

Only a few of the 18,000 students in the school system wore the black armbands. Only five students were suspended for wearing them. There is no indication that the work of the schools or any class was disrupted. Outside the classrooms, a few students made hostile remarks to the children wearing armbands, but there were no threats or acts of violence on school premises.

The District Court concluded that the action of the school authorities was reasonable because it was based upon their fear of a disturbance from the wearing of the armbands. But, in our system, undifferentiated fear or apprehension of disturbance is not enough to overcome the right to freedom of expression. Any departure from absolute regimentation may cause trouble. Any variation from the majority's opinion may inspire fear. Any word spoken, in class, in the lunchroom, or on the campus, that deviates from the views of another person may start an argument or cause a disturbance. But our Constitution says we must take this risk . . .

In order for the State in the person of school officials to justify prohibition of a particular expression of opinion, it must be able to show that its action was caused by something more than a mere desire to avoid the discomfort and unpleasantness that always accompany an unpopular viewpoint. Certainly where there is no finding and no showing that engaging in the forbidden conduct would "materially and substantially interfere with the requirements of appropriate discipline in the operation of the school,"[6] the prohibition cannot be sustained.

In the present case, the District Court made no such finding, and our independent examination of the record fails to yield evidence[7] that the school authorities had reason to anticipate that the wearing of the armbands would substantially interfere with the work of the school or impinge upon the rights of other students. Even an official memorandum prepared after the suspension that listed the reasons for the ban on wearing the armbands made no reference to the anticipation of such disruption.

[6] The Court determined that school officials could limit student speech if they could show that the student speech would "materially and substantially interfere" with school activities. This is sometimes known as the "substantial disruption" test. This has become the leading test in student speech cases.

[7] In this case, the Court determined that school officials had no reason to anticipate that the students wearing the armbands would cause a substantial disruption of school activities. Because there was no such reason, the Court determined that the students had the right to wear the armbands.

. . .

It is also relevant that the school authorities did not purport to prohibit the wearing of all symbols of political or controversial significance.[8] The record shows that students in some of the schools wore buttons relating to national political campaigns, and some even wore the Iron Cross, traditionally a symbol of Nazism. The order prohibiting the wearing of armbands did not extend to these. Instead, a particular symbol—black armbands worn to exhibit opposition to this Nation's involvement in Vietnam—was singled out for prohibition. Clearly, the prohibition of expression of one particular opinion, at least without evidence that it is necessary to avoid material and substantial interference with schoolwork or discipline, is not constitutionally permissible.

[8] School officials allowed students to wear other symbols, such as campaign buttons and the Iron Cross. But school officials singled out the black armbands for regulation. This raises the distinct possibility that school officials selectively targeted the black armband because of the antiwar viewpoint.

In our system, state-operated schools may not be enclaves of totalitarianism. School officials do not possess absolute authority over their students. Students in school as well as out of school are "persons" under our Constitution. They are possessed of fundamental rights which the State must respect, just as they themselves must respect their obligations to the State. In our system, students may not be regarded as closed-circuit recipients of only that which the State chooses to communicate.[9] . . .

[9] Parts of Justice Fortas's opinion read like a paean to student speech. Some of the language seems lofty. Certainly, some school officials have questioned whether *Tinker* gave too many rights to public school students.

But conduct by the student, in class or out of it, which for any reason—whether it stems from time, place, or type of behavior—materially disrupts classwork or involves substantial disorder or invasion of the rights of others is, of course, not immunized by the constitutional guarantee of freedom of speech.

. . .

As we have discussed, the record does not demonstrate any facts which might reasonably have led school authorities to forecast substantial disruption of or material interference with school activities, and no disturbances or disorders on the school premises in fact occurred. These petitioners merely went about their ordained rounds in school. Their deviation consisted only in wearing on their sleeve a band of black cloth, not more than two inches wide. They wore it to exhibit their disapproval of the Vietnam hostilities and their advocacy of a truce, to make their views known, and, by their example, to influence others to adopt them. They neither interrupted school activities nor sought to intrude in the school affairs or the lives of others.[10] They caused discussion outside of the classrooms, but no interference with work and no disorder. In the circumstances, our Constitution does not permit officials of the State to deny their form of expression.

[10] Once again, the Court emphasizes that the students engaged in passive, peaceful political speech. The wearing of the armbands did not interfere with school activities or cause any substantial disruptions.

Source: *Tinker v. Des Moines Independent Community School District*, 393 U.S. 503 (1969).

Watts v. United States

April 21, 1969

INTRODUCTION

We know that the First Amendment does not protect all forms of speech. For example, in *Chaplinsky v. New Hampshire* (1942), the Supreme Court created the "fighting words" exception to the First Amendment. The Court also determined that speech that incites imminent lawless action is not protected, in *Brandenburg v. Ohio* (1969).

Related to fighting words and incitement to imminent lawless action is another category of unprotected expression called "true threats." The Court first addressed the topic of true threats in *Watts v. United States* (1969), a case involving a young African American who was protesting the Vietnam War.

PER CURIAM.[1]

After a jury trial in the United States District Court for the District of Columbia, petitioner was convicted of violating a 1917 statute which prohibits any person from "knowingly and willfully . . . [making] any threat to take the life of or to inflict bodily harm upon the President of the United States[2] . . . ."

The incident which led to petitioner's arrest occurred on August 27, 1966, during a public rally on the Washington Monument grounds. The crowd present broke up into small discussion groups and petitioner joined a gathering scheduled to discuss police brutality. Most of those in the group were quite young, either in their teens or early twenties. Petitioner, who himself was 18 years old, entered into the discussion after one member of the group suggested that the young people present should get more education before expressing their views. According to an investigator for the Army Counter Intelligence Corps who was present, petitioner responded: "They always holler at us to get an education. And now I have already received my draft classification as 1-A and I have got to report for my physical this Monday coming. I am not going. If they ever make me carry a rifle the first man I want to get in my sights is L. B. J." "They are

[1] "Per curiam" is Latin meaning "for the court." Usually, the Court identifies the justice who authored the opinion. A per curiam opinion is an opinion that the justices wrote together or as a whole.

[2] Mr. Watts was convicted of violating a 1917 law that specifically prohibits making threatening statements about the president of the United States.

not going to make me kill my black brothers."[3] On the basis of this statement, the jury found that petitioner had committed a felony by knowingly and willfully threatening the President. The United States Court of Appeals for the District of Columbia Circuit affirmed by a two-to-one vote. We reverse.

[3] "L. B. J." refers to the sitting U.S. president at the time, Lyndon Baines Johnson. Mr. Watts, who was only 18 years old, objected to the idea of being drafted to serve in the Vietnam War. Many believed that a disproportionate number of young black men were being forced to go overseas and fight in Vietnam.

At the close of the Government's case, petitioner's trial counsel moved for a judgment of acquittal. He contended that there was "absolutely no evidence on the basis of which the jury would be entitled to find that [petitioner] made a threat against the life of the President." He stressed the fact that petitioner's statement was made during a political debate, that it was expressly made conditional upon an event—induction into the Armed Forces—which petitioner vowed would never occur, and that both petitioner and the crowd laughed after the statement was made. He concluded, "Now actually what happened here in all this was a kind of very crude offensive method of stating a political opposition to the President.[4] What he was saying, he says, I don't want to shoot black people because I don't consider them my enemy, and if they put a rifle in my hand it is the people that put the rifle in my hand, as symbolized by the President, who are my real enemy." We hold that the trial judge erred in denying this motion.

[4] Mr. Watts's lawyers argued that he did not utter a true threat. Instead, he merely expressed political opposition to the president and the president's policies on the draft and Vietnam. The U.S. Supreme Court essentially agreed with Mr. Watts's argument.

Certainly the statute under which petitioner was convicted is constitutional on its face. The Nation undoubtedly has a valid, even an overwhelming, interest in protecting the safety of its Chief Executive and in allowing him to perform his duties without interference from threats of physical violence. See H. R. Rep. No. 652, 64th Cong., 1st Sess. (1916). Nevertheless, a statute such as this one, which makes criminal a form of pure speech, must be interpreted with the commands of the First Amendment clearly in mind. What is a threat must be distinguished from what is constitutionally protected speech.[5]

[5] The Supreme Court explains that the antithreat statute is constitutional. However, the Court also recognizes that the statute criminalizes certain forms of speech. The Court explains that while the First Amendment protects a great deal of speech, it does not protect true threats. In other words, true threats are one of the narrow unprotected categories of speech in First Amendment law.

. . .

But . . . the statute initially requires the Government to prove a true "threat." We do not believe that the kind of political hyperbole indulged in by petitioner fits within that statutory term. For we must interpret the language Congress chose "against the background of a profound national commitment to the principle that debate on public issues should be uninhibited, robust, and wide-open, and that it may well include vehement, caustic, and sometimes unpleasantly sharp attacks on government and public officials." . . . We agree with petitioner that his only offense here was "a kind of very crude offensive method of stating a political opposition to the President." Taken in context, and regarding the expressly conditional nature of the statement and the reaction of the listeners,[6] we do not see how it could be interpreted otherwise.

[6] The Supreme Court in its *Watts* decision did not define "true threats." However, the Court did identify what came to be known as the "Watts factors" to help lower court judges determine when speech crossed the line into a true threat. These factors are (1) the context of the speech, (2) whether the threatening statement was conditional or unconditional, and (3) the reaction of the listeners. In *Watts*, the Court believed that these factors cut in favor of Mr. Watts. He was speaking at a public political rally. His statement was conditional rather than unconditional. Furthermore, the people who heard Mr. Watts laughed instead of taking him seriously.

The motion for leave to proceed *in forma pauperis* and the petition for a writ of certiorari are granted and the judgment of the Court of Appeals is reversed. The case is remanded with instructions that it be returned to the District Court for entry of a judgment of acquittal.

It is so ordered.

Source: *Watts v. United States*, 394 U.S. 705 (1969).

Brandenburg v. Ohio

June 8, 1969

INTRODUCTION

A key aspect of First Amendment jurisprudence is categorization—determining whether speech falls into narrow unprotected categories of expression. Some of these unprotected categories are obscenity, fighting words, true threats, defamation, and false advertising.

In *Brandenburg v. Ohio*, the Supreme Court articulated another unprotected category that it called "incitement to imminent lawless action." It generally applies when a speaker urges a crowd or many other people to engage in immediate lawless action. Many state and local laws are based on this standard, which often is called "inciting a riot."

Incitement to imminent lawless action is a more modern version of what the Court used to describe as speech that creates a clear and present danger. Notice that much of the Court's language in *Brandenburg* is similar to Justice Louis Brandeis's famous concurring opinion in *Whitney v. California* (1927).

The other aspect of the *Brandenburg* decision is that it protects a speaker who engages in vile and hateful speech. The defendant in the case, Clarence Brandenburg, was a Ku Klux Klan leader who uttered repugnant speech about racial and ethnic minorities. The decision shows that the First Amendment often protects offensive and even hateful speech.

PER CURIAM.

The appellant, a leader of a Ku Klux Klan group, was convicted under the Ohio Criminal Syndicalism statute[1] for "advocat[ing] . . . the duty, necessity, or propriety of crime, sabotage, violence, or unlawful methods of terrorism as a means of accomplishing industrial or political reform" and for "voluntarily assembl[ing] with any society, group, or assemblage of persons formed to teach or advocate the doctrines of criminal syndicalism." He was fined $1,000 and sentenced to one to 10 years' imprisonment. The appellant challenged the constitutionality of the criminal syndicalism statute under the First and Fourteenth Amendments to the United States Constitution, but the intermediate appellate court of Ohio affirmed his conviction without opinion. The Supreme Court of Ohio dismissed his appeal, *sua sponte*, "for the reason that no substantial constitutional

[1] Clarence Brandenburg, a Ku Klux Klan leader, was prosecuted and convicted under Ohio's criminal syndicalism law. This law was very similar to the law that Charlotte Anita Whitney was convicted under in *Whitney v. California* (1927). The Ohio law allowed individuals to be prosecuted for advocating unlawful acts.

question exists herein." It did not file an opinion or explain its conclusions. Appeal was taken to this Court, and we noted probable jurisdiction. We reverse.

The record shows that a man, identified at trial as the appellant, telephoned an announcer-reporter on the staff of a Cincinnati television station and invited him to come to a Ku Klux Klan "rally" to be held at a farm in Hamilton County. With the cooperation of the organizers, the reporter and a cameraman attended the meeting and filmed the events. Portions of the films were later broadcast on the local station and on a national network.

The prosecution's case rested on the films and on testimony identifying the appellant as the person who communicated with the reporter and who spoke at the rally. The State also introduced into evidence several articles appearing in the film, including a pistol, a rifle, a shotgun, ammunition, a Bible, and a red hood worn by the speaker in the films.

One film showed 12 hooded figures, some of whom carried firearms. They were gathered around a large wooden cross, which they burned. No one was present other than the participants and the newsmen who made the film. Most of the words uttered during the scene were incomprehensible when the film was projected, but scattered phrases could be understood that were derogatory of Negroes and, in one instance, of Jews. Another scene on the same film showed the appellant, in Klan regalia, making a speech. The speech, in full, was as follows:

> "This is an organizers' meeting. We have had quite a few members here today which are—we have hundreds, hundreds of members throughout the State of Ohio. I can quote from a newspaper clipping from the Columbus, Ohio Dispatch, five weeks ago Sunday morning. The Klan has more members in the State of Ohio than does any other organization. We're not a revengent organization, but if our President, our Congress, our Supreme Court, continues to suppress the white, Caucasian race, it's possible that there might have to be some revengeance taken.[2]
>
> "We are marching on Congress July the Fourth, four hundred thousand strong. From there we are dividing into two groups, one group to march on St. Augustine, Florida, the other group to march into Mississippi. Thank you."

[2] In his speech, Mr. Brandenburg claimed that if political leaders (including all three branches of the federal government) do not start supporting the white race, "it's possible that there might have to be some revengeance taken." In other words, the statements by Mr. Brandenburg hint that the group might do something drastic if policy changes are not made. Note that there does not seem to be any evidence of an actual unlawful plan or any immediate illegal action.

The second film showed six hooded figures one of whom, later identified as the appellant, repeated a speech very similar to that recorded on the first film. The reference to the possibility of "revengeance" was omitted, and one sentence was added: "Personally, I believe the nigger should be returned to Africa, the Jew returned to Israel."[3] Though some of the figures in the films carried weapons, the speaker did not.

[3] Mr. Brandenburg engaged in hate speech, spewing racial slurs at both African Americans and Jewish Americans. In many countries, hate speech is outlawed. In the United States, hate speech is a form of protected speech unless the speech is a true threat, incites imminent lawless action, or consists of "fighting words." The United States is an outlier in the world community on hate speech. In many countries, the speech uttered by Mr. Brandenburg could be punished.

The Ohio Criminal Syndicalism Statute was enacted in 1919. From 1917 to 1920, identical or quite similar laws were adopted by 20 States and two territories. In 1927, this Court sustained the constitutionality of California's Criminal Syndicalism Act, Cal. Penal Code §§ 11400–11402, the text of which is quite similar to that of the laws of Ohio. *Whitney v. California*, 274 U.S. 357 (1927). The Court upheld the statute on the ground that, without more, "advocating" violent means to effect political and economic change involves such danger to the security of the State that the State may outlaw it. But *Whitney* has been thoroughly discredited by later decisions.[4] These later decisions have fashioned the principle that the constitutional guarantees of free speech and free press do not permit a State to forbid or proscribe advocacy of the use of force or of law violation except where such advocacy is directed to inciting or producing imminent lawless action[5] and is likely to incite or produce such action. . . . "The mere abstract teaching . . . of the moral propriety or even moral necessity for a resort to force and violence, is not the same as preparing a group for violent action and steeling it to such action." A statute which fails to draw this distinction impermissibly intrudes upon the freedoms guaranteed by the First and Fourteenth Amendments. It sweeps within its condemnation speech which our Constitution has immunized from governmental control.

[4] Note that the Court refers to its earlier decision in *Whitney v. California* as a "discredited" decision; this decision officially overruled it.

[5] The U.S. Supreme Court establishes a new standard or test to be applied. The Court declares that even advocacy of illegal conduct is protected speech unless it incites imminent lawless action and is likely to incite such action. Under this ruling, there is an unprotected category of speech called "incitement to imminent lawless action." This category is the Court's modern iteration of the "clear and present danger" standard.

Measured by this test, Ohio's Criminal Syndicalism Act cannot be sustained. The Act punishes persons who "advocate or teach the duty, necessity, or propriety" of violence "as a means of accomplishing industrial or political reform"; or who publish or circulate or display any book or paper containing such advocacy; or who "justify" the commission of violent acts "with intent to exemplify, spread or advocate the propriety of the doctrines of criminal syndicalism"; or who "voluntarily assemble" with a group formed "to teach or advocate the doctrines of criminal syndicalism." Neither the indictment nor the trial judge's instructions to the jury in any way refined the statute's bald definition of the crime in terms of mere advocacy not distinguished from incitement to imminent lawless action.[6]

Accordingly, we are here confronted with a statute which, by its own words and as applied, purports to punish mere advocacy and to forbid, on pain of criminal punishment, assembly with others merely to advocate the described type of action. Such a statute falls within the condemnation of the First and Fourteenth Amendments. The contrary teaching of *Whitney v. California*, *supra*, cannot be supported, and that decision is therefore overruled.[7]

[6] The Court reasons that the Ohio criminal syndicalism statutes create a crime for "mere advocacy" instead of "incitement to imminent lawless action." Much advocacy does not cross the line into incitement. Thus, the Court invalidates the Ohio law and thereby reverses Mr. Brandenburg's conviction.

[7] The Court specifically overrules its decision in *Whitney v. California* (1927). The Court's opinion in *Brandenburg* actually adopts much of the reasoning from Justice Louis Brandeis's famous concurring opinion in *Whitney*.

Source: *Brandenburg v. Ohio*, 395 U.S. 444 (1969).

Cohen v. California

June 7, 1971

INTRODUCTION

One of the more interesting First Amendment decisions from the U.S. Supreme Court involved the punishment of a man who wore a jacket with a profane word on it. Paul Robert Cohen went into a Los Angeles courthouse wearing a jacket with the message "F**k the Draft." Cohen was opposed to the Vietnam War and the draft.

A police officer arrested Cohen for disturbing the peace through "offensive conduct." The state pointed out that there were women and children in the courthouse. Cohen contended that he had a First Amendment right to display his political message.

The state argued that Cohen's profane message was obscene, that it infringed on the privacy rights of those who didn't want to see such profanity, and that it constituted "fighting words."

The most important aspect of this opinion is the Court's limitation on the fighting-words doctrine. Notice how the Court explains that "fighting words" requires there to be a direct, face-to-face personal confrontation.

An interesting aspect of this decision is the closeness of the case. The Court ruled in favor of Cohen by a single vote, 5–4. Justice John Marshall Harlan II, often a conservative jurist, wrote the majority opinion in favor of Mr. Cohen.

This case may seem at first blush too inconsequential to find its way into our books, but the issue it presents is of no small constitutional significance.

Appellant Paul Robert Cohen was convicted in the Los Angeles Municipal Court of violating that part of California Penal Code 415 which prohibits "maliciously and willfully disturb[ing] the peace or quiet of any neighborhood or person . . . by . . . offensive conduct . . . ." [1] He was given 30 days' imprisonment.

. . .

"On April 26, 1968, the defendant was observed in the Los Angeles County Courthouse in the corridor outside of division 20 of the municipal court wearing a jacket bearing the words 'Fuck the Draft' which were plainly visible. There were women and children present in the corridor. The defendant was arrested.[1] The defendant testified that he wore the jacket knowing that the words were on the jacket as a means of informing the public of the depth of his feelings against the Vietnam War and the draft."

[1] A police officer asked a judge to charge Mr. Cohen with contempt. The judge refused to do so. The officer then arrested Mr. Cohen after he was in the hallway.

. . .

In affirming the conviction, the Court of Appeal held that "offensive conduct" means "behavior which has a tendency to provoke others to acts of violence or to in turn disturb the peace," and that the State had proved this element . . .

I

The conviction quite clearly rests upon the asserted offensiveness of the words Cohen used to convey his message to the public. The only "conduct" which the State sought to punish is the fact of communication.[2] Thus, we deal here with a conviction resting solely upon "speech." . . .

[2] In First Amendment law, there is something known as the speech-conduct dichotomy. This means that there is a difference between protected speech and unprotected conduct. The distinction is one that bothers many First Amendment scholars, because speech is a form of conduct. Justice Harlan emphasized that Cohen was punished for his speech, not any conduct.

Appellant's conviction, then, rests squarely upon his exercise of the "freedom of speech" protected from arbitrary governmental interference by the Constitution and can be justified, if at all, only as a valid regulation of the manner in which he exercised that freedom, not as a permissible prohibition on the substantive message it conveys. This does not end the inquiry, of course, for the First and Fourteenth Amendments have never been thought to give absolute protection to every individual to speak whenever or wherever he pleases, or to use any form of address in any circumstances that he chooses.[3] . . .

[3] Justice Harlan explains that the First Amendment doesn't protect all forms of speech. Furthermore, individuals cannot engage in their preferred form of speech wherever they please.

In the first place, Cohen was tried under a statute applicable throughout the entire State. Any attempt to support this conviction on the ground that the statute seeks to preserve an appropriately decorous atmosphere in the courthouse[4] where Cohen was arrested must fail in the absence of any language in the statute that would have put appellant on notice that certain kinds of otherwise permissible speech or conduct would nevertheless, under California law, not be tolerated in certain places. . . .

[4] This means that Cohen probably would not have a First Amendment claim to wear whatever he wanted to inside a courtroom. Judges have more power to control conduct, including dress, inside their courtrooms. Here, Cohen was charged with violating a state law.

In the second place, as it comes to us, this case cannot be said to fall within those relatively few categories of instances where prior decisions have established the power of government to deal more comprehensively with certain forms of individual expression simply upon a showing that such a form was employed. This is not, for example, an obscenity case. Whatever else may be necessary to give rise to the States' broader power to prohibit obscene expression, such expression must be, in some significant way, erotic.[5] . . .

[5] Obscenity is a form of unprotected speech. It consists of hardcore, sexually explicit materials that have no serious artistic value. While the word on the jacket may be obscene to many, the message was not obscenity, because it was not "in some significant way, erotic."

This Court has also held that the States are free to ban the simple use, without a demonstration of additional justifying circumstances, of so-called "fighting words,"[6] those personally abusive epithets which, when addressed to the ordinary citizen, are, as a matter of common knowledge, inherently likely to provoke violent reaction. While the four-letter word displayed by Cohen in relation to the draft is not uncommonly employed in a personally provocative fashion, in this instance it was clearly not "directed to the person of the hearer."[7] No individual actually or likely to be present could reasonably have regarded the words on appellant's jacket as a direct personal insult. Nor do we have here an instance of the exercise of the State's police power to prevent a speaker from intentionally provoking a given group to hostile reaction. . . .

[6] "Fighting words" are words that inflict injury or cause an immediate breach of the peace. They are direct, face-to-face personal insults.

[7] The Supreme Court explained that Cohen's jacket with the profane word could not be considered "fighting words," because Cohen was not directing the message on the jacket to a particular individual. The Court's decision is a key limitation on the fighting-words doctrine.

Finally, in arguments before this Court, much has been made of the claim that Cohen's distasteful mode of expression was thrust upon unwilling or unsuspecting viewers, and that the State might therefore legitimately act as it did in order to protect the sensitive from otherwise unavoidable exposure to appellant's crude form of protest. Of course, the mere presumed presence of unwitting listeners or viewers does not serve automatically to justify curtailing all speech capable of giving offense.[8]

[8] The Court explains that often in society, we have to confront speech that we don't like. The proper response is to "avert our eyes." Individuals have a greater privacy interest in the home than they do when they are out in public.

. . .

II

Against this background, the issue flushed by this case stands out in bold relief. It is whether California can excise, as "offensive conduct," one particular scurrilous epithet from the public discourse, either upon the theory of the court below that its use is inherently likely to cause violent reaction or upon a more general assertion that the States, acting as guardians of public morality, may properly remove this offensive word from the public vocabulary.

. . .

Equally important to our conclusion is the constitutional backdrop against which our decision must be made. The constitutional right of free expression is powerful medicine in a society as diverse and populous as ours. It is designed and intended to remove governmental restraints from the arena of public discussion, putting the decision as to what views shall be voiced largely into the hands of each of us, in the hope that use of such freedom will ultimately produce a more capable citizenry and more perfect polity and in the belief that no other approach would comport with the premise of individual dignity and choice upon which our political system rests.

. . .

How is one to distinguish this from any other offensive word? Surely the State has no right to cleanse public debate to the point where it is grammatically palatable to the most squeamish among us. Yet no readily ascertainable general principle exists for stopping short of that result were we to affirm the judgment below. For, while the particular four-letter word being litigated here is perhaps more distasteful than most others of its genre, it is nevertheless often true that one man's vulgarity is another's lyric.[9] Indeed, we think it is largely because governmental officials cannot make principled distinctions in this area that the Constitution leaves matters of taste and style so largely to the individual.

[9] Perhaps the most memorable line from the entire opinion is the phrase "one man's vulgarity is another's lyric." This passage has become First Amendment lore. It means that what is offensive to one person may not be offensive to another person. There is an "eye of the beholder" phenomenon.

. . .

Finally, and in the same vein, we cannot indulge the facile assumption that one can forbid particular words without also running a substantial risk of suppressing ideas[10] in the process. Indeed, governments might soon seize upon the censorship of particular words as a convenient guise for banning the expression of unpopular views. We have been able, as noted above, to discern little social benefit that might result from running the risk of opening the door to such grave results.

[10] Justice Harlan warns that if the government can ban particular words, the government could use that power selectively and target those individuals with unpopular viewpoints. Many see this passage as a basis for the concept of viewpoint discrimination. The idea is that the government should not have the power to silence private speakers because it disagrees with the viewpoint of the speech.

It is, in sum, our judgment that, absent a more particularized and compelling reason for its actions, the State may not, consistently with the First and Fourteenth Amendments, make the simple public display here involved of this single four-letter expletive a criminal offense. Because that is the only arguably sustainable rationale for the conviction here at issue, the judgment below must be reversed.

Dissenting Opinion by Justice Harry Blackmun

Cohen's absurd and immature antic, in my view, was mainly conduct and little speech,[11] and I cannot characterize it otherwise. Further, the case appears to me to be well within the sphere of *Chaplinsky v. New Hampshire*, where Mr. Justice Murphy,[12] a known champion of First Amendment freedoms, wrote for a unanimous bench.

[11] This is an example of the application of the speech-conduct dichotomy.

[12] *Chaplinksy*, for which Justice Frank Murphy was the main author, is the original "fighting words" case. Justice Blackmun writes that Cohen's profanity clearly qualifies as fighting words under the *Chaplinsky* ruling.

Source: *Cohen v. California*, 403 U.S. 15 (1971).

New York Times Co. v. United States

June 30, 1971

INTRODUCTION

One of the seminal freedom-of-expression cases involved the United States government attempting to prevent the *New York Times* and the *Washington Post* from publishing excerpts of a government report called the Pentagon Papers.

The Pentagon Papers was a secret government study on American involvement in Vietnam. There were only 15 copies of the report. The U.S. government wanted to keep the report silent, allegedly for security reasons, but Daniel Ellsberg, a RAND Corporation employee who had worked on the study, released it to the newspapers.

Ultimately, the Court ruled 6–3 in favor of the newspapers. However, there was no majority opinion. Nearly every justice wrote separately. Justice Hugo Black, a passionate defender of the First Amendment, wrote a particularly powerful opinion that was protective of First Amendment values.

MR. JUSTICE BLACK, with whom MR. JUSTICE DOUGLAS joins, concurring.

I adhere to the view that the Government's case against the Washington Post should have been dismissed and that the injunction against the New York Times should have been vacated without oral argument when the cases were first presented to this Court. I believe that every moment's continuance of the injunctions against these newspapers amounts to a flagrant, indefensible, and continuing violation of the First Amendment.[1] Furthermore, after oral argument, I agree completely that we must affirm the judgment of the Court of Appeals for the District of Columbia Circuit and reverse the judgment of the Court of Appeals for the Second Circuit for the reasons stated by my Brothers DOUGLAS and BRENNAN. In my view it is unfortunate that some of my Brethren are apparently willing to hold that the publication of news may sometimes be enjoined. Such a holding would make a shambles of the First Amendment.

[1] Justice Black was the most adamant of all the justices that the actions of the federal government violated the First Amendment. He abhorred the concept of prior restraint – or pre-publication hurdles imposed by the government on expression.

Our Government was launched in 1789 with the adoption of the Constitution. The Bill of Rights, including the First Amendment, followed in 1791. Now, for the first time in the 182 years since the founding of the Republic, the federal courts are asked to hold that the First Amendment does not mean what it says, but rather means that the Government can halt the publication of current news of vital importance to the people of this country.

In seeking injunctions against these newspapers and in its presentation to the Court, the Executive Branch seems to have forgotten the essential purpose and history of the First Amendment. When the Constitution was adopted, many people strongly opposed it because the document contained no Bill of Rights to safeguard certain basic freedoms. They especially feared that the new powers granted to a central government might be interpreted to permit the government to curtail freedom of religion, press, assembly, and speech. In response to an overwhelming public clamor, James Madison[2] offered a series of amendments to satisfy citizens that these great liberties would remain safe and beyond the power of government to abridge. Madison proposed what later became the First Amendment in three parts, two of which are set out below, and one of which proclaimed: "The people shall not be deprived or abridged of their right to speak, to write, or to publish their sentiments; and the freedom of the press, as one of the great bulwarks of liberty, shall be inviolable." The amendments were offered to curtail and restrict the general powers granted to the Executive, Legislative, and Judicial Branches two years before in the original Constitution. The Bill of Rights changed the original Constitution into a new charter under which no branch of government could abridge the people's freedoms of press, speech, religion, and assembly. Yet the Solicitor General argues and some members of the Court appear to agree that the general powers of the Government adopted in the original Constitution should be interpreted to limit and restrict the specific and emphatic guarantees of the Bill of Rights adopted later. I can imagine no greater perversion of history. Madison and the other Framers of the First Amendment, able men that they were, wrote in language they earnestly believed could never be misunderstood: "Congress shall make no law . . . abridging the freedom . . . of the press . . . ." Both the history and language of the First Amendment support the view that the press must be left free to publish news, whatever the source, without censorship, injunctions, or prior restraints.[3]

[2] James Madison, the fourth president of the United States, is often called "the Father of the Bill of Rights." It was Madison who introduced what became the First Amendment and the other provisions of the Bill of Rights into Congress on June 8, 1789. Madison referred to these as the "Great Rights of Mankind."

[3] A prior restraint is a type of censorship in which a governmental body prevents publication or imposes a burdensome series of restrictions on publication. The classic type of prior restraint is an injunction barring publication or a gag order imposed by a judge. In this passage, Justice Black explains that the concept of prior restraint is anathema to the vision of James Madison and the other framers who supported the Bill of Rights.

In the First Amendment the Founding Fathers gave the free press the protection it must have to fulfill its essential role in our democracy. The press was to serve the governed, not the governors. The Government's power to censor the press was abolished so that the press would remain forever free to censure the Government. The press was protected so that it could bare the secrets of government and inform the people.[4] Only a free and unrestrained press can effectively expose deception in government. And paramount among the responsibilities of a free press is the duty to prevent any part of the government from deceiving the people and sending them off to distant lands to die of foreign fevers and foreign shot and shell. In my view, far from deserving condemnation for their courageous reporting, the New York Times, the Washington Post, and other newspapers should be commended for serving the purpose that the Founding Fathers saw so clearly. In revealing the workings of government that led to the Vietnam war, the newspapers nobly did precisely that which the Founders hoped and trusted they would do.

[4] Justice Black references the role of the press as the people's watchdog, or the watchdog of a free society. The press is supposed to serve as the fourth estate, a separate entity that can "bare the secrets" of the government and expose wrongdoing.

The Government's case here is based on premises entirely different from those that guided the Framers of the First Amendment.

. . .

The word "security" is a broad, vague[5] generality whose contours should not be invoked to abrogate the fundamental law embodied in the First Amendment. The guarding of military and diplomatic secrets at the expense of informed representative government provides no real security for our Republic. The Framers of the First Amendment, fully aware of both the need to defend a new nation and the abuses of the English and Colonial governments, sought to give this new society strength and security by providing that freedom of speech, press, religion, and assembly should not be abridged.

[5] In the Pentagon Papers case, the U.S. government argued that suppression of the papers was necessary in order to protect national security. However, Justice Black warns that the term "security" can be used and abused by the government as a post hoc justification for its conduct. He refers to it as both a "broad" and a "vague" term. These two terms refer to overbreadth and vagueness, two of the most important words in all of constitutional law. In fact, overbreadth and vagueness are the chief tools of constitutional litigators when challenging laws, rules, or regulations. A law is too broad if it sweeps too broadly and prohibits protected speech. A law is too vague when people cannot understand naturally what those words mean.

Source: *New York Times Co. v. United States*, 403 U.S. 713 (1971).

Police Department of Chicago v. Mosley

June 26, 1972

INTRODUCTION

A primary principle of First Amendment law is that the government generally may not censor speech based on content. This is known as the content discrimination principle. Under First Amendment law, content-based laws are subject to strict scrutiny, the highest form of judicial review. Meanwhile, content-neutral laws are subject to a lesser form of judicial review known as intermediate scrutiny.

The Supreme Court explained the content discrimination principle quite beautifully in *Police Department of Chicago v. Mosley* (1972). Justice Thurgood Marshall wrote, "If the First Amendment means anything, it means that the government may not censor speech because of its message, its ideas, its subject matter, or its content."

The Mosley case involved a federal postal employee named Earl Mosley, who protested within 150 feet of a school about racial discrimination. He feared arrest for violating a Chicago ordinance that prohibited such protesting. However, the law did allow for peaceful picketing about labor.

Because the law selectively favored some picketers and disfavored other picketers, Earl Mosley challenged the law under both the First Amendment and the Equal Protection Clause of the Fourteenth Amendment.

MR. JUSTICE MARSHALL delivered the opinion of the Court.

At issue in this case is the constitutionality of the following Chicago ordinance:

> "A person commits disorderly conduct when he knowingly:
>
> . . .
>
> "(i) Pickets or demonstrates on a public way within 150 feet of any primary or secondary school building while the school is in session and one-half hour before the school is in session and one-half hour after the school session has been concluded, provided that this subsection does not prohibit the peaceful picketing of any school involved in a labor dispute[1] . . . ."
>
> Municipal Code, c. 193-1 (i).

[1] The Chicago ordinance prohibited picketing within 150 feet of a school but provided an exemption for peaceful labor picketers. In other words, picketing about race discrimination in hiring was disallowed, but picketing about labor issues was allowed. This selective treatment of different picketers based on subject matter presents a First Amendment problem.

The suit was brought by Earl Mosley, a federal postal employee, who for seven months prior to the enactment of the ordinance had frequently picketed Jones Commercial High School in Chicago. During school hours and usually by himself, Mosley would walk the public sidewalk adjoining the school, carrying a sign that read: "Jones High School practices black discrimination. Jones High School has a black quota."[2] His lonely crusade was always peaceful, orderly, and quiet, and was conceded to be so by the city of Chicago.

[2] Earl Mosley protested outside Jones High School and was charged with violating the anti-picketing ordinance. Mosley picketed about racial discrimination, not labor. Thus, Mr. Mosley was at risk of being arrested.

. . .

He alleged a violation of constitutional rights in that (1) the statute punished activity protected by the First Amendment; and (2) by exempting only peaceful labor picketing from its general prohibition against picketing, the statute denied him "equal protection of the law[3] in violation of the First and Fourteenth Amendments . . . ."

[3] Mosley sued, alleging a violation of two constitutional rights: (1) the right to free speech under the First Amendment and (2) the right to equal protection of the laws. The Equal Protection Clause often prohibits government officials from treating similarly situated individuals or classes differently. Mosley alleged an equal protection violation, because the ordinance treated one class of picketers (labor) much better than other classes of picketers.

. . .

We hold that the ordinance is unconstitutional because it makes an impermissible distinction between labor picketing and other peaceful picketing.

The city of Chicago exempts peaceful labor picketing from its general prohibition on picketing next to a school. The question we consider here is whether this selective exclusion from a public place is permitted. Our answer is "No."

Because Chicago treats some picketing differently from others, we analyze this ordinance in terms of the Equal Protection Clause of the Fourteenth Amendment. Of course, the equal protection claim in this case is closely intertwined with First Amendment interests;[4] the Chicago ordinance affects picketing, which is expressive conduct; moreover, it does so by classifications formulated in terms of the subject of the picketing. As in all equal protection cases, however, the crucial question is whether there is an appropriate governmental interest suitably furthered by the differential treatment.

[4] The First Amendment and the Equal Protection Clause often work hand in hand. When the government discriminates among different types of speakers, that obviously violates the right to free speech. However, it can also violate the Equal Protection Clause, because the government is selectively favoring some groups and disfavoring other groups.

The central problem with Chicago's ordinance is that it describes permissible picketing in terms of its subject matter. Peaceful picketing on the subject of a school's labor-management dispute is permitted, but all other peaceful picketing is prohibited. The operative distinction is the message on a picket sign. But, above all else, the First Amendment means that government has no power to restrict expression because of its message, its ideas, its subject matter, or its content.[5] To permit the continued building of our politics and culture, and to assure self-fulfillment for each individual, our people are guaranteed the right to express any thought, free from government censorship. The essence of this forbidden censorship is content control. Any restriction on expressive activity because of its content would completely undercut the "profound national commitment to the principle that debate on public issues should be uninhibited, robust, and wide-open."

Necessarily, then, under the Equal Protection Clause, not to mention the First Amendment itself, government may not grant the use of a forum to people whose views it finds acceptable, but deny use to those wishing to express less favored or more controversial views. And it may not select which issues are worth discussing or debating in public facilities. There is an "equality of status in the field of ideas," and government must afford all points of view an equal opportunity to be heard. Once a forum is opened up to assembly or speaking by some groups, government may not prohibit others from assembling or speaking on the basis of what they intend to say. Selective exclusions from a public forum[6] may not be based on content alone, and may not be justified by reference to content alone.

Guided by these principles, we have frequently condemned such discrimination among different users of the same medium for expression. . . . Similarly, because of their potential use as instruments for selectively suppressing some points of view, this Court has condemned licensing schemes that lodge broad discretion[7] in a public official to permit speech-related activity.

. . .

This is not to say that all picketing must always be allowed. We have continually recognized that reasonable "time, place and manner" regulations[8] of picketing may be necessary to further significant governmental interests. Similarly, under an equal protection analysis, there may be sufficient regulatory interests justifying selective exclusions or distinctions among pickets. Conflicting demands on the

[5] This is one of the most oft-quoted passages in all of First Amendment law. Justice Marshall explains that when the government discriminates against speech based on its "message, subject matter, ideas, or content," the government has violated the First Amendment. This statement forms the basis of the content discrimination principle in First Amendment jurisprudence. In First Amendment law, there is a presumption that content-based laws are unconstitutional.

[6] A public forum is a piece of government property that traditionally has been open to the public for expressive activities. The classic examples of public forums are public parks and public streets. Justice Marshall warns that the government should not selectively exclude people from public forums.

[7] A key term in First Amendment law is "unbridled discretion." When government officials have unbridled discretion to deny persons the opportunity to speak, problems arise. Generally, an ordinance or licensing scheme should provide clear standards so that people know when they can speak on government property and when they cannot. Government officials can enact licensing schemes; they just need to make sure that these schemes have clear standards.

[8] A reasonable time, place, and manner restriction on speech is one that applies across the board to all speakers at certain times. For example, an ordinance that prohibited picketing near a school between the hours of 7:00 a.m.–8:00 a.m. and 2:00 p.m.–3:00 p.m. likely would be considered a reasonable time, place, and manner restriction on speech. This ordinance only prohibits picketers at the times when children are being dropped off at school and there would be increased traffic. Furthermore, this type of ordinance does not discriminate between different types of picketers.

same place may compel the State to make choices among potential users and uses. And the State may have a legitimate interest in prohibiting some picketing to protect public order. But these justifications for selective exclusions from a public forum must be carefully scrutinized. Because picketing plainly involves expressive conduct within the protection of the First Amendment, discriminations among pickets must be tailored to serve a substantial governmental interest.

In this case, the ordinance itself describes impermissible picketing not in terms of time, place, and manner, but in terms of subject matter. The regulation "thus slip[s] from the neutrality of time, place, and circumstance into a concern about content." This is never permitted. In spite of this, Chicago urges that the ordinance is not improper content censorship, but rather a device for preventing disruption of the school. Cities certainly have a substantial interest in stopping picketing which disrupts a school. "The crucial question, however, is whether [Chicago's ordinance] advances that objective in a manner consistent with the command of the Equal Protection Clause." It does not.

Although preventing school disruption is a city's legitimate concern, Chicago itself has determined that peaceful labor picketing during school hours is not an undue interference with school. Therefore, under the Equal Protection Clause, Chicago may not maintain that other picketing disrupts the school unless that picketing is clearly more disruptive than the picketing Chicago already permits. If peaceful labor picketing is permitted, there is no justification for prohibiting all nonlabor picketing,[9] both peaceful and nonpeaceful. "Peaceful" nonlabor picketing, however the term "peaceful" is defined, is obviously no more disruptive than "peaceful" labor picketing. But Chicago's ordinance permits the latter and prohibits the former. . . .

[9]This passage means that the city of Chicago has no justification for treating peaceful labor picketing differently from peaceful picketing on other subjects. The bottom line is that this ordinance discriminates against certain speakers and favors others. This violates both the First Amendment and the Equal Protection Clause.

Similarly, we reject the city's argument that, although it permits peaceful labor picketing, it may prohibit all nonlabor picketing because, as a class, nonlabor picketing is more prone to produce violence than labor picketing. Predictions about imminent disruption from picketing involve judgments appropriately made on an individualized basis, not by means of broad classifications, especially those based on subject matter. Freedom of expression, and its intersection with the guarantee of equal protection, would rest on a soft foundation indeed if government could distinguish among picketers on such a wholesale and categorical basis. "[I]n our system, undifferentiated fear or apprehension of disturbance is not enough to overcome the right to freedom of expression." Some labor picketing is peaceful, some disorderly; the same is true of picketing on other themes. No labor picketing could be more peaceful or less prone to violence than Mosley's solitary vigil. In seeking to restrict nonlabor picketing that is clearly more disruptive than peaceful labor picketing, Chicago may not prohibit all nonlabor picketing at the school forum.

The Equal Protection Clause requires that statutes affecting First Amendment interests be narrowly tailored[10] to their legitimate objectives. Chicago may not vindicate its interest in preventing disruption by the wholesale exclusion of picketing on all but one preferred subject. Given what Chicago tolerates from labor picketing, the excesses of some nonlabor picketing may not be controlled by a broad ordinance prohibiting both peaceful and violent picketing. Such excesses "can be controlled by narrowly drawn statutes," focusing on the abuses and dealing even-handedly with picketing regardless of subject matter. Chicago's ordinance imposes a selective restriction on expressive conduct far "greater than is essential to the furtherance of [a substantial governmental] interest." Far from being tailored to a substantial governmental interest, the discrimination among pickets is based on the content of their expression. Therefore, under the Equal Protection Clause, it may not stand.

The judgment is affirmed.

[10]"Narrowly tailored" is a term used to describe a law that is drafted narrowly enough to address a particular problem but not drafted so broadly that it infringes on too much speech. In this case, the Supreme Court explained that Chicago's ordinance was not narrowly tailored, because it prohibited many different types of peaceful picketing.

Source: *Police Department of Chicago v. Mosley*, 408 U.S. 92 (1972).

Miller v. California

June 21, 1973

INTRODUCTION

In First Amendment law, there are a few narrow categories of speech not entitled to free-speech protection. One of these unprotected categories is obscenity: hardcore pornography that has no serious value. Obscenity remains a controversial area of free-speech law, as critics warn that it is difficult to draw a constitutional line between unprotected and protected speech.

The U.S. Supreme Court first ruled explicitly that obscenity was not protected speech in *Roth v. United States* (1957). The Court created the following test for obscenity: "whether to the average person, applying contemporary community standards, the dominant theme of the material taken as a whole appeals to prurient interest." However, the Court struggled mightily with obscenity through the 1960s, with different justices using different tests.

In 1973, the Court again addressed the subject of obscenity in *Miller v. California* and created a new test for obscenity that is still used today.

MR. CHIEF JUSTICE BURGER delivered the opinion of the Court.

This is one of a group of "obscenity-pornography" cases being reviewed by the Court in a re-examination of standards enunciated in earlier cases involving what Mr. Justice Harlan called "the intractable obscenity problem."[1]

Appellant conducted a mass mailing campaign to advertise the sale of illustrated books, euphemistically called "adult" material. After a jury trial, he was convicted of violating California Penal Code 311.2 (a), a misdemeanor, by knowingly distributing obscene matter, and the Appellate Department, Superior Court of California, County of Orange, summarily affirmed the judgment without opinion. Appellant's conviction was specifically based on his conduct in causing five unsolicited advertising brochures to be sent through the mail in an envelope addressed to a restaurant in Newport Beach, California.

[1] Chief Justice Warren Burger quotes his colleague John Marshall Harlan II on obscenity as "the intractable obscenity problem." The Supreme Court struggled through the years on how to deal with and define obscenity. Chief Justice Burger is acknowledging that this issue has proven to be very difficult for the Court to resolve.

The envelope was opened by the manager of the restaurant and his mother. They had not requested the brochures; they complained to the police.

The brochures advertise four books[2] entitled "Intercourse," "Man-Woman," "Sex Orgies Illustrated," and "An Illustrated History of Pornography," and a film entitled "Marital Intercourse." While the brochures contain some descriptive printed material, primarily they consist of pictures and drawings very explicitly depicting men and women in groups of two or more engaging in a variety of sexual activities, with genitals often prominently displayed.

[2] Marvin Miller, the appellant, had mailed advertisements of four books that depicted men and women in sexual positions and poses. In other words, Mr. Miller trafficked in what we call pornography. However, not all pornography falls into the unprotected category of obscenity. For adults, the only types of pornography that are not protected are obscenity and child pornography.

This case involves the application of a State's criminal obscenity statute to a situation in which sexually explicit materials have been thrust by aggressive sales action upon unwilling recipients who had in no way indicated any desire to receive such materials. . . .

Apart from the initial formulation in the Roth case, no majority of the Court has at any given time been able to agree on a standard[3] to determine what constitutes obscene, pornographic material subject to regulation under the States' police power. We have seen "a variety of views among the members of the Court unmatched in any other course of constitutional adjudication." This is not remarkable, for in the area of freedom of speech and press the courts must always remain sensitive to any infringement on genuinely serious literary, artistic, political, or scientific expression. This is an area in which there are few eternal verities.

[3] The Court initially agreed on a standard for obscenity in *Roth v. United States* (1957). However, in the 1960s, the Court could not agree on a consistent standard for this type of material. Chief Justice Burger recognizes the difficulties of providing such a definition.

. . .

This much has been categorically settled by the Court, that obscene material is unprotected by the First Amendment. . . . As a result, we now confine the permissible scope of such regulation to works which depict or describe sexual conduct. That conduct must be specifically defined by the applicable state law, as written or authoritatively construed. A state offense must also be limited to works which, taken as a whole, appeal to the prurient interest in sex, which portray sexual conduct in a patently offensive way, and which, taken as a whole, do not have serious literary, artistic, political, or scientific value.

The basic guidelines for the trier of fact[4] must be: (a) whether "the average person, applying contemporary community standards" would find that the work, taken as a whole, appeals to the prurient interest, (b) whether the work depicts or describes, in a patently offensive way, sexual conduct specifically defined by the applicable state law; and (c) whether the work, taken as a whole, lacks serious literary, artistic, political, or scientific value.

[4] The Court majority adopts "basic guidelines" for jurors to use in obscenity cases. These three guidelines, or prongs, form what is called the "Miller test." The first prong is the "prurient interest" prong—the material must appeal to a shameful, or morbid, interest in sex, as opposed to a healthy interest in sex. The second prong is the "patently offensive" prong. The final prong is sometimes called by the acronym "SLAPS"—no serious literary, artistic, political, or scientific value. The Miller test remains the governing standard for obscenity in the United States. It has never been overruled.

. . .

Under the holdings announced today, no one will be subject to prosecution for the sale or exposure of obscene materials unless these materials depict or describe patently offensive "hard core" sexual conduct[5] specifically defined by the regulating state law, as written or construed. We are satisfied that these specific prerequisites will provide fair notice to a dealer in such materials that his public and commercial activities may bring prosecution.

[5] The Court explains that people should be charged with obscenity only if the material in question constitutes hardcore pornography as defined by state law. This means that standard pornography is not obscenity. There is a significant legal difference between pornography and obscenity. In other words, only a narrow range of pornography can be classified as obscenity.

. . .

Under a National Constitution, fundamental First Amendment limitations on the powers of the States do not vary from community to community, but this does not mean that there are, or should or can be, fixed, uniform national standards of precisely what appeals to the "prurient interest" or is "patently offensive." These are essentially questions of fact, and our Nation is simply too big and too diverse for this Court to reasonably expect that such standards could be articulated for all 50 States in a single formulation, even assuming the prerequisite consensus exists. . . . To require a State to structure obscenity proceedings around evidence of a national "community standard"[6] would be an exercise in futility.

[6] One of the arguments asserted by Marvin Miller was that there needed to be a national community standard for obscenity. He argued that it did not make sense that a producer of sexual materials could be prosecuted in one state but be fine in another state. Chief Justice Burger rejected that argument, noting that it would be "an exercise in futility" to force a national standard.

. . .

It is neither realistic nor constitutionally sound to read the First Amendment as requiring that the people of Maine or Mississippi accept public depiction of conduct found tolerable in Las Vegas, or New York City. People in different States vary in their tastes and attitudes, and this diversity is not to be strangled by the absolutism of imposed uniformity.[7] . . .

[7] Chief Justice Burger once again emphasizes that local community standards are more realistic and preferable in our legal system than a forced national standard. He explains that people in Maine or Mississippi may be less tolerant of sexually based conduct than people in Las Vegas or New York City. He values this as "diversity" and criticizes the idea of a national standard as "the absolutism of imposed uniformity."

In sum, we (a) reaffirm the *Roth* holding that obscene material is not protected[8] by the First Amendment; (b) hold that such material can be regulated by the States, subject to the specific safeguards enunciated above, without a showing that the material is "utterly without redeeming social value"; and (c) hold that obscenity is to be determined by applying "contemporary community standards" . . .

[8] Chief Justice Burger concludes his opinion by explaining that obscenity remains a category of unprotected expression in First Amendment jurisprudence. States can regulate such material by applying "contemporary community standards" and the guidelines articulated in the so-called Miller test.

Source: *Miller v. California*, 413 U.S. 15 (1973).

Erznoznik v. City of Jacksonville

June 23, 1975

INTRODUCTION

One of the more underappreciated First Amendment free-speech decisions is *Erznoznik v. City of Jacksonville* (1975). The case involved a city ordinance that prohibited the display in drive-in movie theaters of any movies that contained nudity. The city claimed that the law was necessary to protect minors from harmful material. Richard Erznoznik was the manager of a local drive-in movie theater.

The Supreme Court struck down the law and discussed many important First Amendment concepts, including content discrimination, protection for offensive speech, and overbreadth. The city vigorously tried to defend its law, but ultimately the Court found that the law was not drafted precisely enough to satisfy constitutional standards.

MR. JUSTICE POWELL delivered the opinion of the Court.

This case presents a challenge to the facial validity[1] of a Jacksonville, Fla., ordinance that prohibits showing films containing nudity by a drive-in movie theater when its screen is visible from a public street or place.

[1] "Facial validity" refers to whether a law, by its very language, is constitutional or unconstitutional. If a law is facially invalid, the law is no longer enforceable.

Appellant, Richard Erznoznik, is the manager of the University Drive-In Theatre in Jacksonville. On March 13, 1972, he was charged with violating 330.313 of the municipal code for exhibiting a motion picture, visible from public streets, in which "female buttocks and bare breasts were shown." The ordinance, adopted January 14, 1972, provides:

"330.313 Drive-In Theaters, Films Visible From Public Streets or Public Places. It shall be unlawful and it is hereby declared a public nuisance[2] for any ticket seller, ticket taker, usher, motion picture projection machine operator, manager, owner, or any other person connected with or employed by any drive-in theater in the City to exhibit, or aid or assist in exhibiting, any motion picture, slide, or other exhibit in which the human male or female bare buttocks,

[2] The Jacksonville city ordinance challenged in this case banned drive-in movie theaters from showing movies featuring any public nudity. The ordinance declared such conduct to be a public nuisance. A public nuisance is something that harms the community, such as a house that features illegal drug sales or a house of prostitution.

human female bare breasts, or human bare pubic areas are shown, if such motion picture, slide, or other exhibit is visible from any public street or public place. Violation of this section shall be punishable as a Class C offense."

Appellant, with the consent of the city prosecutor, successfully moved to stay his prosecution so that the validity of the ordinance could be tested in a separate declaratory action. In that action, appellee, the city of Jacksonville, introduced evidence showing that the screen of appellant's theater is visible from two adjacent public streets and a nearby church parking lot.[3] There was also testimony indicating that people had been observed watching films while sitting outside the theater in parked cars and in the grass.

[3] One reason why this became a controversy is that apparently some youths would park in the church parking lot across from the drive-in movie theater and watch movies, including movies that featured nudity.

The trial court upheld the ordinance as a legitimate exercise of the municipality's police power,[4] and ruled that it did not infringe upon appellant's First Amendment rights. The District Court of Appeal, First District of Florida, affirmed, 288 So.2d 260 (1974), relying exclusively on *Chemline, Inc. v. City of Grand Prairie*, 364 F.2d 721 (CA5 1966), which had sustained a similar ordinance. The Florida Supreme Court denied certiorari, three judges dissenting. We noted probable jurisdiction and now reverse.

[4] State and local governments have police powers. This means that they can pass laws or ordinances that serve the public's health, safety, and welfare interests.

Appellee concedes that its ordinance sweeps far beyond the permissible restraints on obscenity,[5] and thus applies to films that are protected by the First Amendment. Nevertheless, it maintains that any movie containing nudity which is visible from a public place may be suppressed as a nuisance. Several theories are advanced to justify this contention.

[5] Obscenity is a narrow category of hardcore sexual materials that are not protected by the First Amendment. The Supreme Court established a test for obscenity in *Miller v. California* (1973). The Court explains that the movies covered under this Jacksonville ordinance are not legally obscene. The vast majority of movies that contain nudity are not obscene under the law.

Appellee's primary argument is that it may protect its citizens against unwilling exposure to materials that may be offensive. Jacksonville's ordinance, however, does not protect citizens from all movies that might offend; rather it singles out films containing nudity, presumably because the lawmakers considered them especially offensive to passersby.

This Court has considered analogous issues—pitting the First Amendment rights of speakers against the privacy rights of those who may be unwilling viewers or auditors—in a variety of contexts. . . .

Although each case ultimately must depend on its own specific facts, some general principles have emerged. A State or municipality may protect individual privacy by enacting reasonable time, place, and manner regulations applicable to all speech irrespective of content. But when the government, acting as censor, undertakes selectively to shield the public[6] from some kinds of speech on the ground that they are more offensive than others, the First Amendment strictly limits its power. Such selective restrictions have been upheld only when the speaker intrudes on the privacy of the home, or the degree of captivity makes it impractical for the unwilling viewer or auditor to avoid exposure. . . .

[6] The Court is troubled by the Jacksonville ordinance because it seeks to shield the public from offensive material that is not unprotected speech. In other words, the First Amendment protects a great deal of offensive, obnoxious, and even repugnant speech. The city argued that the law was necessary to protect privacy, but the Court said that privacy is an interest most protected in the home, not out in the general public.

The plain, if at times disquieting, truth is that in our pluralistic society, constantly proliferating new and ingenious forms of expression, "we are inescapably captive audiences for many purposes." Much that we encounter offends our esthetic, if not our political and moral, sensibilities. Nevertheless, the Constitution does not permit government to decide which types of otherwise protected speech are sufficiently offensive to require protection for the unwilling listener or viewer. Rather, absent the narrow circumstances described above, the burden normally falls upon the viewer to "avoid further bombardment of [his] sensibilities simply by averting [his] eyes."[7]

[7] When individuals are confronted with offensive speech, they can "avert their eyes." The Court explains that this is the proper response in our legal system, not the government overstepping its bounds and over-regulating all forms of speech that might be offensive to some.

The Jacksonville ordinance discriminates among movies solely on the basis of content.[8] Its effect is to deter drive-in theaters from showing movies containing any nudity, however innocent or even educational. This discrimination cannot be justified as a means of preventing significant intrusions on privacy. The ordinance seeks only to keep these films from being seen from public streets and places where the offended viewer readily can avert his eyes. In short, the screen of a drive-in theater is not "so obtrusive as to make it impossible for an unwilling individual to avoid exposure to it." Thus, we conclude that the limited privacy interest of persons on the public streets cannot justify this censorship of otherwise protected speech on the basis of its content.

[8] The Court views this Jacksonville law as content-based, because it treats movies differently based on whether they contain nudity. In other words, the law treats some movies differently than others. This is clearly content-based.

Appellee also attempts to support the ordinance as an exercise of the city's undoubted police power to protect children. Appellee maintains that even though it cannot prohibit the display of films containing nudity to adults, the present ordinance is a reasonable means of protecting minors from this type of visual influence.

It is well settled that a State or municipality can adopt more stringent controls on communicative materials available to youths than on those available to adults. Nevertheless, minors are entitled to a significant measure of First Amendment protection,[9] and only in relatively narrow and well-defined circumstances may government bar public dissemination of protected materials to them.

[9] The city argued that the ordinance was necessary to protect minors from harmful material. The Court responds that minors have a significant degree of free-speech rights. The Court cites the Court's decision in *Tinker v. Des Moines Independent Community School District* (1969) for this point. In that case, the Court held that students had free-speech rights at school.

In this case, assuming the ordinance is aimed at prohibiting youths from viewing the films, the restriction is broader than permissible. The ordinance is not directed against sexually explicit nudity, nor is it otherwise limited. Rather, it sweepingly forbids display of all films containing any uncovered buttocks or breasts, irrespective of context or pervasiveness. Thus it would bar a film containing a picture of a baby's buttocks, the nude body of a war victim, or scenes from a culture in which nudity is indigenous. The ordinance also might prohibit newsreel scenes of the opening of an art exhibit as well as shots of bathers on a beach. Clearly all nudity cannot be deemed obscene, even as to minors. Nor can such a broad restriction be justified by any other governmental interest pertaining to minors. Speech that is neither obscene as to youths nor subject to some other legitimate proscription cannot be suppressed solely to protect the young from ideas or images that a legislative body thinks unsuitable for them. In most circumstances, the values protected by the First Amendment are no less applicable when government seeks to control the flow of information to minors. Thus, if Jacksonville's ordinance is intended to regulate expression accessible to minors, it is overbroad[10] in its proscription.

[10] The Court finds that the Jacksonville ordinance is too broad, or overbroad, because it prohibits the showing of films that contain nudity that is not harmful in any way. For example, the Court explains that the ordinance could prohibit the showing of a movie that shows the nude body of a war victim.

At oral argument, appellee, for the first time, sought to justify its ordinance as a traffic regulation.[11] It claimed that nudity on a drive-in movie screen distracts passing motorists, thus slowing the flow of traffic and increasing the likelihood of accidents.

[11] The city even argued that the ordinance would protect traffic safety, because a driver could see nudity and then crash his or her vehicle. The Court found this argument specious, pointing out that a wide variety of movie scenes could distract viewers, such as violent scenes.

Nothing in the record or in the text of the ordinance suggests that it is aimed at traffic regulation. Indeed, the ordinance applies to movie screens visible from public places as well as public streets, thus indicating that it is not a traffic regulation. But even if this were the purpose of the ordinance, it nonetheless would be invalid. By singling out movies containing even the most fleeting and innocent glimpses of nudity, the legislative classification is strikingly underinclusive. There is no reason to think that a wide variety of other scenes in the customary screen diet, ranging from soap opera to violence, would be any less distracting to the passing motorist.

...

Even though none of the reasons advanced by appellee will sustain the Jacksonville ordinance, it remains for us to decide whether the ordinance should be invalidated on its face. This Court has long recognized that a demonstrably overbroad statute or ordinance may deter the legitimate exercise of First Amendment rights. Nonetheless, when considering a facial challenge, it is necessary to proceed with caution and restraint, as invalidation may result in unnecessary interference with a state regulatory program. In accommodating these competing interests, the Court has held that a state statute should not be deemed facially invalid unless it is not readily subject to a narrowing construction by the state courts, and its deterrent effect on legitimate expression is both real and substantial.

In the present case, the possibility of a limiting construction appears remote.[12] Appellee explicitly joined in this test of the facial validity of its ordinance by agreeing to stay appellant's prosecution. Moreover, the ordinance, by its plain terms, is not easily susceptible of a narrowing construction. Indeed, when the state courts were presented with this overbreadth challenge, they made no effort to restrict its application. In these circumstances, particularly where, as here, appellee offers several distinct justifications for the ordinance in its broadest terms, there is no reason to assume that the ordinance can or will be decisively narrowed.

[12] Sometimes courts will apply a narrowing, or limiting, construction to interpret a law in a way that saves it from being invalidated. In *Chaplinsky v. New Hampshire* (1942), the U.S. Supreme Court accepted the limiting construction of a disorderly conduct law done by the New Hampshire Supreme Court. In this case, the Court finds it difficult to think of a limiting construction, particularly when the city advanced so many arguments defending the ordinance.

Moreover, the deterrent effect of this ordinance is both real and substantial. Since it applies specifically to all persons employed by or connected with drive-in theaters, the owners and operators of these theaters are faced with an unwelcome choice: to avoid prosecution of themselves and their employees, they must either restrict their movie offerings or construct adequate protective fencing which may be extremely expensive or even physically impracticable.

In concluding that this ordinance is invalid, we do not deprecate the legitimate interests asserted by the city of Jacksonville. We hold only that the present ordinance does not satisfy the rigorous constitutional standards that apply when government attempts to regulate

[13] The Court explains that lawmakers must be precise and clear when they draft laws impacting individual freedoms. The city had good intentions in trying to protect minors from nudity. However, the law they drafted was way too broad.

expression. Where First Amendment freedoms are at stake, we have repeatedly emphasized that precision of drafting and clarity of purpose are essential.[13] These prerequisites are absent here. Accordingly the judgment below is

Reversed.

Source: *Erznoznik v. City of Jacksonville*, 422 U.S. 205 (1975).

Bates v. State Bar of Arizona

June 27, 1977

INTRODUCTION

The text of the First Amendment does not mention that different types of speech should be treated differently. But the U.S. Supreme Court repeatedly has indicated that pure political speech is the core type of speech that the amendment was designed to protect. Other forms of speech receive less protection. One of these forms of lesser-protected speech is commercial speech, or advertising.

Until the mid-1970s, advertising received no First Amendment protection. The Supreme Court had declared in 1942 that the Constitution imposed no limitations on the regulation of advertising. However, the Court changed the equation in a 1976 decision, *Virginia Pharmacy v. Virginia Consumer Council.* That case involved a ban on pharmacists advertising X drug for Y price.

The Court reasoned that consumers have a strong interest in the free flow of commercial information. However, the Court did not rule that all professions had a right to advertise. Some believed that there was a difference between business advertising and advertising by those in a learned profession, such as law.

In 1977, the Court examined the case of *Bates v. State Bar of Arizona*. Two young lawyers, John Bates and Van O'Steen, had started a law practice based on the delivery of routine, low-cost legal services. They quickly found out that they needed a larger client base to survive economically. The two lawyers placed an ad in the *Arizona Republic*, advertising their prices for wills, no-contest divorces, and other services.

The problem for Bates and O'Steen was that the Arizona rules governing attorneys prohibited lawyer advertising. The lawyers turned to their former constitutional law professor, William Canby. Professor Canby called his good friend and noted attorney, John P. Frank. Professor Canby started to inform Mr. Frank about the situation of his two former students. Mr. Frank informed Professor Canby that he had been retained by the Arizona Bar. Professor Canby then decided that he would represent his former students.

Thus, these two good friends—John P. Frank and William Canby—opposed each other in this precedent-setting case.

MR. JUSTICE BLACKMUN delivered the opinion of the Court.

As part of its regulation of the Arizona Bar,[1] the Supreme Court of that State has imposed and enforces a disciplinary rule that restricts advertising by attorneys. This case presents two issues: whether 1 and 2 of the Sherman Act, 15 U.S.C. 1 and 2, forbid such state regulation, and whether the operation of the rule violates the First Amendment, made applicable to the States through the Fourteenth.

[1] The legal profession is self-regulating. The high court in each state has the authority to dictate the rules of professional conduct for lawyers. The states delegate much of the responsibility to boards of professional responsibility, which review complaints against lawyers. In this case, the local committee recommended a six-month suspension for John Bates and Van O'Steen. The Board of Governors then reduced the suspension to one week. Bates and O'Steen then appealed to the Arizona Supreme Court, which affirmed the suspension.

Appellants John R. Bates and Van O'Steen are attorneys licensed to practice law in the State of Arizona. As such, they are members of the appellee, the State Bar of Arizona. After admission to the bar in 1972, appellants worked as attorneys with the Maricopa County Legal Aid Society.

In March 1974, appellants left the Society and opened a law office, which they call a "legal clinic," in Phoenix. Their aim was to provide legal services at modest fees to persons of moderate income who did not qualify for governmental legal aid. In order to achieve this end, they would accept only routine matters, such as uncontested divorces, uncontested adoptions, simple personal bankruptcies, and changes of name, for which costs could be kept down by extensive use of paralegals, automatic typewriting equipment, and standardized forms and office procedures. More complicated cases, such as contested divorces, would not be accepted. Because appellants set their prices so as to have a relatively low return on each case they handled, they depended on substantial volume.

After conducting their practice in this manner for two years, appellants concluded that their practice and clinical concept could not survive unless the availability of legal services at low cost was advertised and, in particular, fees were advertised. Consequently, in order to generate the necessary flow of business, that is, "to attract clients," appellants on February 22, 1976, placed an advertisement in the Arizona Republic, a daily newspaper of general circulation in the Phoenix metropolitan area. As may be seen, the advertisement stated that appellants were offering "legal services at very reasonable fees," and listed their fees for certain services.

Appellants concede that the advertisement constituted a clear violation of Disciplinary Rule 2-101 (B), incorporated in Rule 29 (a) of the Supreme Court of Arizona, 17A Ariz. Rev. Stat., p. 26 (Supp. 1976). The disciplinary rule provides in part:

"(B) A lawyer shall not publicize himself, or his partner, or associate, or any other lawyer affiliated with him or his firm, as a lawyer through newspaper or magazine advertisements, radio or television announcements, display advertisements in the city or telephone directories or other means of commercial publicity, nor shall he authorize or permit others to do so in his behalf."

Upon the filing of a complaint initiated by the president of the State Bar, a hearing was held before a three-member Special Local Administrative Committee, as prescribed by Arizona Supreme Court Rule 33. Although the committee took the position that it could not consider an attack on the validity of the rule, it allowed the parties to develop a record on which such a challenge could be based. The committee recommended that each of the appellants be suspended from the practice of law for not less than six months. Upon further review by the Board of Governors of the State Bar, pursuant to the Supreme Court's Rule 36, the Board recommended only a one-week suspension[2] for each appellant, the weeks to run consecutively.

[2] The Board recommended a one-week suspension. The typical punishments in lawyer discipline cases are disbarment, suspension, public reprimand, and private reprimand. Disbarment means that a lawyer loses his or her license. The disbarred lawyer can reapply for a license, usually after a period of five years. A suspension means that a lawyer loses his or her license for a period of time, but normally it is not as permanent as a disbarment. Reprimands, or censures, are where the court imposes discipline but the lawyer does not lose his or her license even temporarily. However, a lawyer never wants to receive professional discipline.

Appellants, as permitted by the Supreme Court's Rule 37, then sought review in the Supreme Court of Arizona, arguing, among other things . . . that the rule infringed their First Amendment rights. . . .

Turning to the First Amendment issue, the plurality . . . held that commercial speech was entitled to certain protection under the First Amendment, the plurality focused on passages in those opinions acknowledging that special considerations might bear on the advertising of professional services by lawyers. . . . The plurality apparently was of the view that the older decisions dealing with professional advertising survived these recent cases unscathed, and held that Disciplinary Rule 2-101 (B) passed First Amendment muster. Because the court, in agreement with the Board of Governors, felt that appellants' advertising "was done in good faith to test the constitutionality of DR 2-101 (B)," it reduced the sanction to censure only.

. . .

We noted probable jurisdiction.

. . .

The First Amendment

Last Term, in *Virginia Pharmacy Board v. Virginia Consumer Council* (1976), the Court considered the validity under the First Amendment of a Virginia statute declaring that a pharmacist was guilty of "unprofessional conduct" if he advertised prescription drug prices. The pharmacist would then be subject to a monetary penalty or the suspension or revocation of his license. The statute thus effectively prevented the advertising of prescription drug price information. We recognized that the pharmacist who desired to advertise did not wish to report any particularly newsworthy fact or to comment on any cultural, philosophical, or political subject; his desired communication was characterized simply: "I will sell you the X prescription drug at the Y price."[3] Nonetheless, we held that commercial speech of that kind was entitled to the protection of the First Amendment.

[3] "X drug for Y price" is a classic example of commercial speech, or advertising. In the Bates case, there was no question that John Bates and Van O'Steen engaged in commercial speech when they advertised their prices for certain routine legal services.

Our analysis began with the observation that our cases long have protected speech even though it is in the form of a paid advertisement; in a form that is sold for profit; or in the form of a solicitation to pay or contribute money. If commercial speech is to be distinguished, it "must be distinguished by its content." But a consideration of competing interests reinforced our view that such speech should not be withdrawn from protection merely because it proposed a mundane commercial transaction. Even though the speaker's interest is largely economic, the Court has protected such speech in certain contexts. The listener's interest is substantial: the consumer's concern for the free flow of commercial speech often may be far keener than his concern for urgent political dialogue.[4] Moreover, significant societal interests are served by such speech. Advertising, though entirely commercial, may often carry information of import to significant issues of the day. And commercial speech serves to inform the public of the availability, nature, and prices of products and services, and thus performs an indispensable role in the allocation of resources in a free enterprise system. In short, such speech serves individual and societal interests in assuring informed and reliable decision-making.

[4] Justice Blackmun points out that consumers have a "keen" interest in price advertising. In fact, he writes that consumers may care more about price advertising than about current political issues of the day. This is a key reason why the Court the year before had ruled in the *Virginia Pharmacy* case that commercial speech was entitled to some First Amendment protection.

Arrayed against these substantial interests in the free flow of commercial speech were a number of proffered justifications for the advertising ban. Central among them were claims that the ban was essential to the maintenance of professionalism[5] among licensed pharmacists. It was asserted that advertising would create price competition that might cause the pharmacist to economize at the customer's expense. He might reduce or eliminate the truly professional portions of his services: the maintenance and packaging of drugs so as to assure their effectiveness, and the supplementation on occasion of the prescribing physician's advice as to use. Moreover, it was said, advertising would cause consumers to price-shop, thereby undermining the pharmacist's effort to monitor the drug use of a regular customer so as to ensure that the prescribed drug would not provoke an allergic reaction or be incompatible with another substance the customer was consuming. Finally, it was argued that advertising would reduce the image of the pharmacist as a skilled and specialized craftsman—an image that was said to attract talent to the profession and to reinforce the good habits of those in it—to that of a mere shopkeeper.

[5] The primary argument against various forms of advertising was that they would reduce professionalism. The Court rejected that argument in *Virginia Pharmacy*. A key question in the *Bates* case was whether the professionalism argument is stronger when it comes to lawyers.

. . .

The issue presently before us is a narrow one. First, we need not address the peculiar problems associated with advertising claims relating to the quality of legal services.[6] Such claims probably are not susceptible of precise measurement or verification and, under some circumstances, might well be deceptive or misleading to the public, or even false. . . .

[6] The Court points out that the issue it reviews concerns lawyers advertising prices, not making statements as to the quality of their legal services. A lawyer's prices are more easily verified than a subjective statement that the lawyer "is the best" or "better than other lawyers."

The heart of the dispute before us today is whether lawyers also may constitutionally advertise the prices at which certain routine services will be performed. Numerous justifications are proffered for the restriction of such price advertising. We consider each in turn:

1. The Adverse Effect on Professionalism. Appellee places particular emphasis on the adverse effects that it feels price advertising will have on the legal profession. The key to professionalism, it is argued, is the sense of pride that involvement in the discipline generates. It is claimed that price advertising will bring about commercialization, which will undermine the attorney's sense of dignity and self-worth. The hustle of the marketplace will adversely affect the profession's

service orientation, and irreparably damage the delicate balance between the lawyer's need to earn and his obligation selflessly to serve. . . .

We recognize, of course, and commend the spirit of public service with which the profession of law is practiced and to which it is dedicated. The present Members of this Court, licensed attorneys all, could not feel otherwise. And we would have reason to pause if we felt that our decision today would undercut that spirit. But we find the postulated connection between advertising and the erosion of true professionalism to be severely strained.[7] At its core, the argument presumes that attorneys must conceal from themselves and from their clients the real-life fact that lawyers earn their livelihood at the bar. We suspect that few attorneys engage in such self-deception. . . .

[7] Here, the U.S. Supreme Court majority rejects the connection between advertising and a decline in professionalism. Some attorneys and members of the public don't like attorney advertising, but the reality is that many attorneys who advertise are also quite professional.

Moreover, the assertion that advertising will diminish the attorney's reputation in the community is open to question. Bankers and engineers advertise, and yet these professions are not regarded as undignified.[8] In fact, it has been suggested that the failure of lawyers to advertise creates public disillusionment with the profession. The absence of advertising may be seen to reflect the profession's failure to reach out and serve the community:[9] studies reveal that many persons do not obtain counsel even when they perceive a need, because of the feared price of services or because of an inability to locate a competent attorney. Indeed, cynicism with regard to the profession may be created by the fact that it long has publicly eschewed advertising, while condoning the actions of the attorney who structures his social or civic associations so as to provide contacts with potential clients.

[8] Justice Blackmun explains that advertising by lawyers may help the profession's image with the public. He cites studies showing that many people do not seek legal counsel because they cannot locate a competent attorney. He also points out that other professions, such as bankers and engineers, have advertised without an apparent loss of public esteem.

[9] Here, the U.S. Supreme Court identifies that legal advertising does reach out to people and services the legal needs of the public. A key aspiration of the legal profession is to ensure that people have access to the legal system. Advertising can help in this matter.

It appears that the ban on advertising originated as a rule of etiquette and not as a rule of ethics. Early lawyers in Great Britain viewed the law as a form of public service, rather than as a means of earning a living, and they looked down on "trade" as unseemly. . . . But habit and tradition are not in themselves an adequate answer to a constitutional challenge. In this day, we do not belittle the person who earns his living by the strength of his arm or the force of his mind. Since the belief that lawyers are somehow "above" trade has become an anachronism, the historical foundation for the advertising restraint has crumbled.

2. The Inherently Misleading Nature of Attorney Advertising.[10] It is argued that advertising of legal services inevitably will be misleading (a) because such services are so individualized with regard to content and quality as to prevent informed comparison on the basis of an advertisement, (b) because the consumer of legal services is unable to determine in advance just what services he needs, and (c) because advertising by attorneys will highlight irrelevant factors and fail to show the relevant factor of skill.

[10] Justice Blackmun rejects the idea that advertising by lawyers is inherently misleading. Many lawyer price ads could be quite truthful. As long as the lawyer performs the legal tasks at the advertised price, there is no valid argument that the advertising was misleading.

We are not persuaded that restrained professional advertising by lawyers inevitably will be misleading. Although many services performed by attorneys are indeed unique, it is doubtful that any attorney would or could advertise fixed prices for services of that type. The only services that lend themselves to advertising are the routine ones: the uncontested divorce, the simple adoption, the uncontested personal bankruptcy, the change of name, and the like—the very services advertised by appellants. Although the precise service demanded in each task may vary slightly, and although legal services are not fungible, these facts do not make advertising misleading so long as the attorney does the necessary work at the advertised price.

. . .

3. The Adverse Effect on the Administration of Justice. Advertising is said to have the undesirable effect of stirring up litigation. The judicial machinery is designed to serve those who feel sufficiently aggrieved to bring forward their claims. Advertising, it is argued, serves to encourage the assertion of legal rights in the courts, thereby undesirably unsettling societal repose. There is even a suggestion of barratry.

But advertising by attorneys is not an unmitigated source of harm to the administration of justice. It may offer great benefits. Although advertising might increase the use of the judicial machinery, we cannot accept the notion that it is always better for a person to suffer a wrong silently than to redress it by legal action.[11] . . . Advertising can help to solve this acknowledged problem: advertising is the traditional mechanism in a free-market economy for a supplier to inform a potential purchaser of the availability and terms of exchange. The disciplinary rule at issue likely has served to burden access to legal services, particularly for the not-quite-poor and the unknowledgeable.

[11] Justice Blackmun also rejects the argument that allowing lawyers to advertise will lead to unnecessary litigation, or too many lawsuits. Instead, he explains that allowing lawyers to advertise will inform consumers of their legal rights and may provide greater access to those who traditionally cannot afford legal services. For example, many lawyers who advertise provide for contingency fees. This means that the consumer-client only pays the lawyer if the client prevails in the litigation.

A rule allowing restrained advertising would be in accord with the bar's obligation to "facilitate the process of intelligent selection of lawyers, and to assist in making legal services fully available."

4. The Undesirable Economic Effects of Advertising.[12] It is claimed that advertising will increase the overhead costs of the profession, and that these costs then will be passed along to consumers in the form of increased fees. Moreover, it is claimed that the additional cost of practice will create a substantial entry barrier, deterring or preventing young attorneys from penetrating the market and entrenching the position of the bar's established members.

[12] The Arizona Bar also argued that lawyer advertising would increase the prices for consumers. Justice Blackmun flatly rejects this argument. Instead, he points out that advertising by lawyers may well lower the prices of competitors.

These two arguments seem dubious at best. . . . The ban on advertising serves to increase the difficulty of discovering the lowest cost seller of acceptable ability. As a result, to this extent attorneys are isolated from competition, and the incentive to price competitively is reduced. Although it is true that the effect of advertising on the price of services has not been demonstrated, there is revealing evidence with regard to products; where consumers have the benefit of price advertising, retail prices often are dramatically lower than they would be without advertising. It is entirely possible that advertising will serve to reduce, not advance, the cost of legal services to the consumer.

The entry-barrier argument is equally unpersuasive. In the absence of advertising, an attorney must rely on his contacts with the community to generate a flow of business. In view of the time necessary to develop such contacts, the ban in fact serves to perpetuate the market position of established attorneys.[13] Consideration of entry-barrier problems would urge that advertising be allowed so as to aid the new competitor in penetrating the market.

[13] He also mentions that opposition to lawyer advertising may come from lawyers who already have an established "market position." These attorneys do not want to lose business to newer lawyers like John Bates and Van O'Steen.

. . .

In sum, we are not persuaded that any of the proffered justifications rise to the level of an acceptable reason for the suppression of all advertising by attorneys.

In the usual case involving a restraint on speech, a showing that the challenged rule served unconstitutionally to suppress speech would end our analysis. In the First Amendment context, the Court has permitted attacks on overly broad statutes without requiring that the person making the attack demonstrate that in fact his specific conduct was protected. . . .

The First Amendment overbreadth doctrine,[14] however, represents a departure from the traditional rule that a person may not challenge a statute on the ground that it might be applied unconstitutionally in circumstances other than those before the court. . . . Indeed, such a person might choose not to speak because of uncertainty whether his claim of privilege would prevail if challenged. The use of overbreadth analysis reflects the conclusion that the possible harm to society from allowing unprotected speech to go unpunished is outweighed by the possibility that protected speech will be muted.

[14] An important concept in First Amendment law is the overbreadth doctrine. This doctrine means that laws can sweep too broadly and prohibit protected speech in addition to speech that should be prohibited. Thus, if a law is overbroad, it is unconstitutional. However, Justice Blackmun explains that the overbreadth doctrine should not apply in cases involving commercial speech.

But the justification for the application of overbreadth analysis applies weakly, if at all, in the ordinary commercial context. As was acknowledged in *Virginia Pharmacy Board v. Virginia Consumer Council*, there are "commonsense differences" between commercial speech and other varieties. Since advertising is linked to commercial well-being, it seems unlikely that such speech is particularly susceptible to being crushed by overbroad regulation. Moreover, concerns for uncertainty in determining the scope of protection are reduced; the advertiser seeks to disseminate information about a product or service that he provides, and presumably he can determine more readily than others whether his speech is truthful and protected. Since overbreadth has been described by this Court as "strong medicine," which "has been employed . . . sparingly and only as a last resort," we decline to apply it to professional advertising, a context where it is not necessary to further its intended objective.

. . .

In holding that advertising by attorneys may not be subjected to blanket suppression, and that the advertisement at issue is protected, we, of course, do not hold that advertising by attorneys may not be regulated in any way. We mention some of the clearly permissible limitations on advertising not foreclosed by our holding.

Advertising that is false, deceptive, or misleading[15] of course is subject to restraint. Since the advertiser knows his product and has a commercial interest in its dissemination, we have little worry that

[15] Justice Blackmun explains that the Court's ruling only applies to truthful lawyer price advertising. It does not apply to lawyer advertising about the quality of legal services, to advertisements that are misleading, or to in-person, direct face-to-face solicitations.

regulation to assure truthfulness will discourage protected speech. And any concern that strict requirements for truthfulness will undesirably inhibit spontaneity seems inapplicable, because commercial speech generally is calculated. Indeed, the public and private benefits from commercial speech derive from confidence in its accuracy and reliability. Thus, the leeway for untruthful or misleading expression that has been allowed in other contexts has little force in the commercial arena. In fact, because the public lacks sophistication concerning legal services, misstatements that might be overlooked or deemed unimportant in other advertising may be found quite inappropriate in legal advertising. For example, advertising claims as to the quality of services—a matter we do not address today—are not susceptible of measurement or verification; accordingly, such claims may be so likely to be misleading as to warrant restriction. Similar objections might justify restraints on in-person solicitation. We do not foreclose the possibility that some limited supplantation, by way of warning or disclaimer or the like, might be required of even an advertisement of the kind ruled upon today so as to assure that the consumer is not misled. In sum, we recognize that many of the problems in defining the boundary between deceptive and nondeceptive advertising remain to be resolved, and we expect that the bar will have a special role to play in assuring that advertising by attorneys flows both freely and cleanly.

. . .

The constitutional issue in this case is only whether the State may prevent the publication in a newspaper of appellants' truthful advertisement concerning the availability and terms of routine legal services. We rule simply that the flow of such information may not be restrained, and we therefore hold the present application of the disciplinary rule against appellants to be violative of the First Amendment.

Source: *Bates v. State Bar of Arizona,* 433 U.S. 350 (1977).

Renton v. Playtime Theatres, Inc.

February 25, 1986

INTRODUCTION

In First Amendment law, the content discrimination principle often controls. Laws are classified as content-based or content-neutral. A law is content-based if it treats a particular type of speech differently than other types of speech.

On the surface, a law that singles out adult businesses would appear to be a content-based law. However, the Supreme Court has determined that a zoning law impacting only adult businesses can be considered content-neutral. The Court reasoned that the law was not designed to suppress offensive speech but instead to address harmful, adverse secondary effects allegedly associated with those businesses. These secondary effects include increased crime and decreased property values.

The secondary effects doctrine is controversial in First Amendment law. Justice William Brennan warned that it could lead to "an evisceration of First Amendment freedoms." All speech causes effects. However, the Court consistently has upheld zoning regulations on adult businesses based on the secondary effects doctrine.

The leading secondary effects Supreme Court case is *Renton v. Playtime Theatres, Inc.* (1986).

Justice Rehnquist delivered the opinion of the Court.

This case involves a constitutional challenge to a zoning ordinance,[1] enacted by appellant city of Renton, Washington, that prohibits adult motion picture theaters from locating within 1,000 feet of any residential zone, single- or multiple-family dwelling, church, park, or school. Appellees, Playtime Theatres, Inc., and Sea-First Properties, Inc., filed an action in the United States District Court for the Western District of Washington seeking a declaratory judgment that the Renton ordinance violated the First and Fourteenth Amendments and a permanent injunction against its enforcement. The District Court ruled in favor of Renton and denied the permanent injunction, but the Court of Appeals for the Ninth Circuit reversed and remanded for reconsideration. We noted probable jurisdiction and now reverse the judgment of the Ninth Circuit.

[1] Cities often impose zoning laws that regulate the location of adult businesses. This ordinance enacted by the city of Renton imposed a 1,000-foot restriction on adult businesses from being located in a residential zone, school, church, or park. The idea is to prohibit a conglomeration of adult businesses into a red-light district.

In May 1980, the Mayor of Renton, a city of approximately 32,000 people located just south of Seattle, suggested to the Renton City Council that it consider the advisability of enacting zoning legislation dealing with adult entertainment uses. No such uses existed in the city at that time. Upon the Mayor's suggestion, the City Council referred the matter to the city's Planning and Development Committee. The Committee held public hearings, reviewed the experiences of Seattle and other cities,[2] and received a report from the City Attorney's Office advising as to developments in other cities. The City Council, meanwhile, adopted Resolution No. 2368, which imposed a moratorium on the licensing of "any business . . . which . . . has as its primary purpose the selling, renting or showing of sexually explicit materials." The resolution contained a clause explaining that such businesses "would have a severe impact upon surrounding businesses and residences."

[2] The Renton City Council looked at studies done in other cities on adult businesses. This was a major issue in the case, as the city of Renton did not conduct its own study but instead relied on studies from other cities. The resolution adopted by the city focused on the adverse impacts such adult businesses would have on the community.

. . .

The District Court then vacated the preliminary injunction, denied respondents' requested permanent injunction, and entered summary judgment in favor of Renton. The court found that the Renton ordinance did not substantially restrict First Amendment interests, that Renton was not required to show specific adverse impact on Renton from the operation of adult theaters but could rely on the experiences of other cities, that the purposes of the ordinance were unrelated to the suppression of speech, and that the restrictions on speech imposed by the ordinance were no greater than necessary to further the governmental interests involved. Relying on *Young v. American Mini Theatres, Inc.* (1976),[3] and *United States v. O'Brien* (1968), the court held that the Renton ordinance did not violate the First Amendment.

[3] Ten years earlier, the U.S. Supreme Court in *Young v. American Mini Theatres, Inc.* (1976) had upheld the constitutionality of an ordinance in Detroit limiting the locations of adult businesses. In a footnote, the Court had said that the purpose of the ordinance was not to silence offensive expression but instead to combat harmful secondary effects associated with the adult businesses.

The Court of Appeals for the Ninth Circuit reversed. The Court of Appeals first concluded, contrary to the finding of the District Court, that the Renton ordinance constituted a substantial restriction on First Amendment interests. Then, using the standards set forth in *United States v. O'Brien*,[4] the Court of Appeals held that Renton had improperly relied on the experiences of other cities in lieu of evidence about the effects of adult theaters on Renton, that Renton had thus failed to establish adequately the existence of a substantial governmental interest in support of its ordinance, and that in any event Renton's asserted

[4] The District Court upheld the constitutionality of the ordinance, but on appeal the Ninth Circuit reversed. Note that the Ninth Circuit relied on the O'Brien test from *United States v. O'Brien* (1968). In *O'Brien*, the Court created a test for when there were speech and non-speech elements combined together. Recall that *O'Brien* involved the punishment of a man for burning his draft card.

interests had not been shown to be unrelated to the suppression of expression. The Court of Appeals remanded the case to the District Court for reconsideration of Renton's asserted interests.

In our view, the resolution of this case is largely dictated by our decision in *Young v. American Mini Theatres, Inc.*, supra. There, although five Members of the Court did not agree on a single rationale for the decision, we held that the city of Detroit's zoning ordinance, which prohibited locating an adult theater within 1,000 feet of any two other "regulated uses" or within 500 feet of any residential zone, did not violate the First and Fourteenth Amendments. *Id.*, at 72–73 (plurality opinion of STEVENS, J., joined by BURGER, C. J., and WHITE and REHNQUIST, JJ.); *id.*, at 84 (POWELL, J., concurring). The Renton ordinance, like the one in *American Mini Theatres*, does not ban adult theaters altogether, but merely provides that such theaters may not be located within 1,000 feet of any residential zone, single- or multiple-family dwelling, church, park, or school. The ordinance is therefore properly analyzed as a form of time, place, and manner regulation.[5]

Describing the ordinance as a time, place, and manner regulation is, of course, only the first step in our inquiry. This Court has long held that regulations enacted for the purpose of restraining speech on the basis of its content presumptively violate the First Amendment. On the other hand, so-called "content-neutral"[6] time, place, and manner regulations are acceptable so long as they are designed to serve a substantial governmental interest and do not unreasonably limit alternative avenues of communication.

At first glance, the Renton ordinance, like the ordinance in *American Mini Theatres*, does not appear to fit neatly into either the "content-based" or the "content-neutral" category. To be sure, the ordinance treats theaters that specialize in adult films differently from other kinds of theaters. Nevertheless, as the District Court concluded, the Renton ordinance is aimed not at the content of the films shown at "adult motion picture theatres," but rather at the secondary effects[7] of such theaters on the surrounding community. The District Court found that the City Council's "*predominate* concerns" were with the secondary effects of adult theaters, and not with the content of adult films themselves.

...

[5] In First Amendment cases, courts have to assess whether a regulation on speech is directed at the content of the speech or is merely a "time, place, and manner" regulation of speech. In his opinion Justice Rehnquist views this ordinance as a time, place, and manner restriction on speech, since the ordinance does not ban adult businesses; rather, it simply limits their location.

[6] Recall that in First Amendment cases, we ask whether laws are content-based or content-neutral. Content-based laws are viewed much more rigorously than content-neutral laws. A key issue in this case was whether an ordinance regulating the location of adult businesses was content-based or content-neutral.

[7] Here, Justice Rehnquist reasons that the ordinance impacting only adult businesses can be considered content-neutral because it is not designed to silence speech but instead to address the harmful secondary effects associated with these adult businesses. This is the essence of the secondary effects doctrine—that regulations on adult businesses are treated as content-neutral instead of as content-based.

The District Court's finding as to "predominate" intent, left undisturbed by the Court of Appeals, is more than adequate to establish that the city's pursuit of its zoning interests here was unrelated to the suppression of free expression. The ordinance by its terms is designed to prevent crime, protect the city's retail trade, maintain property values,[8] and generally "protec[t] and preserv[e] the quality of [the city's] neighborhoods, commercial districts, and the quality of urban life," not to suppress the expression of unpopular views. As JUSTICE POWELL observed in *American Mini Theatres*, "[i]f [the city] had been concerned with restricting the message purveyed by adult theaters, it would have tried to close them or restrict their number rather than circumscribe their choice as to location."

[8] The two chief secondary effects associated with adult businesses are that they lead to more crime and to lower property values. Here, Justice Rehnquist explains that the district court found that the city of Renton passed this ordinance in order to address these secondary effects.

In short, the Renton ordinance is completely consistent with our definition of "content-neutral" speech regulations as those that "are justified without reference to the content of the regulated speech." The ordinance does not contravene the fundamental principle[9] that underlies our concern about "content-based" speech regulations: that "government may not grant the use of a forum to people whose views it finds acceptable, but deny use to those wishing to express less favored or more controversial views."

[9] A fundamental principle in First Amendment law is that the government may not punish individuals merely because they engage in controversial speech. Justice Rehnquist explains that the Renton ordinance does not violate this fundamental principle.

It was with this understanding in mind that, in *American Mini Theatres*, a majority of this Court decided that, at least with respect to businesses that purvey sexually explicit materials, zoning ordinances designed to combat the undesirable secondary effects of such businesses are to be reviewed under the standards applicable to "content-neutral" time, place, and manner regulations. JUSTICE STEVENS, writing for the plurality, concluded that the city of Detroit was entitled to draw a distinction between adult theaters and other kinds of theaters "without violating the government's paramount obligation of neutrality in its regulation of protected communication," noting that "[i]t is th[e] secondary effect which these zoning ordinances attempt to avoid, not the dissemination of 'offensive' speech" . . .

The appropriate inquiry in this case, then, is whether the Renton ordinance is designed to serve a substantial governmental interest and allows for reasonable alternative avenues of communication.[10] It is clear that the ordinance meets such a standard. As a majority of this Court recognized in *American Mini Theatres*, a city's "interest in attempting to preserve the quality of urban life is one that must be

[10] Even content-neutral laws can violate the First Amendment if they do not allow for "reasonable alternative avenues of communication." In this context, the question is whether the Renton ordinance limiting the location of adult businesses still affords enough places in the city for the businesses to locate. A city could pass a zoning law so restrictive that it does not allow enough places to operate.

accorded high respect." Exactly the same vital governmental interests are at stake here.

The Court of Appeals ruled, however, that because the Renton ordinance was enacted without the benefit of studies specifically relating to "the particular problems or needs of Renton," the city's justifications for the ordinance were "conclusory and speculative." We think the Court of Appeals imposed on the city an unnecessarily rigid burden of proof. The record in this case reveals that Renton relied heavily on the experience of, and studies produced by, the city of Seattle. In Seattle, as in Renton, the adult theater zoning ordinance was aimed at preventing the secondary effects caused by the presence of even one such theater in a given neighborhood.

. . .

We hold that Renton was entitled to rely on the experiences of Seattle and other cities, and in particular on the "detailed findings" summarized in the Washington Supreme Court's *Northend Cinema* opinion, in enacting its adult theater zoning ordinance. The First Amendment does not require a city, before enacting such an ordinance, to conduct new studies[11] or produce evidence independent of that already generated by other cities, so long as whatever evidence the city relies upon is reasonably believed to be relevant to the problem that the city addresses. That was the case here. Nor is our holding affected by the fact that Seattle ultimately chose a different method of adult theater zoning than that chosen by Renton, since Seattle's choice of a different remedy to combat the secondary effects of adult theaters does not call into question either Seattle's identification of those secondary effects or the relevance of Seattle's experience to Renton.

We also find no constitutional defect in the method chosen by Renton to further its substantial interests. Cities may regulate adult theaters by dispersing them, as in Detroit, or by effectively concentrating them, as in Renton. "It is not our function to appraise the wisdom of [the city's] decision to require adult theaters to be separated rather than concentrated in the same areas. . . . [T]he city must be allowed a reasonable opportunity to experiment with solutions to admittedly serious problems." *American Mini Theatres*, 427 U.S., at 71 (plurality opinion). Moreover, the Renton ordinance is

[11] Justice Rehnquist determined that the city of Renton did not have to create its own study on adult businesses. Instead, the city of Renton could rely on the experiences of other cities, including Seattle, in determining that adult businesses cause adverse secondary effects.

[12] "Narrowly tailored" is another important term in First Amendment law. A law is narrowly tailored when it is not too broad and does not impact too much speech. In other words, when a court finds that a law is "narrowly tailored," it generally means that it approves of the law.

"narrowly tailored"[12] to affect only that category of theaters shown to produce the unwanted secondary effects . . .

Respondents contend that the Renton ordinance is "underinclusive," in that it fails to regulate other kinds of adult businesses that are likely to produce secondary effects similar to those produced by adult theaters. On this record the contention must fail. There is no evidence that, at the time the Renton ordinance was enacted, any other adult business was located in, or was contemplating moving into, Renton. In fact, Resolution No. 2368, enacted in October 1980, states that "the City of Renton does not, at the present time, have any business whose primary purpose is the sale, rental, or showing of sexually explicit materials." That Renton chose first to address the potential problems created by one particular kind of adult business in no way suggests that the city has "singled out" adult theaters for discriminatory treatment. We simply have no basis on this record for assuming that Renton will not, in the future, amend its ordinance to include other kinds of adult businesses that have been shown to produce the same kinds of secondary effects as adult theaters.

Finally, turning to the question whether the Renton ordinance allows for reasonable alternative avenues of communication, we note that the ordinance leaves some 520 acres, or more than five percent of the entire land area of Renton, open to use as adult theater sites. The District Court found, and the Court of Appeals did not dispute the finding, that the 520 acres of land consists of "[a]mple, accessible real estate," including "acreage in all stages of development from raw land to developed, industrial, warehouse, office, and shopping space that is crisscrossed by freeways, highways, and roads."

Respondents argue, however, that some of the land in question is already occupied by existing businesses, that "practically none" of the undeveloped land is currently for sale or lease, and that in general there are no "commercially viable" adult theater sites within the 520 acres left open by the Renton ordinance. The Court of Appeals accepted these arguments, concluded that the 520 acres was not truly "available" land, and therefore held that the Renton ordinance "would result in a substantial restriction" on speech.

We disagree with both the reasoning and the conclusion of the Court of Appeals. That respondents must fend for themselves in the real estate market, on an equal footing with other prospective purchasers and lessees, does not give rise to a First Amendment violation. And although we have cautioned against the enactment of zoning regulations that have "the effect of suppressing, or greatly restricting access to, lawful speech," *American Mini Theatres*, 427 U.S., at 71, n. 35 (plurality opinion), we have never suggested that the First Amendment compels the Government to ensure that adult theaters, or any other kinds of speech-related businesses for that matter, will be able to obtain sites at bargain prices. In our view, the First Amendment requires only that Renton refrain from effectively denying respondents a reasonable opportunity to open[13] and operate an adult theater within the city, and the ordinance before us easily meets this requirement.

[13] As indicated, the adult businesses contended that the city ordinance did not provide them with reasonable alternative locations to open. The businesses argued that the city relegated them to potential areas of undeveloped land. Justice Rehnquist was not sympathetic to that view, explaining that all a city has to do is offer an adult business "a reasonable opportunity to open."

In sum, we find that the Renton ordinance represents a valid governmental response to the "admittedly serious problems" created by adult theaters. Renton has not used "the power to zone as a pretext for suppressing expression," but rather has sought to make some areas available for adult theaters and their patrons, while at the same time preserving the quality of life in the community at large by preventing those theaters from locating in other areas. This, after all, is the essence of zoning.[14] Here, as in *American Mini Theatres*, the city has enacted a zoning ordinance that meets these goals while also satisfying the dictates of the First Amendment. The judgment of the Court of Appeals is therefore

[14] Justice Rehnquist concludes that Renton's ordinance is a typical zoning law not designed to suppress free expression. Instead, the law is designed to address harmful secondary effects. He calls this the "essence of zoning."

Reversed.

Source: *Renton v. Playtime Theatres, Inc.*, 475 U.S. 41 (1986).

Bethel School District v. Fraser

July 7, 1986

INTRODUCTION

In 1969, the U.S. Supreme Court had ruled in *Tinker v. Des Moines Independent Community School District* that public school students do not "shed their constitutional rights to freedom of speech and expression at the schoolhouse gates." The Court created the "substantial disruption" standard.

In the 1980s, a more conservative Court cut back on protection for student speech. In 1986, the Court decided a case that created an exception to *Tinker* for student speech that was vulgar, lewd, or plainly offensive. That case was *Bethel School District v. Fraser*. It involved a high school student from the state of Washington who delivered a speech before the school assembly that contained sexual references.

When school officials suspended the student, he and his father sued, alleging a violation of his free-speech rights. The lower courts ruled in favor of the student. However, the U.S. Supreme Court reversed and ruled 7–2 in favor of the school district.

CHIEF JUSTICE BURGER[1] delivered the opinion of the Court.

We granted certiorari to decide whether the First Amendment prevents a school district from disciplining a high school student for giving a lewd speech at a school assembly.

On April 26, 1983, respondent Matthew N. Fraser, a student at Bethel High School in Pierce County, Washington, delivered a speech nominating a fellow student for student elective office.[2] Approximately 600 high school students, many of whom were 14-year-olds, attended the assembly. Students were required to attend the assembly or to report to the study hall. The assembly was part of a school-sponsored educational program in self-government. Students who elected not to attend the assembly were required to report to study hall. During the entire speech, Fraser referred to his candidate in terms of an elaborate, graphic, and explicit sexual metaphor.

[1] Chief Justice Warren Burger was the 15th chief justice of the U.S. Supreme Court. Nominated by President Richard Nixon, Burger came to the Court with a reputation as a law-and-order judge. In his career, Chief Justice Burger wrote several opinions protective of the press. His opinion in *Bethel School District v. Fraser* was the last opinion he ever wrote. He retired and was ultimately replaced by William Rehnquist.

[2] Fraser was nominating fellow student Jeff Kuhlman for student vice president. His speech read in part, "I know a man who is firm—he's firm in his pants, he's firm in his shirt . . . Jeff Kuhlman is a man who takes his point and pounds it in. . . . Jeff is a man who will go to the every end—even the climax." School officials were not pleased with the speech, which, as the Court described it, referred to the candidate in terms of "an elaborate, graphic, and explicit sexual metaphor."

Two of Fraser's teachers, with whom he discussed the contents of his speech in advance, informed him that the speech was "inappropriate and that he probably should not deliver it," and that his delivery of the speech might have "severe consequences."

During Fraser's delivery of the speech, a school counselor observed the reaction of students to the speech. Some students hooted and yelled; some by gestures graphically simulated the sexual activities pointedly alluded to in respondent's speech. Other students appeared to be bewildered and embarrassed by the speech.[3] One teacher reported that on the day following the speech, she found it necessary to forgo a portion of the scheduled class lesson in order to discuss the speech with the class.

[3] Fraser's speech caused some people embarrassment. Other students giggled during the speech. However, it is questionable to say that Fraser's speech caused any type of "substantial disruption."

A Bethel High School disciplinary rule prohibiting the use of obscene language in the school provides:

"Conduct which materially and substantially interferes[4] with the educational process is prohibited, including the use of obscene, profane language or gestures."

[4] The school's no-disruption rule appears to be modeled after the Supreme Court's standard in the *Tinker v. Des Moines Independent Community School District* case. In *Tinker*, the Court held that public school officials could censor student speech only if they could reasonably forecast that the student speech would cause a "substantial disruption" of school activities or invade the rights of others.

The morning after the assembly, the Assistant Principal called Fraser into her office and notified him that the school considered his speech to have been a violation of this rule. Fraser was presented with copies of five letters submitted by teachers, describing his conduct at the assembly; he was given a chance to explain his conduct, and he admitted to having given the speech described and that he deliberately used sexual innuendo in the speech. Fraser was then informed that he would be suspended for three days, and that his name would be removed from the list of candidates for graduation speaker at the school's commencement exercises.

Fraser sought review of this disciplinary action through the School District's grievance procedures. The hearing officer determined that the speech given by respondent was "indecent, lewd, and offensive to the modesty and decency of many of the students and faculty in attendance at the assembly." The examiner determined that the speech fell within the ordinary meaning of "obscene," as used in the disruptive-conduct rule, and affirmed the discipline in its entirety. Fraser served two days of his suspension, and was allowed to return to school on the third day.

Respondent, by his father as guardian *ad litem*, then brought this action in the United States District Court for the Western District of Washington. Respondent alleged a violation of his First Amendment right to freedom of speech and sought both injunctive relief and monetary damages under 42 U.S.C. 1983. The District Court held that the school's sanctions violated respondent's right to freedom of speech under the First Amendment to the United States Constitution, that the school's disruptive-conduct rule is unconstitutionally vague and overbroad,[5] and that the removal of respondent's name from the graduation speaker's list violated the Due Process Clause of the Fourteenth Amendment because the disciplinary rule makes no mention of such removal as a possible sanction. The District Court awarded respondent $278 in damages, $12,750 in litigation costs and attorney's fees, and enjoined the School District from preventing respondent from speaking at the commencement ceremonies. Respondent, who had been elected graduation speaker[6] by a write-in vote of his classmates, delivered a speech at the commencement ceremonies on June 8, 1983.

[5] Fraser prevailed in the federal district court, which invalidated the school's no-disruption rule as both vague and overbroad. A rule is too vague when people have to guess at its meaning. A rule is too broad when it sweeps too broadly and prohibits speech that ought to be protected.

[6] A great irony in this case is that Fraser was elected graduation speaker by his peers and delivered the speech. As Matthew Fraser later told the author in an interview, school officials made him a martyr. (See David L. Hudson, Jr., *Let The Students Speak!: A History of the Fight for Free Expression in American Schools* [Beacon Press, 2011], p. 87.) He got to deliver the graduation speech in part because he had prevailed before the federal district court.

The Court of Appeals for the Ninth Circuit[7] affirmed the judgment of the District Court, holding that respondent's speech was indistinguishable from the protest armband in *Tinker v. Des Moines Independent Community School Dist.*, 393 U.S. 503 (1969). The court explicitly rejected the School District's argument that the speech, unlike the passive conduct of wearing a black armband, had a disruptive effect[8] on the educational process. The Court of Appeals also rejected the School District's argument that it had an interest in protecting an essentially captive audience of minors from lewd and indecent language in a setting sponsored by the school, reasoning that the School District's "unbridled discretion" to determine what discourse is "decent" would "increase the risk of cementing white, middle-class standards for determining what is acceptable and proper speech and behavior in our public schools." Finally, the Court of Appeals rejected the School District's argument that, incident to its responsibility for the school curriculum, it had the power to control the language used to express ideas during a school-sponsored activity.

[7] The school district appealed the decision to the 9th U.S. Circuit Court of Appeals, which also ruled in Matthew Fraser's favor.

[8] The appeals court said that the case was controlled by the *Tinker* decision. The appeals court did not believe that the speech was disruptive.

We granted certiorari. We reverse.

This Court acknowledged in *Tinker v. Des Moines Independent Community School Dist.*, supra, that students do not "shed their constitutional rights to freedom of speech or expression at the schoolhouse gate." The Court of Appeals read that case as precluding any discipline of Fraser for indecent speech and lewd conduct in the school assembly. That court appears to have proceeded on the theory that the use of lewd and obscene speech in order to make what the speaker considered to be a point in a nominating speech for a fellow student was essentially the same as the wearing of an armband in *Tinker* as a form of protest or the expression of a political position.

The marked distinction[9] between the political "message" of the armbands in *Tinker* and the sexual content of respondent's speech in this case seems to have been given little weight by the Court of Appeals. In upholding the students' right to engage in a nondisruptive, passive expression of a political viewpoint in *Tinker*, this Court was careful to note that the case did "not concern speech or action that intrudes upon the work of the schools or the rights of other students."

[9] Chief Justice Burger found a "marked distinction" between Matthew Fraser's speech and the expression of the students in the *Tinker* case. The Chief Justice characterized Fraser's speech as sexual and the speech of the *Tinker* kids as political. It should be noted, however, that Matthew Fraser was delivering a speech nominating a fellow student for a political office.

It is against this background that we turn to consider the level of First Amendment protection accorded to Fraser's utterances and actions before an official high school assembly attended by 600 students.

The role and purpose of the American public school system were well described by two historians, who stated: "[P]ublic education must prepare pupils for citizenship in the Republic. . . . It must inculcate the habits and manners of civility[10] as values in themselves conducive to happiness and as indispensable to the practice of self-government in the community and the nation." . . .

[10] Chief Justice Burger explains that school officials have the responsibility to teach students "manners of civility." Fraser's speech crossed the bounds of social decency for the chief justice and most of his colleagues on the Court.

These fundamental values of "habits and manners of civility" essential to a democratic society must, of course, include tolerance of divergent political and religious views, even when the views expressed may be unpopular. But these "fundamental values" must also take into account consideration of the sensibilities of others, and, in the case of a school, the sensibilities of fellow students. The undoubted freedom to advocate unpopular and controversial views in schools and classrooms must be balanced against the society's countervailing interest in teaching students the boundaries of socially appropriate behavior.[11] Even the most heated political discourse in a democratic society requires consideration for the personal sensibilities of the other participants and audiences.

[11] The Court writes that the freedom to engage in controversial speech must be balanced against "teaching students the boundaries of socially appropriate behavior." Chief Justice Burger's opinion is replete with this idea that school officials have the power to teach and inculcate moral values and civility.

. . .

The First Amendment guarantees wide freedom in matters of adult public discourse. A sharply divided Court upheld the right to express an antidraft viewpoint in a public place, albeit in terms highly offensive to most citizens. It does not follow, however, that simply because the use of an offensive form of expression may not be prohibited to adults making what the speaker considers a political point, the same latitude must be permitted to children in a public school. In *New Jersey v. T. L. O.* (1985), we reaffirmed that the constitutional rights of students in public school are not automatically coextensive with the rights of adults[12] in other settings. As cogently expressed by Judge Newman, "the First Amendment gives a high school student the classroom right to wear Tinker's armband, but not Cohen's jacket."[13]

[12] The year before it decided the *Fraser* case, the Supreme Court had decided the Fourth Amendment case of *New Jersey v. T.L.O.* (1985). In that decision, the Court upheld an assistant school principal's action of searching a student's purse. In its decision, the Court said that minors do not have the same level of constitutional rights as adults. The Court in *Fraser* reiterated this point.

[13] Chief Justice Burger quotes a famous passage from Judge Jon Newman of the 2nd U.S. Circuit Court of Appeals. He famously wrote that a public school student can "wear Tinker's armband, but not Cohen's jacket." In other words, a student can wear a black armband but not a jacket with the words "F**k the Draft."

Surely it is a highly appropriate function of public school education to prohibit the use of vulgar and offensive terms[14] in public discourse. Indeed, the "fundamental values necessary to the maintenance of a democratic political system" disfavor the use of terms of debate highly offensive or highly threatening to others. Nothing in the Constitution prohibits the states from insisting that certain modes of expression are inappropriate and subject to sanctions. The inculcation of these values is truly the "work of the schools." The determination of what manner of speech in the classroom or in school assembly is inappropriate properly rests with the school board.

[14] A key rule from the *Fraser* decision is that public school officials can prohibit student speech that is vulgar, lewd, or plainly offensive. To the Court majority, Matthew Fraser's speech was vulgar and lewd.

The process of educating our youth for citizenship in public schools is not confined to books, the curriculum, and the civics class; schools must teach by example the shared values of a civilized social order. Consciously or otherwise, teachers—and indeed the older students—demonstrate the appropriate form of civil discourse[15] and political expression by their conduct and deportment in and out of class. Inescapably, like parents, they are role models. The schools, as instruments of the state, may determine that the essential lessons of civil, mature conduct cannot be conveyed in a school that tolerates lewd, indecent, or offensive speech and conduct such as that indulged in by this confused boy.

[15] Chief Justice Burger once again reiterates that public school officials have the power to teach the "appropriate form of civil discourse." Note also that the chief justice refers to Fraser as a "confused boy."

The pervasive sexual innuendo in Fraser's speech was plainly offensive to both teachers and students—indeed, to any mature person. By glorifying male sexuality, and in its verbal content, the speech was acutely insulting to teenage girl students. The speech could well be seriously damaging to its less mature audience, many of whom were only 14 years old[16] and on the threshold of awareness of human sexuality. Some students were reported as bewildered by the speech and the reaction of mimicry it provoked.

[16] The chief justice notes that many of the students in the school assembly audience for Fraser's speech were only 14 years old. Again, the Court believes that the students should not be exposed to this type of speech at school.

This Court's First Amendment jurisprudence has acknowledged limitations on the otherwise absolute interest of the speaker in reaching an unlimited audience where the speech is sexually explicit and the audience may include children. In *Ginsberg v. New York* (1968), this Court upheld a New York statute banning the sale of sexually oriented material to minors, even though the material in question was entitled to First Amendment protection with respect to adults. And in addressing the question whether the First Amendment places any limit on the authority of public schools to remove books from a public school library, all Members of the Court, otherwise sharply divided, acknowledged that the school board has the authority to remove books that are vulgar.[17] These cases recognize the obvious concern on the part of parents, and school authorities acting *in loco parentis*, to protect children—especially in a captive audience—from exposure to sexually explicit, indecent, or lewd speech.

[17] The Court cites *Board of Education v. Pico* (1982), a library censorship case. In that case, a public middle school had removed nine books from library shelves, in part because they found that the books contained offensive ideas. The Court held that public school officials could not remove books simply because they did not like the ideas in the books. However, the Court also said that public school officials could remove books because they were vulgar.

We have also recognized an interest in protecting minors from exposure to vulgar and offensive spoken language. In FCC v. Pacifica Foundation (1978),[18] we dealt with the power of the Federal Communications Commission to regulate a radio broadcast described as "indecent but not obscene." . . . We concluded that the broadcast was properly considered "obscene, indecent, or profane" within the meaning of the statute. The plurality opinion went on to reject the radio station's assertion of a First Amendment right to broadcast vulgarity.

[18] In *FCC v. Pacifica Foundation* (1978), the Supreme Court narrowly held that the Federal Communications Commission had the power to fine a radio station for playing comedian George Carlin's "Seven Dirty Words" monologue during daytime hours. Burger cites the case for the principle that the government has the power in certain circumstances to punish indecent speech.

. . .

We hold that petitioner School District acted entirely within its permissible authority in imposing sanctions upon Fraser in response to his offensively lewd and indecent speech. Unlike the sanctions imposed on the students wearing armbands in *Tinker*, the penalties imposed in this case were unrelated to any political viewpoint.[19] The First Amendment does not prevent the school officials from determining that to permit a vulgar and lewd speech such as respondent's would undermine the school's basic educational mission. A high school assembly or classroom is no place for a sexually explicit

[19] In the *Tinker* case, school officials had punished the armband-wearing students because they did not like the antiwar viewpoint. In this case, Chief Justice Burger points out that Matthew Fraser was punished not because of his viewpoint but instead because he used profanity.

monologue directed towards an unsuspecting audience of teenage students. Accordingly, it was perfectly appropriate for the school to disassociate itself to make the point to the pupils that vulgar speech and lewd conduct is wholly inconsistent with the "fundamental values" of public school education. . . .

Respondent contends that the circumstances of his suspension violated due process[20] because he had no way of knowing that the delivery of the speech in question would subject him to disciplinary sanctions. This argument is wholly without merit. We have recognized that "maintaining security and order in the schools requires a certain degree of flexibility in school disciplinary procedures, and we have respected the value of preserving the informality of the student-teacher relationship." . . . The school disciplinary rule proscribing "obscene" language and the prespeech admonitions of teachers gave adequate warning to Fraser that his lewd speech could subject him to sanctions.

[20] Fraser contended that his due-process rights were violated because he did not have fair notice that his speech would be in violation of the school's rule. Due process is about fundamental fairness. The Court majority determined that the rule gave Fraser adequate notice that his speech would be a problem.

The judgment of the Court of Appeals for the Ninth Circuit is

Reversed.

Source: *Bethel School District v. Fraser*, 478 U.S. 675 (1986).

Hazelwood School District v. Kuhlmeier

January 13, 1988

INTRODUCTION

In *Tinker v. Des Moines Independent Community School District* (1969), the U.S. Supreme Court famously had declared that public school students do not "shed their constitutional rights to freedom of speech or expression" at school. The Court determined that public school officials could censor student speech only if they reasonably forecast that the student speech would cause a substantial disruption of school activities or would invade the rights of others. This was a very speech-protective standard for students, and it led to many lawsuits.

In the 1980s, a more conservative Supreme Court created exceptions to the *Tinker* standard. In *Bethel School District v. Fraser* (1986), the Court held that public school officials could punish students for vulgar and lewd expression. The Court explained that minors don't have the same level of constitutional rights as adults.

Two years later, the Court addressed another student-speech case, *Hazelwood School District v. Kuhlmeier* (1988), involving the censorship of two articles in a student newspaper. The two articles concerned teen pregnancy and divorce. The school's principal determined that the articles were inappropriate and ordered them deleted.

Three female student editors challenged the principal's action in federal court. They had a good argument at the time. Their articles were not substantially disruptive under *Tinker*, and they were not vulgar within the meaning of *Fraser*. Instead, the Court created another new rule for so-called school-sponsored student speech.

The black armbands in *Tinker* were student-initiated expression. However, the articles in the *Hazelwood* case were produced in connection with a high school journalism class. Thus, these articles were school-sponsored.

JUSTICE WHITE delivered the opinion of the Court.

This case concerns the extent to which educators may exercise editorial control over the contents of a high school newspaper produced as part of the school's journalism curriculum.

Petitioners are the Hazelwood School District in St. Louis County, Missouri; various school officials; Robert Eugene Reynolds, the principal of Hazelwood East High School; and Howard Emerson, a teacher in the school district. Respondents are three former Hazelwood East students who were staff members of Spectrum, the school newspaper.[1] They contend that school officials violated their First Amendment rights by deleting two pages of articles from the May 13, 1983, issue of Spectrum.

Spectrum was written and edited by the Journalism II class at Hazelwood East. The newspaper was published every three weeks or so during the 1982–1983 school year. More than 4,500 copies of the newspaper were distributed during that year to students, school personnel, and members of the community.

. . .

The practice at Hazelwood East during the spring 1983 semester was for the journalism teacher to submit page proofs of each Spectrum issue to Principal Reynolds for his review prior to publication. On May 10, Emerson delivered the proofs of the May 13 edition to Reynolds, who objected to two of the articles scheduled to appear in that edition. One of the stories described three Hazelwood East students' experiences with pregnancy; the other discussed the impact of divorce on students at the school.[2]

. . .

Reynolds believed that there was no time to make the necessary changes in the stories before the scheduled press run, and that the newspaper would not appear before the end of the school year if printing were delayed to any significant extent. He concluded that his only options under the circumstances were to publish a four-page newspaper instead of the planned six-page newspaper, eliminating the two pages[3] on which the offending stories appeared, or to publish no newspaper at all. Accordingly, he directed Emerson to withhold from publication the two pages containing the stories on pregnancy and divorce. He informed his superiors of the decision, and they concurred.

Respondents subsequently commenced this action in the United States District Court for the Eastern District of Missouri, seeking a declaration that their First Amendment rights had been violated,

[1] A key to the *Hazelwood* case is that the newspaper in question was a school-sponsored newspaper produced as part of a journalism class. This newspaper class was part of the school's curriculum. It was not an "underground" student newspaper produced by students off campus apart from the school curriculum.

[2] Principal Robert Reynolds believed that these stories were not appropriate for younger students to read. There were several pregnant students at school, and Principal Reynolds feared that those students would be ostracized by the article. He also worried that the article about divorce did not adequately consider the response of parents.

[3] Principal Reynolds decided that the two articles in question, concerning pregnancy and divorce, needed to be cut from the newspaper. It was this act of censorship that caused three female student editors to sue in court. The three students argued that the elimination of these articles violated the First Amendment.

injunctive relief, and monetary damages. After a bench trial,[4] the District Court denied an injunction, holding that no First Amendment violation had occurred.

. . .

The Court of Appeals for the Eighth Circuit reversed. The court held at the outset that Spectrum was not only "a part of the school adopted curriculum," but also a public forum,[5] because the newspaper was "intended to be and operated as a conduit for student viewpoint." The court then concluded that Spectrum's status as a public forum precluded school officials from censoring its contents except when "necessary to avoid material and substantial interference with school work or discipline . . . or the rights of others."

. . .

We granted certiorari, and we now reverse.

Students in the public schools do not "shed their constitutional rights to freedom of speech or expression at the schoolhouse gate."[6] They cannot be punished merely for expressing their personal views on the school premises—whether "in the cafeteria, or on the playing field, or on the campus during the authorized hours," unless school authorities have reason to believe that such expression will "substantially interfere with the work of the school or impinge upon the rights of other students."

We have nonetheless recognized that the First Amendment rights of students in the public schools "are not automatically coextensive with the rights of adults in other settings,"[7] and must be "applied in light of the special characteristics of the school environment." A school need not tolerate student speech that is inconsistent with its "basic educational mission," *Fraser*, *supra*, at 685, even though the government could not censor similar speech outside the school. Accordingly, we held in *Fraser* that a student could be disciplined for having delivered a speech that was "sexually explicit" but not legally obscene at an official school assembly, because the school was entitled to "disassociate itself" from the speech in a manner that would demonstrate to others that such vulgarity is "wholly inconsistent with the 'fundamental values' of public school education." We thus

[4] There are two types of trials in American law: jury trials and bench trials. A jury trial is where there are a group of citizens, often twelve persons, who sit as the factfinders and determine the result of the case. A bench trial has no jury. In a bench trial, the judge is both judge and jury. In this case, the trial judge determined that Principal Reynolds acted reasonably in censoring the articles.

[5] The intermediate appellate court, the Eighth Circuit, reversed the trial judge's decision, finding that the newspaper was a "public forum." This is an important concept in First Amendment law. A public forum is a place or entity that invites different speakers or points of view. In other words, when a governmental body creates a public forum, the government has less control over the content of the speech. The Eighth Circuit determined that the principal only could censor the articles if he could reasonably establish that the articles would cause a substantial disruption of school activities.

[6] In this text from *Tinker*, the U.S. Supreme Court ruled that public school officials could censor student expression if they could reasonably forecast that the student expression would cause a substantial disruption of school activities or invade the rights of others. In the *Hazelwood* case, the three student editors contended that Principal Reynolds could not show that the articles were disruptive or invasive of the rights of others. In other words, under the *Tinker* rule, the students claimed that they should win.

[7] In *Bethel School District v. Fraser* (1986), the U.S. Supreme Court ruled that school officials could punish a student who gave a sexually laced speech before the school assembly. In that decision, the Court reasoned that public school students don't have the same level of free-speech rights as adults.

recognized that "[t]he determination of what manner of speech in the classroom or in school assembly is inappropriate properly rests with the school board," *id.*, at 683, rather than with the federal courts. It is in this context that respondents' First Amendment claims must be considered.

We deal first with the question whether Spectrum may appropriately be characterized as a forum for public expression. The public schools do not possess all of the attributes of streets, parks, and other traditional public forums that "time out of mind, have been used for purposes of assembly, communicating thoughts between citizens, and discussing public questions." Hence, school facilities may be deemed to be public forums only if school authorities have "by policy or by practice" opened those facilities "for indiscriminate use by the general public," or by some segment of the public, such as student organizations.[8] If the facilities have instead been reserved for other intended purposes, "communicative or otherwise," then no public forum has been created, and school officials may impose reasonable restrictions on the speech of students, teachers, and other members of the school community. "The government does not create a public forum by inaction or by permitting limited discourse, but only by intentionally opening a nontraditional forum for public discourse."

[8] The students in *Hazelwood* argued that school officials had created a public forum with the school newspaper. The U.S. Supreme Court majority determined that a school creates a public forum only when it, by "policy or by practice," has opened up the newspaper for competing viewpoints and for general use by the public. The Court explains that the newspaper is not a public forum; instead it is part of the school's journalism class. School officials had a practice of reviewing each article prior to publication.

. . .

Educators are entitled to exercise greater control[9] over this second form of student expression to assure that participants learn whatever lessons the activity is designed to teach, that readers or listeners are not exposed to material that may be inappropriate for their level of maturity, and that the views of the individual speaker are not erroneously attributed to the school. Hence, a school may, in its capacity as publisher of a school newspaper or producer of a school play, "disassociate itself," not only from speech that would "substantially interfere with [its] work . . . or impinge upon the rights of other students," but also from speech that is, for example, ungrammatical, poorly written, inadequately researched, biased or prejudiced, vulgar or profane, or unsuitable for immature audiences. A school must be able to set high standards for the student speech that is disseminated under its auspices—standards that may be higher than those demanded by some newspaper publishers or theatrical producers in

[9] Justice White writes that public school officials must have the authority to "exercise greater control" over school-sponsored speech, such as speech from the curriculum. He claims that school officials must be able to set high standards in order to teach students responsibility and to prepare them for the professional world.

the "real" world—and may refuse to disseminate student speech that does not meet those standards. In addition, a school must be able to take into account the emotional maturity of the intended audience in determining whether to disseminate student speech on potentially sensitive topics, which might range from the existence of Santa Claus in an elementary school setting to the particulars of teenage sexual activity in a high school setting. A school must also retain the authority to refuse to sponsor student speech that might reasonably be perceived to advocate drug or alcohol use, irresponsible sex, or conduct otherwise inconsistent with "the shared values of a civilized social order," or to associate the school with any position other than neutrality on matters of political controversy.[10] Otherwise, the schools would be unduly constrained from fulfilling their role as "a principal instrument in awakening the child to cultural values, in preparing him for later professional training, and in helping him to adjust normally to his environment."

Accordingly, we conclude that the standard articulated in *Tinker* for determining when a school may punish student expression need not also be the standard for determining when a school may refuse to lend its name and resources to the dissemination of student expression. Instead, we hold that educators do not offend the First Amendment by exercising editorial control over the style and content of student speech in school-sponsored expressive activities, so long as their actions are reasonably related to legitimate pedagogical concerns.[11]

. . .

We also conclude that Principal Reynolds acted reasonably[12] in requiring the deletion from the May 13 issue of Spectrum of the pregnancy article, the divorce article, and the remaining articles that were to appear on the same pages of the newspaper.

. . .

In sum, we cannot reject as unreasonable Principal Reynolds' conclusion that neither the pregnancy article nor the divorce article was suitable for publication in Spectrum. Reynolds could reasonably have concluded that the students who had written and edited these articles had not sufficiently mastered those portions of the Journalism

[10] Justice White then lists several examples of what school officials may reasonably do in exercising this greater control. One of the more controversial is the idea that the school may disassociate itself from "any position other than neutrality on matters of political controversy." Critics of this decision contend that this turns the First Amendment on its head. After all, one of the high principles of First Amendment law is that the government generally should not discriminate against different speakers based on viewpoint. The First Amendment protects a great deal of controversial speech.

[11] The Court in *Hazelwood* created a new rule, one often considered an exception to the *Tinker* standard. Under this new rule, school officials can censor school-sponsored student speech if they act reasonably pursuant to a legitimate "pedagogical," or educational, purpose. This "reasonableness" standard is more deferential to school officials than the substantial disruption standard articulated in the *Tinker* case. If the student speech is student-initiated, the *Tinker* rule generally controls. If the student speech is school-sponsored, the *Hazelwood* rule controls.

[12] Applying its new rule, the Supreme Court determines that Principal Reynolds "acted reasonably" in ordering the deletion of the two articles. The Court explains that the principal reasonably believed that the pregnant students at the school could be harmed by the article. He also acted reasonably in considering the privacy interests of parents mentioned in the divorce article. The Court also believed that some of the topics in these articles were not appropriate for all the students, some of whom were only 14 years old.

II curriculum that pertained to the treatment of controversial issues and personal attacks, the need to protect the privacy of individuals whose most intimate concerns are to be revealed in the newspaper, and "the legal, moral, and ethical restrictions imposed upon journalists within [a] school community" that includes adolescent subjects and readers. Finally, we conclude that the principal's decision to delete two pages of Spectrum, rather than to delete only the offending articles or to require that they be modified, was reasonable under the circumstances as he understood them. Accordingly, no violation of First Amendment rights occurred.

The judgment of the Court of Appeals for the Eighth Circuit is therefore

Reversed.

CONCLUSION

The *Hazelwood* decision is controversial to First Amendment advocates. Several states have responded to the decision by passing "anti-*Hazelwood*" statutes that provide greater free-speech protection under a state law than the U.S. Supreme Court provided in its decision.

Source: *Hazelwood School District et al. v. Kuhlmeier*, 484 U.S. 260 (1988).

Hustler Magazine, Inc. v. Falwell

February 24, 1988

INTRODUCTION

One of the more celebrated and fascinating First Amendment free-speech decisions ever decided by the U.S. Supreme Court was *Hustler Magazine, Inc. v. Falwell* (1988). The case featured a battle between pornographer Larry Flynt and televangelist Jerry Falwell, two powerful personalities.

In his *Hustler* magazine, Flynt liked to poke fun of public figures that he viewed as pompous or hypocritical. He found his target in Jerry Falwell, known for heading the Moral Majority. In one issue of his magazine, Flynt lampooned Falwell through a play on a series of ads by Campari Liqueur that were running on television at the time. In these ads, various celebrities talked about "their first time"—the first time they sampled Campari. However, the ads clearly played on the sexual double entendre of a first sexual encounter.

Flynt seized upon this and created a parody of Falwell talking about his first time with his mother in an outhouse. This outraged Falwell, who responded with a federal lawsuit. The lawsuit alleged that Flynt had invaded his privacy, libeled him, and committed intentional infliction of emotional distress.

A jury ruled in favor of Falwell on the intentional infliction of emotional distress claim. A federal appeals court affirmed the jury's verdict. Flynt appealed to the U.S. Supreme Court, contending that this jury verdict threatened freedom of speech.

Much of the mainstream media was nervous about this case. They were not very fond of supporting Flynt the pornographer, but they feared that the verdict, if allowed to stand, could threaten freedom of speech and freedom of the press.

Surprisingly to many, the U.S. Supreme Court unanimously ruled in favor of Larry Flynt. Perhaps an even greater surprise was that Chief Justice William Rehnquist—not considered a great defender of individual rights—wrote the opinion protecting the free-speech rights of Larry Flynt.

CHIEF JUSTICE REHNQUIST delivered the opinion of the Court.

Petitioner Hustler Magazine, Inc., is a magazine of nationwide circulation. Respondent Jerry Falwell, a nationally known minister who has been active as a commentator on politics and public affairs, sued petitioner and its publisher, petitioner Larry Flynt, to recover damages for invasion of privacy, libel, and intentional infliction of emotional distress. The District Court directed a verdict against respondent on the privacy claim, and submitted the other two claims to a jury. The jury found for petitioners on the defamation claim, but found for respondent on the claim for intentional infliction of emotional distress[1] and awarded damages. We now consider whether this award is consistent with the First and Fourteenth Amendments of the United States Constitution.

The inside front cover of the November 1983 issue of Hustler Magazine featured a "parody"[2] of an advertisement for Campari Liqueur that contained the name and picture of respondent and was entitled "Jerry Falwell talks about his first time." This parody was modeled after actual Campari ads that included interviews with various celebrities about their "first times." Although it was apparent by the end of each interview that this meant the first time they sampled Campari, the ads clearly played on the sexual double entendre of the general subject of "first times." Copying the form and layout of these Campari ads, Hustler's editors chose respondent as the featured celebrity and drafted an alleged "interview" with him in which he states that his "first time" was during a drunken incestuous rendezvous with his mother in an outhouse. The Hustler parody portrays respondent and his mother as drunk and immoral, and suggests that respondent is a hypocrite who preaches only when he is drunk. In small print at the bottom of the page, the ad contains the disclaimer, "ad parody—not to be taken seriously." The magazine's table of contents also lists the ad as "Fiction; Ad and Personality Parody."

. . .

The jury ruled for respondent on the intentional infliction of emotional distress claim, however, and stated that he should be awarded $100,000 in compensatory damages, as well as $50,000 each in punitive damages[3] from petitioners. Petitioners' motion for judgment notwithstanding the verdict was denied.

. . .

This case presents us with a novel question involving First Amendment limitations upon a State's authority to protect its citizens from the intentional infliction of emotional distress. We must decide whether

[1] Intentional infliction of emotional distress (IIED) is a cause of action involving intentional and outrageous conduct that causes serious emotional harm. The elements of this cause of action are as follows: (1) intentional or reckless conduct; (2) extreme and outrageous conduct, which means conduct beyond the pale of social decency; and (3) severe emotional harm. To constitute IIED, the conduct must be extreme and outrageous. It must be conduct that would cause a reasonable person to exclaim, "That's an outrage!"

[2] "Parody" refers to expression that is a distorted imitation of an original work, often meant to poke fun or provoke social commentary. In this case, the pornographer Larry Flynt created a parody of the Campari liqueur ads to make fun of televangelist Jerry Falwell. Note that the magazine did contain the following disclaimer: "Fiction; Ad and Personality Parody."

[3] Compensatory damages are damages designed to compensate the plaintiff, in this case Jerry Falwell, for the harm that he suffered. Compensatory damages include damages for pain and suffering. Punitive damages are damages that are designed to punish the wrongdoer, or the person who committed the intentional infliction of emotional distress. In this case, the federal jury determined that Jerry Falwell should be awarded both compensatory and punitive damages from *Hustler Magazine* and its publisher, Larry Flynt.

a public figure[4] may recover damages for emotional harm caused by the publication of an ad parody offensive to him, and doubtless gross and repugnant in the eyes of most. Respondent would have us find that a State's interest in protecting public figures from emotional distress is sufficient to deny First Amendment protection to speech that is patently offensive and is intended to inflict emotional injury, even when that speech could not reasonably have been interpreted as stating actual facts about the public figure involved. This we decline to do.

At the heart of the First Amendment is the recognition of the fundamental importance of the free flow of ideas and opinions on matters of public interest and concern.[5] ... We have therefore been particularly vigilant to ensure that individual expressions of ideas remain free from governmentally imposed sanctions. The First Amendment recognizes no such thing as a "false" idea....

...

Of course, this does not mean that any speech about a public figure is immune from sanction in the form of damages. Since *New York Times Co. v. Sullivan*, we have consistently ruled that a public figure may hold a speaker liable for the damage to reputation caused by publication of a defamatory falsehood, but only if the statement was made "with knowledge that it was false or with reckless disregard of whether it was false or not." ... "Freedoms of expression require "breathing space." This breathing space[6] is provided by a constitutional rule that allows public figures to recover for libel or defamation only when they can prove both that the statement was false and that the statement was made with the requisite level of culpability.

...

Generally speaking the law does not regard the intent to inflict emotional distress as one which should receive much solicitude, and it is quite understandable that most if not all jurisdictions have chosen to make it civilly culpable where the conduct in question is sufficiently "outrageous." But in the world of debate about public affairs, many things done with motives that are less than admirable are protected by the First Amendment....

Were we to hold otherwise, there can be little doubt that political cartoonists and satirists would be subjected to damages awards

[4] A public figure is an individual who has achieved general fame or prominence in the community or the larger world. A public figure is considered in a different light than a private person. The distinction between a public figure and a private person is important in defamation law. The idea is that it should be more difficult for a public figure to recover damages, because public figures have greater access to the media to counter false statements than private persons. Also, public figures must accept some of the downside that goes with fame and notoriety. A key question in this case is whether it makes a difference that Jerry Falwell is a public figure, as opposed to a private person.

[5] Another important distinction in First Amendment law is between speech that impacts matters of public importance or public concern versus speech that only impacts a private matter. Speech on matters of public importance is entitled to greater free-speech protection from government censorship.

[6] "Breathing space" is an important concept in the U.S. Supreme Court's defamation decisions. The idea is that a speaker should not be punished for every single mistake or falsehood. It is inevitable that speakers will make mistakes, and there must be some allowance—some "breathing space"—for individuals to speak in a free society.

without any showing that their work falsely defamed its subject.... The appeal of the political cartoon[7] or caricature is often based on exploitation of unfortunate physical traits or politically embarrassing events—an exploitation often calculated to injure the feelings of the subject of the portrayal. The art of the cartoonist is often not reasoned or evenhanded, but slashing and one-sided....

Several famous examples of this type of intentionally injurious speech were drawn by Thomas Nast,[8] probably the greatest American cartoonist to date, who was associated for many years during the post-Civil War era with Harper's Weekly. In the pages of that publication Nast conducted a graphic vendetta against William M. "Boss" Tweed and his corrupt associates in New York City's "Tweed Ring." It has been described by one historian of the subject as "a sustained attack which in its passion and effectiveness stands alone in the history of American graphic art." Another writer explains that the success of the Nast cartoon was achieved "because of the emotional impact of its presentation. It continuously goes beyond the bounds of good taste and conventional manners."

Despite their sometimes caustic nature, from the early cartoon portraying George Washington as an ass down to the present day, graphic depictions and satirical cartoons have played a prominent role in public and political debate. Nast's castigation of the Tweed Ring, Walt McDougall's characterization of Presidential candidate James G. Blaine's banquet with the millionaires at Delmonico's as "The Royal Feast of Belshazzar," and numerous other efforts have undoubtedly had an effect on the course and outcome of contemporaneous debate. Lincoln's tall, gangling posture, Teddy Roosevelt's glasses and teeth, and Franklin D. Roosevelt's jutting jaw and cigarette holder have been memorialized by political cartoons with an effect that could not have been obtained by the photographer or the portrait artist. From the viewpoint of history it is clear that our political discourse would have been considerably poorer without them.

Respondent contends, however, that the caricature in question here was so "outrageous" as to distinguish it from more traditional political cartoons. There is no doubt that the caricature of respondent and his mother published in Hustler is at best a distant cousin of the political cartoons described above, and a rather poor relation at that. If it were possible by laying down a principled standard to separate

[7] In his opinion, Chief Justice William Rehnquist emphasizes that political cartoons often make fun of public officials and public figures. Rehnquist was a collector of political cartoons, and he even posted, in his office, copies of cartoons making fun of him. Political cartoons often engage in parody in an effort to comment on social and political issues.

[8] Thomas Nast was a famous American cartoonist best known for his cartoons of William "Boss" Tweed and other New York City politicians. Nast is sometimes called the "Father of the American Cartoon."

the one from the other, public discourse would probably suffer little or no harm. But we doubt that there is any such standard, and we are quite sure that the pejorative description "outrageous" does not supply one. "Outrageousness" in the area of political and social discourse has an inherent subjectiveness about it which would allow a jury to impose liability on the basis of the jurors' tastes or views, or perhaps on the basis of their dislike of a particular expression. An "outrageousness" standard[9] thus runs afoul of our longstanding refusal to allow damages to be awarded because the speech in question may have an adverse emotional impact on the audience.

[9] Chief Justice Rehnquist explains that an "outrageousness standard" is far too subjective a standard when it comes to determining whether speech is protected or unprotected. Much important political speech could be considered outrageous by some people. Outrageousness is often in the eye of the beholder.

. . .

We conclude that public figures and public officials may not recover for the tort of intentional infliction of emotional distress by reason of publications such as the one here at issue without showing in addition that the publication contains a false statement of fact which was made with "actual malice,"[10] i.e., with knowledge that the statement was false or with reckless disregard as to whether or not it was true. This is not merely a "blind application" of the *New York Times* standard, it reflects our considered judgment that such a standard is necessary to give adequate "breathing space" to the freedoms protected by the First Amendment.

[10] "Actual malice" means that a person acted knowing a statement was false or in reckless disregard as to whether the statement was true or false. The U.S. Supreme Court adopted the actual malice standard in the defamation case *New York Times Co. v. Sullivan* (1964). Chief Justice Rehnquist explains that the actual malice standard is necessary, because it provides needed "breathing space" to free speech.

Here it is clear that respondent Falwell is a "public figure" for purposes of First Amendment law. The jury found against respondent on his libel claim when it decided that the Hustler ad parody could not "reasonably be understood as describing actual facts about [respondent] or actual events in which [he] participated." The Court of Appeals interpreted the jury's finding to be that the ad parody "was not reasonably believable," 797 F.2d, at 1278, and in accordance with our custom we accept this finding. Respondent is thus relegated to his claim for damages awarded by the jury for the intentional infliction of emotional distress by "outrageous" conduct. But for reasons heretofore stated this claim cannot, consistently with the First Amendment, form a basis for the award of damages when the conduct in question is the publication of a caricature such as the ad parody involved here. The judgment of the Court of Appeals is accordingly

Reversed.

Source: *Hustler Magazine, Inc. v. Falwell*, 485 U.S. 46 (1988).

Texas v. Johnson

June 21, 1989

INTRODUCTION

One of the more controversial First Amendment decisions in recent memory was *Texas v. Johnson* (1989), often called the flag burning case. The state of Texas prosecuted Gregory Lee Johnson for violating its flag desecration law. Johnson had burned an American flag outside of the Republican National Convention in Dallas, Texas, to express his dissatisfaction with certain political policies.

In other words, Johnson's act of burning the flag was a form of political protest. The state of Texas contended that it had the right to protect the flag, because the flag is a special symbol. The Supreme Court was deeply divided in this case, splitting 5–4 in favor of Johnson.

After the decision, the U.S. Congress passed the Flag Protection Act of 1989. A challenge was filed to that law as well. In *United States v. Eichman* (1990), the U.S. Supreme Court also invalidated that federal law by a similar 5–4 vote.

Some federal legislators responded by introducing a proposed amendment to the U.S. Constitution. Several times, such amendments cleared the U.S. House of Representatives by the necessary two-thirds margins but fell just a vote or two short in the U.S. Senate. The country was very close to having a new amendment to the U.S. Constitution that would, for the first time in the country's history, amend the First Amendment.

JUSTICE BRENNAN delivered the opinion of the Court.

After publicly burning an American flag as a means of political protest, Gregory Lee Johnson was convicted of desecrating a flag[1] in violation of Texas law. This case presents the question whether his conviction is consistent with the First Amendment. We hold that it is not.

[1] Mr. Johnson was charged with violating a Texas flag desecration law. Most states have such laws. Johnson argued that his act of burning the flag was a form of political protest protected by the First Amendment.

While the Republican National Convention was taking place in Dallas in 1984, respondent Johnson participated in a political demonstration dubbed the "Republican War Chest Tour." As explained in literature distributed by the demonstrators and in speeches made by them, the purpose of this event was to protest the policies of the Reagan administration and of certain Dallas-based corporations. The demonstrators marched through the Dallas streets, chanting political slogans and stopping at several corporate locations to stage "die-ins" intended to dramatize the consequences of nuclear war. On several occasions they spray-painted the walls of buildings and overturned potted plants, but Johnson himself took no part in such activities. He did, however, accept an American flag handed to him by a fellow protestor who had taken it from a flagpole outside one of the targeted buildings.

The demonstration ended in front of Dallas City Hall, where Johnson unfurled the American flag, doused it with kerosene, and set it on fire. While the flag burned, the protestors chanted: "America, the red, white, and blue, we spit on you." After the demonstrators dispersed, a witness to the flag burning collected the flag's remains and buried them in his backyard. No one was physically injured or threatened with injury, though several witnesses testified that they had been seriously offended by the flag burning.

Of the approximately 100 demonstrators, Johnson alone was charged with a crime.[2] The only criminal offense with which he was charged was the desecration of a venerated object in violation of Tex. Penal Code Ann. 42.09(a)(3) (1989). After a trial, he was convicted, sentenced to one year in prison, and fined $2,000. The Court of Appeals for the Fifth District of Texas at Dallas affirmed Johnson's conviction, 706 S. W. 2d 120 (1986), but the Texas Court of Criminal Appeals reversed, holding that the State could not, consistent with the First Amendment, punish Johnson for burning the flag in these circumstances.

[2] As the facts of the case indicate, some of the protesters engaged in vandalism, including the spray-painting of buildings. Other protesters chanted "America, the red, white, and blue, we spit on you." But Johnson was the only person who faced criminal charges among all of the protesters.

. . .

Johnson was convicted of flag desecration for burning the flag, rather than for uttering insulting words. This fact somewhat complicates our consideration of his conviction under the First Amendment. We must first determine whether Johnson's burning of the flag constituted expressive conduct,[3] permitting him to invoke the First Amendment in challenging his conviction. If his conduct was expressive, we next decide whether the State's regulation is related to the suppression of free expression. If the State's regulation is not related to expression, then the less stringent standard we announced

[3] A key term in First Amendment law is "expressive conduct." The First Amendment protects more than the spoken or printed word; it also protects certain forms of expressive conduct or symbolic speech. The U.S. Supreme Court recognized this as far back as *Stromberg v. California* (1931), when it intimated that the display of a red flag was a form of speech. In this case, the Court has to decide whether Johnson's act of burning the flag was expressive enough to trigger heightened review under the First Amendment.

in *United States v. O'Brien* for regulations of noncommunicative conduct controls. If it is, then we are outside of *O'Brien*'s test, and we must ask whether this interest justifies Johnson's conviction under a more demanding standard. A third possibility is that the State's asserted interest is simply not implicated on these facts, and, in that event, the interest drops out of the picture.

. . .

In deciding whether particular conduct possesses sufficient communicative elements to bring the First Amendment into play, we have asked whether "[a]n intent to convey a particularized message was present, and [whether] the likelihood was great that the message would be understood by those who viewed it." Hence, we have recognized the expressive nature of students' wearing of black armbands[4] to protest American military involvement in Vietnam; of a sit-in by blacks in a "whites only" area to protest segregation; of the wearing of American military uniforms in a dramatic presentation criticizing American involvement in Vietnam; and of picketing about a wide variety of causes.

[4] The Court provides several examples of types of expressive conduct that were expressive enough to merit serious First Amendment concern. One of these examples was from *Tinker v. Des Moines Independent Community School District* (1969). In that decision, the Court ruled that several public school students in Iowa had a First Amendment right to wear black armbands to protest U.S. involvement in Vietnam. The Court determined that the act of wearing the armbands was "akin to pure speech."

. . .

In order to decide whether *O'Brien*'s test applies here, therefore, we must decide whether Texas has asserted an interest in support of Johnson's conviction that is unrelated to the suppression of expression.[5] If we find that an interest asserted by the State is simply not implicated on the facts before us, we need not ask whether *O'Brien*'s test applies. The State offers two separate interests to justify this conviction: preventing breaches of the peace and preserving the flag as a symbol of nationhood and national unity. We hold that the first interest is not implicated on this record and that the second is related to the suppression of expression.

[5] The key question in this case is whether the state of Texas's justifications for its flag-desecration law were related to or unrelated to the suppression of free expression. If the justifications are related to the suppression of free expression, then the state of Texas has to meet a higher burden to justify its law.

Texas claims that its interest in preventing breaches of the peace[6] justifies Johnson's conviction for flag desecration. However, no disturbance of the peace actually occurred or threatened to occur because of Johnson's burning of the flag. Although the State stresses the disruptive behavior of the protestors during their march toward City Hall, it admits that "no actual breach of the peace occurred at the time of the flagburning or in response to

[6] One of the interests the state of Texas asserted was in preventing breaches of the peace. However, the Court pointed out that there was no actual breach of the peace. In fact, the only person criminally charged was Mr. Johnson, who burned the flag. To the Court majority, this seemed like the state was relying on another justification for the law.

the flagburning." The State's emphasis on the protestors' disorderly actions prior to arriving at City Hall is not only somewhat surprising, given that no charges were brought on the basis of this conduct, but it also fails to show that a disturbance of the peace was a likely reaction to Johnson's conduct. The only evidence offered by the State at trial to show the reaction to Johnson's actions was the testimony of several persons who had been seriously offended by the flag burning.

. . .

Nor does Johnson's expressive conduct fall within that small class of "fighting words"[7] that are "likely to provoke the average person to retaliation, and thereby cause a breach of the peace." No reasonable onlooker would have regarded Johnson's generalized expression of dissatisfaction with the policies of the Federal Government as a direct personal insult or an invitation to exchange fisticuffs.

[7] The State argued that the act of burning the American flag was a form of "fighting words"—words that, by their very utterance, inflict injury or cause an immediate breach of the peace. The Supreme Court created the fighting-words exception to the First Amendment in *Chaplinsky v. New Hampshire* (1942). The Court rejects the application of the fighting-words doctrine, because Johnson's act of burning the flag was not directed at a particular person but instead was more of a generalized grievance against the government.

. . .

The State also asserts an interest in preserving the flag as a symbol of nationhood and national unity.[8] In *Spence*, we acknowledged that the government's interest in preserving the flag's special symbolic value "is directly related to expression in the context of activity" such as affixing a peace symbol to a flag. We are equally persuaded that this interest is related to expression in the case of Johnson's burning of the flag. The State, apparently, is concerned that such conduct will lead people to believe either that the flag does not stand for nationhood and national unity, but instead reflects other, less positive concepts, or that the concepts reflected in the flag do not in fact exist, that is, that we do not enjoy unity as a Nation. These concerns blossom only when a person's treatment of the flag communicates some message, and thus are related "to the suppression of free expression" within the meaning of *O'Brien*. We are thus outside of *O'Brien*'s test altogether.

[8] The state of Texas asserted another state interest—preserving the flag as a special symbol of nationhood. Many people do revere the American flag. After all, we often stand and recite the Pledge of Allegiance at major events. The Court explains that protecting the flag as a special symbol is related to the suppression of free expression, as the State is interested in silencing disrespectful treatment of this special symbol.

It remains to consider whether the State's interest in preserving the flag as a symbol of nationhood and national unity justifies Johnson's conviction.

. . .

According to the principles announced in *Boos*, Johnson's political expression was restricted because of the content of the message[9] he conveyed. We must therefore subject the State's asserted interest in preserving the special symbolic character of the flag to "the most exacting scrutiny."

[9] The state of Texas punished Mr. Johnson for the content of his expressive conduct or speech. In other words, Mr. Johnson was punished because the state objected very much to his offensive message. The Court explains that the state acted against Mr. Johnson based on the content of his message. This is akin to a content-based restriction on speech. In First Amendment law, content-based restrictions on speech are subject to the highest form of judicial review, known as strict (or exacting) scrutiny. Content-neutral restrictions on speech are subject to intermediate scrutiny.

. . .

If there is a bedrock principle[10] underlying the First Amendment, it is that the government may not prohibit the expression of an idea simply because society finds the idea itself offensive or disagreeable.

[10] One of the most oft-quoted passages in First Amendment law is Justice Brennan's statement about the "bedrock principle" of the First Amendment. Justice Brennan explains that the First Amendment protects a great deal of offensive, obnoxious, and even repugnant speech. The passage explains that the government cannot punish a speaker just because the government doesn't like the message.

. . .

We are tempted to say, in fact, that the flag's deservedly cherished place in our community will be strengthened, not weakened, by our holding today. Our decision is a reaffirmation of the principles of freedom and inclusiveness that the flag best reflects, and of the conviction that our toleration of criticism such as Johnson's is a sign and source of our strength. Indeed, one of the proudest images of our flag, the one immortalized in our own national anthem, is of the bombardment it survived at Fort McHenry. It is the Nation's resilience, not its rigidity, that Texas sees reflected in the flag—and it is that resilience that we reassert today.

The way to preserve the flag's special role is not to punish those who feel differently about these matters. It is to persuade them that they are wrong.[11] "To courageous, self-reliant men, with confidence in the power of free and fearless reasoning applied through the processes of popular government, no danger flowing from speech can be deemed clear and present, unless the incidence of the evil apprehended is so imminent that it may befall before there is opportunity for full discussion. If there be time to expose through discussion the falsehood and fallacies, to avert the evil by the processes of education, the remedy to be applied is more speech, not enforced silence." . . .

[11] In this paragraph, Justice Brennan says that the better course for government is not to punish the speaker but instead to persuade the speaker that he or she is wrong. This is the essence of the counter-speech doctrine explained by Justice Louis Brandeis in his concurring opinion in *Whitney v. California* (1927). Justice Brennan cites Brandeis's opinion for that very purpose in this passage. The counter-speech doctrine remains a vibrant force in First Amendment law.

Johnson was convicted for engaging in expressive conduct. The State's interest in preventing breaches of the peace does not support his conviction, because Johnson's conduct did not threaten to disturb the peace. Nor does the State's interest in preserving the flag as a symbol of nationhood and national unity justify his criminal conviction for engaging in political expression. The judgment of the Texas Court of Criminal Appeals is therefore

Affirmed.

Source: *Texas v. Johnson*, 491 U.S. 397 (1989).

Reno v. ACLU

June 26, 1997

INTRODUCTION

One of the more significant First Amendment decisions over the past 20 years was *Reno v. ACLU* (1997). This case examined the constitutionality of two provisions of the Communications Decency Act of 1996 (CDA) that criminalized the online transmission of "indecent" or "patently offensive" speech.

The CDA was passed as a late-addition amendment to a larger telecommunications bill. Congress had a palpable fear that the Internet was overrun by pornography and wanted to pass a law that would protect minors from harm. However, a series of civil liberties groups and others challenged the law on First Amendment grounds. They argued that the law suppressed too much constitutionally protected speech and could even apply to online speech about such topics as prison rape, abortion, breast cancer, safe sex practices, and nude art.

Justice Stevens delivered the opinion of the Court.

At issue is the constitutionality of two statutory provisions enacted to protect minors[1] from "indecent" and "patently offensive" communications on the Internet. Notwithstanding the legitimacy and importance of the congressional goal of protecting children from harmful materials, we agree with the three-judge District Court[2] that the statute abridges "the freedom of speech" protected by the First Amendment.

[1] The government argued that the two provisions of this law, called the Communications Decency Act, were designed to protect minors from harmful material on the Internet. Protection of minors is a very important governmental interest.

[2] The lawsuit challenging these provisions was brought in a federal district court. The vast majority of cases heard in a federal district court are handled by a single judge. However, the legislation specifically called for challenges to the law to be examined by a panel of three judges in district court with a direct appeal to the U.S. Supreme Court.

The District Court made extensive findings of fact, most of which were based on a detailed stipulation prepared by the parties. The findings describe the character and the dimensions of the Internet, the availability of sexually explicit material in that medium, and the problems confronting age verification for recipients of Internet communications. Because those findings provide the underpinnings for the legal issues, we begin with a summary of the undisputed facts.

The Internet

The Internet[3] is an international network of interconnected computers. It is the outgrowth of what began in 1969 as a military program called "ARPANET," which was designed to enable computers operated by the military, defense contractors, and universities conducting defense-related research to communicate with one another by redundant channels even if some portions of the network were damaged in a war. While the ARPANET no longer exists, it provided an example for the development of a number of civilian networks that, eventually linking with each other, now enable tens of millions of people to communicate with one another and to access vast amounts of information from around the world. The Internet is "a unique and wholly new medium of worldwide human communication."[4]

[3] Here, the Court reviews the beginnings of the Internet as a 1969 military program called ARPANET. At the time of this case, the Internet was just becoming available to many people; the World Wide Web had been invented less than 10 years previous, and the first Web browser was released in 1993.

[4] The Court acknowledges that the Internet is a powerful new medium of communication unlike any other form of communication. That is part of what made the case of *Reno v. ACLU* so important.

The Internet has experienced "extraordinary growth." The number of "host" computers—those that store information and relay communications—increased from about 300 in 1981 to approximately 9,400,000 by the time of the trial in 1996. Roughly 60% of these hosts are located in the United States. About 40 million people used the Internet at the time of trial, a number that is expected to mushroom to 200 million by 1999.

. . .

Anyone with access to the Internet may take advantage of a wide variety of communication and information retrieval methods. These methods are constantly evolving and difficult to categorize precisely. But, as presently constituted, those most relevant to this case are electronic mail (e-mail), automatic mailing list services ("mail exploders," sometimes referred to as "listservs"), "newsgroups," "chat rooms," and the "World Wide Web." All of these methods can be used to transmit text; most can transmit sound, pictures, and moving video images. Taken together, these tools constitute a unique medium[5]—known to its users as "cyberspace"—located in no particular geographical location but available to anyone, anywhere in the world, with access to the Internet.

[5] The Internet truly is a "unique medium." It empowers the individual to post material for millions to view online. This is revolutionary, in that it gave an unprecedented amount of access to people who previously had to rely on more traditional forms of media. It also allowed individuals the ability to be publishers, instead of merely recipients of information.

. . .

Sexually explicit material on the Internet includes text, pictures, and chat and "extends from the modestly titillating to the hardest-core." These files are created, named, and posted in the same manner as material that is not sexually explicit, and may be accessed either deliberately or unintentionally during the course of an imprecise search. "Once a provider posts its content on the Internet, it cannot prevent that content from entering any community." . . .

Though such material is widely available, users seldom encounter such content accidentally. "A document's title or a description of the document will usually appear before the document itself . . . and in many cases the user will receive detailed information about a site's content before he or she need take the step to access the document. Almost all sexually explicit images are preceded by warnings as to the content." For that reason, the "odds are slim" that a user would enter a sexually explicit site by accident.[6] Unlike communications received by radio or television, "the receipt of information on the Internet requires a series of affirmative steps more deliberate and directed than merely turning a dial. A child requires some sophistication and some ability to read to retrieve material and thereby to use the Internet unattended."

[6] The government warned that these provisions of the Communications Decency Act were necessary to protect people from an overwhelming amount of pornography on the Internet. However, the district court and the Supreme Court determined that individuals rarely encounter sexually explicit material by accident. Most of the time, people who find sexually explicit material are looking for it.

Systems have been developed to help parents control the material that may be available on a home computer with Internet access. A system may either limit a computer's access to an approved list of sources that have been identified as containing no adult material, it may block designated inappropriate sites, or it may attempt to block messages containing identifiable objectionable features. "Although parental control software currently can screen for certain suggestive words or for known sexually explicit sites, it cannot now screen for sexually explicit images." Nevertheless, the evidence indicates that "a reasonably effective method by which parents can prevent their children from accessing sexually explicit and other material which parents may believe is inappropriate for their children[7] will soon be available."

[7] A key question in this litigation was whether Congress should impose a criminal law censoring speech on the Internet or whether this issue was best dealt with by technology—equipping parents and guardians with the tools, such as blocking software, to limit minors' access to pornography.

. . .

The Telecommunications Act of 1996 was an unusually important legislative enactment. As stated on the first of its 103 pages, its primary purpose was to reduce regulation and encourage "the rapid deployment of new telecommunications technologies." The major components of the statute have nothing to do with the Internet; they were designed to promote competition in the local telephone service market, the multichannel video market, and the market for over-the-air broadcasting. The Act includes seven Titles, six of which are the product of extensive committee hearings and the subject of discussion in Reports prepared by Committees of the Senate and the House of Representatives. By contrast, Title V—known as the "Communications Decency Act of 1996" (CDA)—contains provisions that were either added in executive committee after the hearings were concluded or as amendments offered during floor debate on the legislation. An amendment offered in the Senate was the source of the two statutory provisions challenged in this case. They are informally described as the "indecent transmission" provision and the "patently offensive display" provision.[8]

[8] The two provisions of the Communications Decency Act that were the focus of this litigation are identified as the "indecent transmission" and "patently offensive" provisions. The law criminalized the online transmission of indecent or patently offensive speech. Unfortunately, Congress did not define either term in the legislation.

. . .

On February 8, 1996, immediately after the President signed the statute, 20 plaintiffs[9] filed suit against the Attorney General of the United States and the Department of Justice challenging the constitutionality of §§ 223(a)(1) and 223(d). . . .

[9] An array of civil liberty groups and individual plaintiffs challenged the constitutionality of these provisions the day after the measure was signed into law by President Bill Clinton. The lead plaintiff was the American Civil Liberties Union, a consistent defender of individual freedoms since its founding in 1919.

The judgment of the District Court enjoins the Government from enforcing the prohibitions in § 223(a)(1)(B) insofar as they relate to "indecent" communications, but expressly preserves the Government's right to investigate and prosecute the obscenity or child pornography activities prohibited therein. The injunction against enforcement of §§ 223(d)(1) and (2) is unqualified because those provisions contain no separate reference to obscenity or child pornography.

The Government appealed under the Act's special review provisions.

. . .

In arguing for reversal, the Government contends that the CDA is plainly constitutional under three of our prior decisions: (1) Ginsberg v. New York (1968);[10] (2) FCC v. Pacifica Foundation (1978);[11] and (3) Renton v. Playtime Theatres, Inc., (1986).[12] A close look at these cases, however, raises—rather than relieves—doubts concerning the constitutionality of the CDA.

[10] In *Ginsberg*, the Supreme Court had upheld a New York harmful-to-minors law and the concept of variable obscenity. This means that material can be obscene as to minors even if it is acceptable for adults.

[11] *Pacifica* was the case in which the U.S. Supreme Court ruled that the Federal Communications Commission had the authority to fine a radio station for playing a comedian's monologue featuring foul language. *Pacifica* stands for the principle that the government has greater authority to regulate the broadcast medium.

[12] *Renton* was a case in which the Supreme Court upheld a law regulating the location of adult businesses. The Court in *Renton* approved of the zoning law. In *Reno v. ACLU*, the government argued that the CDA provisions amounted to a form of "cyberzoning."

. . .

[13]The Supreme Court explains there are four key differences between the New York law at issue in *Ginsberg* and the CDA provisions in *Reno v. ACLU*. First, the CDA applies even if parents willingly purchase material deemed indecent for their older children. Second, the New York law in *Ginsberg* applied only to commercial materials, while the CDA provisions extended to noncommercial speech. Third, the New York law defined the term "harmful to minors," while the CDA did not define the term "indecent." Fourth, the New York law in *Ginsberg* applied to persons under 17, while the CDA applied to those under 18. The Court found that these four differences were significant enough to reject the government's reliance on this precedent.

In four important respects,[13] the statute upheld in *Ginsberg* was narrower than the CDA. First, we noted in *Ginsberg* that "the prohibition against sales to minors does not bar parents who so desire from purchasing the magazines for their children." Under the CDA, by contrast, neither the parents' consent—nor even their participation—in the communication would avoid the application of the statute. Second, the New York statute applied only to commercial transactions, whereas the CDA contains no such limitation. Third, the New York statute cabined its definition of material that is harmful to minors with the requirement that it be "utterly without redeeming social importance for minors." The CDA fails to provide us with any definition of the term "indecent" as used in § 223(a)(1) and, importantly, omits any requirement that the "patently offensive" material covered by § 223(d) lack serious literary, artistic, political, or scientific value. Fourth, the New York statute defined a minor as a person under the age of 17, whereas the CDA, in applying to all those under 18 years, includes an additional year of those nearest majority.

In *Pacifica*, we upheld a declaratory order of the Federal Communications Commission, holding that the broadcast of a recording of a 12-minute monologue entitled "Filthy Words" that had previously been delivered to a live audience "could have been the subject of administrative sanctions." The Commission had found that the repetitive use of certain words referring to excretory or sexual activities or organs "in an afternoon broadcast when children are in the audience was patently offensive" and concluded that the monologue was indecent "as broadcast." The respondent did not quarrel with the finding that the afternoon broadcast was patently offensive, but contended that it was not "indecent" within the meaning of the relevant statutes because it contained no prurient appeal. . . .

[14] The Court found significant differences between *Pacifica* and the current case. First, *Pacifica* involved an order by the FCC, while the CDA provisions imposed criminal penalties. Second, the FCC rule in *Pacifica* only limited speech during hours when children were likely to be awake, while the CDA provisions applied all the time. Third, *Pacifica* involved the broadcast medium, which historically had been subject to greater regulation than the Internet.

As with the New York statute at issue in Ginsberg, there are significant differences between the order upheld in Pacifica and the CDA.[14] First, the order in *Pacifica*, issued by an agency that had been regulating radio stations for decades, targeted a specific broadcast that represented a rather dramatic departure from traditional program content in order to designate when—rather than whether—it would be permissible to air such a program in that particular medium. The CDA's broad categorical prohibitions are not limited to particular times and are not dependent on any evaluation by an agency familiar with the unique characteristics of the Internet. Second, unlike the CDA, the Commission's declaratory order was not punitive; we expressly refused to decide whether the indecent broadcast "would justify a criminal prosecution." Finally, the Commission's order applied to a medium which as a matter of history had "received the most limited First Amendment protection," in large part because warnings could not adequately protect the listener from unexpected program content. The Internet, however, has no comparable history. Moreover, the District Court found that the risk of encountering indecent material by accident is remote because a series of affirmative steps is required to access specific material.

In *Renton*, we upheld a zoning ordinance that kept adult movie theaters out of residential neighborhoods. The ordinance was aimed, not at the content of the films shown in the theaters, but rather at the "secondary effects"—such as crime and deteriorating property values—that these theaters fostered: "It is th[e] secondary effect which these zoning ordinances attempt to avoid, not the dissemination of 'offensive' speech." According to the Government, the CDA is constitutional because it constitutes a sort of "cyberzoning" on the Internet. But the CDA applies broadly to the entire universe of cyberspace. And the purpose of the CDA is to protect children from the primary effects of "indecent" and "patently offensive" speech, rather than any "secondary" effect[15] of such speech. Thus, the CDA is a content-based blanket restriction on speech, and, as such, cannot be "properly analyzed as a form of time, place, and manner regulation." . . .

These precedents, then, surely do not require us to uphold the CDA and are fully consistent with the application of the most stringent review of its provisions.

. . .

Moreover, the Internet is not as "invasive" as radio or television. The District Court specifically found that "[c]ommunications over the Internet do not 'invade' an individual's home or appear on one's computer screen unbidden. Users seldom encounter content 'by accident.'" . . .

Through the use of Web pages, mail exploders, and newsgroups, the same individual can become a pamphleteer.[16] As the District Court

[15] In *Renton*, the U.S. Supreme Court justified treating adult businesses differently than other businesses based on the secondary effects doctrine. The Court reasoned that adult businesses caused adverse, harmful effects—known as secondary effects—such as increased crime and decreased property values. However, the Court explains here that the CDA provisions did not limit speech because of secondary effects, but instead they regulated the primary effects that the speech had on children. Thus, the *Renton* case did not apply, because the CDA was related to the primary effects of speech, not the secondary effects of speech.

[16] The Supreme Court notes that with the Internet, any "individual can become a pamphleteer." This means that the Internet allows the average person to publish material rather than just being a recipient of information.

found, "the content on the Internet is as diverse as human thought." We agree with its conclusion that our cases provide no basis for qualifying the level of First Amendment scrutiny[17] that should be applied to this medium.

[17] A key question in this case was whether the government had greater power to regulate speech on the Internet, like it had with the broadcast medium. The Court declared that speech on the Internet was entitled to the highest degree of protection, similar to the print medium.

Regardless of whether the CDA is so vague[18] that it violates the Fifth Amendment, the many ambiguities concerning the scope of its coverage render it problematic for purposes of the First Amendment.... Given the absence of a definition[19] of either term, this difference in language will provoke uncertainty among speakers about how the two standards relate to each other and just what they mean....

[18] A law is too vague if it fails to provide notice to people of when they violate the law.

[19] The Court explained that these provisions were vague because the government failed to provide definitions for "indecent" or "patently offensive." Thus, the Court invalidated these two provisions of the CDA.

The vagueness of the CDA is a matter of special concern for two reasons. First, the CDA is a content-based regulation of speech. The vagueness of such a regulation raises special First Amendment concerns because of its obvious chilling effect on free speech. Second, the CDA is a criminal statute. In addition to the opprobrium and stigma of a criminal conviction, the CDA threatens violators with penalties including up to two years in prison for each act of violation. The severity of criminal sanctions may well cause speakers to remain silent rather than communicate even arguably unlawful words, ideas, and images....

The Government argues that the statute is no more vague than the obscenity standard this Court established in Miller v. California (1973).[20] But that is not so. In *Miller*, this Court reviewed a criminal conviction against a commercial vendor who mailed brochures containing pictures of sexually explicit activities to individuals who had not requested such materials.

[20] Recall that in *Miller v. California*, the Supreme Court created guidelines for jurors in obscenity cases. The Court recognized that obscenity was not protected speech. In the CDA case, the government argued that the CDA was based on the obscenity standard. The problem was that the Miller test contained elements that were not found in the CDA provisions. For example, the Miller test had an exception for material that had serious literary, artistic, political, or scientific value. The CDA did not have such an exception.

...

In contrast to *Miller* and our other previous cases, the CDA thus presents a greater threat of censoring speech that, in fact, falls outside the statute's scope. Given the vague contours of the coverage of the statute, it unquestionably silences some speakers[21] whose messages would be entitled to constitutional protection. That danger provides further reason for insisting that the statute not be overly broad. The CDA's burden on protected speech cannot be justified if it could be avoided by a more carefully drafted statute.

[21] The Supreme Court invalidated the CDA provisions because most justices feared that the law would impose a chilling effect on would-be speakers whose speech should be protected. In other words, the law was unconstitutional because it caused people to engage in self-censorship for fear of violating the law. A law is suspect if it has a "chilling effect" on people whose speech should be protected.

We are persuaded that the CDA lacks the precision that the First Amendment requires when a statute regulates the content of speech. In order to deny minors access to potentially harmful speech, the CDA effectively suppresses a large amount of speech[22] that adults have a constitutional right to receive and to address to one another. That burden on adult speech is unacceptable if less restrictive alternatives would be at least as effective in achieving the legitimate purpose that the statute was enacted to serve.

[22] Ultimately, the Supreme Court reasons that the CDA provisions suppress too much protected speech for adults. The Court acknowledges that the protection of minors is a compelling government interest, but it realizes that these provisions will criminalize too much protected speech for adults.

. . .

The breadth of the CDA's coverage is wholly unprecedented.[23] Unlike the regulations upheld in *Ginsberg* and *Pacifica*, the scope of the CDA is not limited to commercial speech or commercial entities. Its open-ended prohibitions embrace all nonprofit entities and individuals posting indecent messages or displaying them on their own computers in the presence of minors. The general, undefined terms "indecent" and "patently offensive" cover large amounts of nonpornographic material with serious educational or other value. . . . It may also extend to discussions about prison rape or safe sexual practices, artistic images that include nude subjects, and arguably the card catalogue of the Carnegie Library.

[23] The CDA provisions are overbroad. Like vagueness, overbreadth is a key concept in First Amendment law. A law is overbroad if it sweeps too widely and prohibits speech that should be protected as well as speech that should be unprotected. In this case, the Court points out that the CDA is too broad because it could criminalize speech about prison rape, safe sexual practices, breast cancer, and other types of speech that should be protected. In other words, the law will apply to more than commercial pornography.

For the purposes of our decision, we need neither accept nor reject the Government's submission that the First Amendment does not forbid a blanket prohibition on all "indecent" and "patently offensive" messages communicated to a 17-year-old—no matter how much value the message may contain and regardless of parental approval. It is at least clear that the strength of the Government's interest in protecting minors is not equally strong throughout the coverage of this broad statute. Under the CDA, a parent allowing her 17-year-old to use the family computer to obtain information on the Internet that she, in her parental judgment, deems appropriate could face a lengthy prison term. Similarly, a parent who sent his 17-year-old college freshman information on birth control via e-mail[24] could be incarcerated even though neither he, his child, nor anyone in their home community found the material "indecent" or "patently offensive," if the college town's community thought otherwise.

[24] The Court provides an illuminating example of why these provisions are too broad. Under this law, a parent could be in trouble for sending an e-mail message about birth control to his 17-year-old child.

. . .

We agree with the District Court's conclusion that the CDA places an unacceptably heavy burden on protected speech, and that the defenses do not constitute the sort of "narrow tailoring"[25] that will save an otherwise patently invalid unconstitutional provision. . . . The CDA, casting a far darker shadow over free speech, threatens to torch a large segment of the Internet community.

[25] The concept of "narrow tailoring" is very important in First Amendment law. If a law is not narrowly tailored, it often is too broad and punishes too much speech. Here, the Court says that these CDA provisions threaten to "torch a large segment of the Internet community."

. . .

We find this argument singularly unpersuasive. The dramatic expansion of this new marketplace of ideas[26] contradicts the factual basis of this contention. The record demonstrates that the growth of the Internet has been and continues to be phenomenal. As a matter of constitutional tradition, in the absence of evidence to the contrary, we presume that governmental regulation of the content of speech is more likely to interfere with the free exchange of ideas than to encourage it. The interest in encouraging freedom of expression in a democratic society outweighs any theoretical but unproven benefit of censorship.

[26] The federal government had argued that without the CDA provisions criminalizing commercial pornography, many people would withdraw from the Internet community. The Supreme Court finds this argument singularly unpersuasive, noting that there has been a "dramatic expansion of this new marketplace of ideas."

For the foregoing reasons, the judgment of the district court is affirmed.

It is so ordered.

CONCLUSION

Ultimately, the Supreme Court invalidated the two provisions, causing attorney Bruce Ennis to say that the decision gave the Internet its "legal birth certificate."

Source: *Reno v. American Civil Liberties Union*, 521 U.S. 844 (1997).

Russ Feingold's Speech on the PATRIOT Act

October 25, 2001

INTRODUCTION

On September 11, 2001, the United States suffered a horrific terrorist attack. Al-Qaeda operatives hijacked airplanes and crashed them into the World Trade Center in New York City and the Pentagon in Washington, DC. More than 3,000 people lost their lives in the deadly terrorist attacks.

The response from the federal government was swift. The United States Congress acted quickly by passing a 342-page bill that amended at least 15 different federal laws. The bill was called the Uniting and Strengthening America by Providing Appropriate Tools Required to Intercept and Obstruct Terrorism. The bill was better known by its acronym—the USA PATRIOT Act. Congress passed the measure a mere 45 days after September 11 by an overwhelming margin. In the United States Senate, the vote was 98–1. The lone dissenting voice was a senator from Wisconsin, Russ Feingold. In this speech, Senator Feingold explained many of his reservations about the bill. A key objection of Feingold's was that the bill trampled on important First Amendment and Fourth Amendment freedoms.

Mr. President, I have asked for this time to speak about the anti-terrorism bill before us, H.R. 3162. As we address this bill, we are especially mindful of the terrible events of September 11 and beyond, which led to the bill's proposal and its quick consideration in the Congress.

This has been a tragic time in our country. Before I discuss this bill, let me first pause to remember, through one small story, how September 11th has irrevocably changed so many lives. In a letter to *The Washington Post* recently, a man wrote that as he went jogging near the Pentagon, he came across the makeshift memorial built for those who lost their lives there. He slowed to a walk as he took in the sight before him—the red, white and blue flowers covering the structure, and then, off to the side, a second, smaller memorial with a card.

The card read, "Happy Birthday Mommy. Although you died and are no longer with me, I feel as if I still have you in my life. I think about you every day."

. . .

We all also had our own initial reactions, and my first and most powerful emotion was a solemn resolve to stop these terrorists.[1] And that remains my principal reaction to these events. But I also quickly realized that two cautions were necessary, and I raised them on the Senate floor the day after the attacks.

The first caution was that we must continue to respect our Constitution and protect our civil liberties[2] in the wake of the attacks. As the chairman of the Constitution Subcommittee of the Judiciary Committee, I recognize that this is a different world with different technologies, different issues, and different threats. Yet we must examine every item that is proposed in response to these events to be sure we are not rewarding these terrorists and weakening ourselves by giving up the cherished freedoms that they seek to destroy.

The second caution I issued was a warning against the mistreatment of Arab Americans, Muslim Americans, South Asians,[3] or others in this country. Already, one day after the attacks, we were hearing news reports that misguided anger against people of these backgrounds had led to harassment, violence, and even death.

I suppose I was reacting instinctively to the unfolding events in the spirit of the Irish statesman John Philpot Curran, who said: "The condition upon which God hath given liberty to man is eternal vigilance."

During those first few hours after the attacks, I kept remembering a sentence from a case I had studied in law school. Not surprisingly, I didn't remember which case it was, who wrote the opinion, or what it was about, but I did remember these words: "While the Constitution protects against invasions of individual rights, it is not a suicide pact."[4] I took these words as a challenge to my concerns about civil liberties at such a momentous time in our history; that we must be careful to not take civil liberties so literally that we allow ourselves to be destroyed.[5]

But upon reviewing the case itself, *Kennedy v. Mendoza-Martinez*, I found that Justice Arthur Goldberg had made this statement but then ruled in favor of the civil liberties position in the case, which was about draft evasion. He elaborated:

"It is fundamental that the great powers of Congress to conduct war and to regulate the Nation's foreign relations are subject to the

[1] The PATRIOT Act passed Congress only 45 days after the terrible attacks on September 11, 2001. The motivation of many who supported the bill was to empower governmental agencies to monitor, stop, and thwart those who would commit future terrorist acts.

[2] Senator Feingold worried that the rush to combat the terrorists and equip the federal government with more surveillance (and other) powers would lead to a diminution of protection for civil liberties. In this passage, Sen. Feingold warns that civil liberties must be protected even in the face of pressure and bad circumstances.

[3] Sadly, the post-9/11 period witnessed a rise in discrimination against and harassment of Arabs and Muslims. Senator Feingold was prescient when he spoke about this issue and the need to ensure that people are not mistreated.

[4] This phrase, in slightly different wordings, appears in Justice Jackson's dissent in *Terminiello v. Chicago* (1949) (a free-speech case to do with inciting a riot) and Justice Goldberg's opinion in *Kennedy v. Mendoza-Martinez* (1963) (on whether the citizenship of draft-dodgers should be stripped).

[5] Senator Feingold urges his colleagues to be eternally vigilant in ensuring that the rush to increase security does not lead to a serious reduction in individual liberty and freedoms. After the passage of time, many came to believe that Senator Feingold's warnings were wise and prescient.

constitutional requirements of due process. The imperative necessity for safeguarding these rights to procedural due process under the gravest of emergencies has existed throughout our constitutional history, for it is then, under the pressing exigencies of crisis, that there is the greatest temptation to dispense with fundamental constitutional guarantees which, it is feared, will inhibit governmental action. The Constitution of the United States is a law for rulers and people, equally in war and peace, and covers with the shield of its protection all classes of men, at all times, and under all circumstances . . . In no other way can we transmit to posterity unimpaired the blessings of liberty, consecrated by the sacrifices of the Revolution."

I have approached the events of the past month and my role in proposing and reviewing legislation relating to it in this spirit. I believe we must redouble our vigilance.[6] We must redouble our vigilance to ensure our security and to prevent further acts of terror. But we must also redouble our vigilance to preserve our values and the basic rights that make us who we are.

The Founders who wrote our Constitution and Bill of Rights exercised that vigilance even though they had recently fought and won the Revolutionary War. They did not live in comfortable and easy times of hypothetical enemies. They wrote a Constitution of limited powers and an explicit Bill of Rights to protect liberty in times of war,[7] as well as in times of peace.

There have been periods in our nation's history when civil liberties have taken a back seat[8] to what appeared at the time to be the legitimate exigencies of war. Our national consciousness still bears the stain and the scars of those events: The Alien and Sedition Acts, the suspension of habeas corpus during the Civil War, the internment of Japanese-Americans, German-Americans, and Italian-Americans during World War II, the blacklisting of supposed communist sympathizers during the McCarthy era, and the surveillance and harassment of antiwar protesters, including Dr. Martin Luther King Jr., during the Vietnam War. We must not allow these pieces of our past to become prologue.

Mr. President, even in our great land, wartime has sometimes brought us the greatest tests of our Bill of Rights.

. . .

[6] Senator Feingold uses the term "redouble our vigilance." He is saying that society should not only take great care to have security but also take great care to ensure that our basic constitutional rights are not infringed.

[7] Senator Feingold references an "explicit Bill of Rights." The Bill of Rights, which includes the First Amendment, was added to the Constitution in 1791, only a few years after the ratification of the Constitution in 1787. Many people wanted a Bill of Rights that specifically listed the most important individual liberties before agreeing to ratify the Constitution.

[8] Senator Feingold references the undeniable fact that during times of war, "civil liberties have taken a back seat." He references the Sedition Act of 1798, the blacklisting of communist Americans that Senator Margaret Chase Smith warned about, and other instances.

[9] The interment of 110,000 Japanese Americans during World War II remains one of the most ignominious stains in American history. The U.S. Supreme Court upheld the internment process in *Korematsu v. United States* (1944).

During World War II, President Roosevelt signed orders to incarcerate more than 110,000[9] people of Japanese origin, as well as some roughly 11,000 of German origin and 3,000 of Italian origin.

. . .

Now some may say, indeed we may hope, that we have come a long way since those days of infringements on civil liberties. But there is ample reason for concern. And I have been troubled in the past six weeks by the potential loss of commitment in the Congress and the country to traditional civil liberties.

[10] The attacks on 9/11 caused the United States government to react with many measures designed to increase security. Some of these measures resulted in a tightening of the immigration process. Critics charged that many of these measures suppressed civil liberties and resulted in discrimination against Arab Americans and others.

As it seeks to combat terrorism, the Justice Department is making extraordinary use of its power[10] to arrest and detain individuals, jailing hundreds of people on immigration violations and arresting more than a dozen "material witnesses" not charged with any crime. Although the government has used these authorities before, it has not done so on such a broad scale. Judging from government announcements, the government has not brought any criminal charges related to the attacks with regard to the overwhelming majority of these detainees.

. . .

[11] Racial profiling remains a hot-button issue in the United States. Senator Feingold references the racial profiling concerns over targeting African Americans and Latino Americans on the highways. He warns that racial profiling has increased.

Now, it so happens that since early 1999, I have been working on another bill that is poignantly relevant to recent events: legislation to prohibit racial profiling,[11] especially the practice of targeting pedestrians or drivers for stops and searches based on the color of their skin. Before September 11th, people spoke of the issue mostly in the context of African-Americans and Latino-Americans who had been profiled. But after September 11, the issue has taken on a new context and a new urgency.

. . .

Of course, given the enormous anxiety and fears generated by the events of September 11th, it would not have been difficult to anticipate some of these reactions, both by our government and some of our people. Some have said rather cavalierly that in these difficult times we must accept some reduction in our civil liberties in order to be secure.

Of course, there is no doubt that if we lived in a police state, it would be easier to catch terrorists. If we lived in a country that allowed the police to search your home at any time for any reason; if we lived in a country that allowed the government to open your mail, eavesdrop on your phone conversations, or intercept your email communications;[12] if we lived in a country that allowed the government to hold people in jail indefinitely based on what they write or think, or based on mere suspicion that they are up to no good, then the government would no doubt discover and arrest more terrorists.

[12] Key criticisms of the USA PATRIOT Act were directed at its impact on Fourth Amendment freedoms. The Fourth Amendment generally prohibits the government from engaging in unreasonable searches and seizures. When the government intercepts e-mail communications, it is triggering the protections of the Fourth Amendment.

But that probably would not be a country in which we would want to live. And that would not be a country for which we could, in good conscience, ask our young people to fight and die. In short, that would not be America.

Preserving our freedom is one of the main reasons that we are now engaged in this new war on terrorism. We will lose that war without firing a shot if we sacrifice the liberties of the American people.

That is why I found the antiterrorism bill originally proposed by Attorney General Ashcroft and President Bush to be troubling.

. . .

Let me take a moment to discuss some of the shortcomings of the bill.

First, the bill contains some very significant changes in criminal procedure that will apply to every federal criminal investigation in this country, not just those involving terrorism. One provision would greatly expand the circumstances in which law enforcement agencies can search homes and offices without notifying the owner prior to the search. The longstanding practice under the Fourth Amendment[13] of serving a warrant prior to executing a search could be easily avoided in virtually every case, because the government would simply have to show that it has "reasonable cause to believe" that providing notice "may" "seriously jeopardize an investigation." This is a significant infringement on personal liberty.

[13] Much of Senator Feingold's opposition to the USA PATRIOT Act revolved around his concerns that the bill would negatively impact Fourth Amendment freedoms. The Fourth Amendment prohibits the government from engaging in unreasonable searches and seizures. Feingold details how several provisions in the bill water down traditional Fourth Amendment protections, such as the requirement for a warrant backed up by probable cause.

. . .

Another very troubling provision has to do with the effort to combat computer crime. The bill allows law enforcement to monitor a computer with the permission of its owner or operator, without the need to get a warrant or show probable cause. That's fine in the case of a so called "denial of service attack" or plain old computer hacking. A computer owner should be able to give the police permission to monitor communications coming from what amounts to a trespasser on the computer.

. . .

And under this new provision all business records can be compelled, including those containing sensitive personal information like medical records from hospitals or doctors, or educational records, or records of what books someone has taken out of the library.[14] This is an enormous expansion of authority, under a law that provides only minimal judicial supervision.

[14] Senator Feingold references a section of the USA PATRIOT Act, later known as Section 215, that gave government officials the power to search various types of records, including the books that individuals checked out of libraries. He notes that the provision enabled government officials to obtain these records with "minimal judicial supervision." Several lawsuits were filed later challenging aspects of this provision.

Under this provision, the government can apparently go on a fishing expedition and collect information on virtually anyone. All it has to allege in order to get an order for these records from the court is that the information is sought for an investigation of international terrorism or clandestine intelligence gathering. That's it. On that minimal showing in an ex parte application to a secret court, with no showing even that the information is relevant to the investigation, the government can lawfully compel a doctor or hospital to release medical records, or a library to release circulation records. This is a truly breathtaking expansion of police power.

. . .

Another provision in the bill that deeply troubles me allows the detention and deportation of people engaging in innocent associational activity. It would allow for the detention and deportation of individuals who provide lawful assistance to groups that are not even designated by the Secretary of State as terrorist organizations, but instead have engaged in vaguely defined "terrorist activity" sometime in the past. To avoid deportation, the immigrant is required to prove a negative: that he or she did not know, and should not have known, that the assistance would further terrorist activity.

This language creates a very real risk that truly innocent individuals could be deported for innocent associations with humanitarian or political groups that the government later chooses to regard as terrorist organizations. Groups that might fit this definition could include Operation Rescue, Greenpeace, and even the Northern Alliance fighting the Taliban in northern Afghanistan. This provision amounts to "guilt by association,"[15] which I believe violates the First Amendment.

And speaking of the First Amendment, under this bill, a lawful permanent resident who makes a controversial speech[16] that the government deems to be supportive of terrorism might be barred from returning to his or her family after taking a trip abroad.

Despite assurances from the Administration at various points in this process that these provisions that implicate associational activity would be improved, there have been no changes in the bill on these points since it passed the Senate.

. . .

We must grant law enforcement the tools that it needs to stop this terrible threat. But we must give them only those extraordinary tools that they need and that relate specifically to the task at hand.

. . .

We must maintain our vigilance to preserve our laws and our basic rights.

[15] Senator Feingold warns that language in the bill prohibits individuals from providing assistance or support to different groups. However, Senator Feingold rightfully raises serious concerns that such a measure could punish people who merely provide lawful help with no intent to support terrorist activities. He warns this could lead to the punishing of people under a process of "guilt by association." The measure, which became law, prohibits the giving of "material support" to groups designated as terrorist organizations. The U.S. Supreme Court later upheld this measure in *Holder v. Humanitarian Law Project* (2010).

[16] Senator Feingold explicitly references the First Amendment in this passage. He warns that people could be accused of being pro-terrorist or wrongfully discriminated against merely for uttering a "controversial speech." That would violate the fundamental right of free speech.

Source: *Congressional Record*, 107th Congress, 1st Session, Vol. 147, No. 144, October 25, 2001, pp. S11019–S11023.

Garcetti v. Ceballos

May 30, 2006

INTRODUCTION

One of the more impactful First Amendment free-speech decisions over the last several decades was *Garcetti v. Ceballos*. This decision fundamentally changed public employee free-speech jurisprudence.

In 1968, the Court had ruled in *Pickering v. Board of Education* that public employees had free-speech rights to speak out on matters of public concern. Under the Pickering test, a court first asks whether a public employee spoke on a matter of public concern or merely uttered a private grievance. If the speech is only a private grievance, the First Amendment does not come into play. If, however, the employee spoke on a matter of public concern, then the court must balance the employee's free-speech rights against the employer's right to an efficient, disruptive-free workplace.

This rule was used for decades until the Supreme Court decided the *Garcetti* case. In this case, the Court created an additional threshold layer of analysis. That threshold question is whether the employee spoke as an employee or as a citizen. If the employee spoke as an employee, or engaged in an official job duty, then the First Amendment offers no protection. If the employee spoke more as a citizen, then the court still applies the rest of the *Pickering* analysis.

It is hard to overstate the significance of the *Garcetti* decision. It has led to a term used by employees' attorneys, called "being Garcettized." Many employees, including many who have tried to blow the whistle on corruption, have lost their free-speech cases because of this decision.

Justice Kennedy delivered the opinion of the Court.

It is well settled that "a State cannot condition public employment on a basis that infringes the employee's constitutionally protected interest in freedom of expression." The question presented by the instant case is whether the First Amendment protects a government employee from discipline based on speech made pursuant to the employee's official duties.

Respondent Richard Ceballos has been employed since 1989 as a deputy district attorney for the Los Angeles County District Attorney's

Office. During the period relevant to this case, Ceballos was a calendar deputy[1] in the office's Pomona branch, and in this capacity he exercised certain supervisory responsibilities[2] over other lawyers. In February 2000, a defense attorney contacted Ceballos about a pending criminal case. The defense attorney said there were inaccuracies in an affidavit used to obtain a critical search warrant. The attorney informed Ceballos that he had filed a motion to traverse, or challenge, the warrant, but he also wanted Ceballos to review the case. According to Ceballos, it was not unusual for defense attorneys to ask calendar deputies to investigate aspects of pending cases.

After examining the affidavit and visiting the location it described, Ceballos determined the affidavit contained serious misrepresentations.[3] The affidavit called a long driveway what Ceballos thought should have been referred to as a separate roadway. Ceballos also questioned the affidavit's statement that tire tracks led from a stripped-down truck to the premises covered by the warrant. His doubts arose from his conclusion that the roadway's composition in some places made it difficult or impossible to leave visible tire tracks.

Ceballos spoke on the telephone to the warrant affiant, a deputy sheriff from the Los Angeles County Sheriff's Department, but he did not receive a satisfactory explanation for the perceived inaccuracies. He relayed his findings to his supervisors, petitioners Carol Najera and Frank Sundstedt, and followed up by preparing a disposition memorandum. The memo explained Ceballos' concerns and recommended dismissal of the case.[4] On March 2, 2000, Ceballos submitted the memo to Sundstedt for his review. A few days later, Ceballos presented Sundstedt with another memo, this one describing a second telephone conversation between Ceballos and the warrant affiant.

Based on Ceballos' statements, a meeting was held to discuss the affidavit. Attendees included Ceballos, Sundstedt, and Najera, as well as the warrant affiant and other employees from the sheriff's department. The meeting allegedly became heated, with one lieutenant sharply criticizing Ceballos for his handling of the case.

Despite Ceballos' concerns, Sundstedt decided to proceed with the prosecution, pending disposition of the defense motion to traverse.

[1] Mr. Ceballos was a "calendar deputy," which meant that he was a supervisor of other assistant district attorneys. This becomes important in this case because Ceballos's superiors stripped him of his supervisory responsibilities after the controversy over his memo.

[2] Stripping an employee of his or her supervisor responsibilities is considered a demotion, or an adverse employment action. In this case, Mr. Ceballos claimed that this demotion occurred in retaliation for his protected speech. Thus, this is a classic public employee First Amendment retaliation case.

[3] When a law enforcement official fills out a form to obtain a search warrant, he or she fills out an affidavit. In an affidavit, the person swears that the information contained in the document is true. In this case, a defense attorney believed that a law enforcement official perjured himself in the search warrant affidavit. The defense attorney contacted Mr. Ceballos and told him about the alleged perjury. The reason this is important in First Amendment law is because speech about perjured law enforcement testimony is clearly speech on a matter of public importance.

[4] Ceballos wrote two memos to his superiors, recommending dismissal of the criminal charges, because of what Ceballos believed to be perjured law enforcement testimony. These memos were the "speech" at issue in this case. Ceballos argued that his superiors took adverse actions against him in retaliation for his writing these memos recommending dismissal of the criminal charges. His employer countered that there is no free-speech protection for speech that an employee is supposed to perform as part of his regular job duties.

The trial court held a hearing on the motion. Ceballos was called by the defense[5] and recounted his observations about the affidavit, but the trial court rejected the challenge to the warrant.

[5] Ceballos's superiors refused to dismiss the criminal charges. At a hearing in the case, the defense attorney called Ceballos to the stand. Apparently, Ceballos testified about his concerns with the affidavit. The trial court sided with the prosecution and did not throw out the warrant.

Ceballos claims that in the aftermath of these events he was subjected to a series of retaliatory employment actions.[6] The actions included reassignment from his calendar deputy position to a trial deputy position, transfer to another courthouse, and denial of a promotion. Ceballos initiated an employment grievance, but the grievance was denied based on a finding that he had not suffered any retaliation. Unsatisfied, Ceballos sued in the United States District Court for the Central District of California, asserting, as relevant here, a claim under Rev. Stat. §1979, 42 U. S. C. §1983. He alleged petitioners violated the First and Fourteenth Amendments by retaliating against him based on his memo of March 2.

[6] Ceballos claimed that after he wrote the memo and testified in the case, his superiors engaged in a pattern of retaliation. He was reassigned or demoted and transferred to a less desirable workplace location. Ceballos then sued, alleging a First Amendment retaliation claim.

Petitioners responded that no retaliatory actions were taken against Ceballos and that all the actions of which he complained were explained by legitimate reasons such as staffing needs. They further contended that, in any event, Ceballos' memo was not protected speech[7] under the First Amendment. Petitioners moved for summary judgment, and the District Court granted their motion. Noting that Ceballos wrote his memo pursuant to his employment duties, the court concluded he was not entitled to First Amendment protection for the memo's contents. It held in the alternative that even if Ceballos' speech was constitutionally protected, petitioners had qualified immunity because the rights Ceballos asserted were not clearly established.

[7] The trial courts in the federal court system are called the federal district courts. In Ceballos's case, the district court ruled that his memo was not a form of protected speech. Ultimately, this is also what a bare majority of the U.S. Supreme Court ruled.

The Court of Appeals for the Ninth Circuit reversed, holding that "Ceballos's allegations of wrongdoing in the memorandum constitute protected speech under the First Amendment." In reaching its conclusion the court looked to the First Amendment analysis set forth in *Pickering v. Board of Ed. of Township High School Dist. 205, Will Cty.*, 391 U.S. 563 (1968),[8] and *Connick*, 461 U.S. 138. *Connick* instructs courts to begin by considering whether the expressions in question were made by the speaker "as a citizen upon matters of public concern." The Court of Appeals determined that Ceballos' memo, which recited what he thought to be governmental misconduct, was "inherently a matter of public concern." The court did not, however, consider whether the speech was

[8] In the *Pickering* case, a high school teacher named Marvin Pickering wrote a letter to the editor of his local newspaper, complaining about his school board. The U.S. Supreme Court ruled that Pickering had a First Amendment right to write that letter and could not be fired for writing it.

made in Ceballos' capacity as a citizen. Rather, it relied on Circuit precedent rejecting the idea that "a public employee's speech is deprived of First Amendment protection whenever those views are expressed, to government workers or others, pursuant to an employment responsibility."

Having concluded that Ceballos' memo satisfied the public-concern requirement, the Court of Appeals proceeded to balance Ceballos' interest in his speech[9] against his supervisors' interest in responding to it. The court struck the balance in Ceballos' favor, noting that petitioners "failed even to suggest disruption or inefficiency in the workings of the District Attorney's Office" as a result of the memo. The court further concluded that Ceballos' First Amendment rights were clearly established and that petitioners' actions were not objectively reasonable.

[9] While the district attorney's office prevailed in the district court, Ceballos won before the 9th U.S. Circuit Court of Appeals, a federal appeals court. The 9th Circuit applied the Pickering balancing test. First, the 9th Circuit determined that Ceballos's memo concerned speech on a matter of public importance. The appeals court also reasoned that his free-speech rights trumped the district attorney's interest in an efficient workplace.

. . .

We granted certiorari and we now reverse.

As the Court's decisions have noted, for many years "the unchallenged dogma was that a public employee had no right to object to conditions placed upon the terms of employment[10]—including those which restricted the exercise of constitutional rights."

[10] For many years, the rule was that public employees had no First Amendment rights. It was best expressed by Justice Oliver Wendell Holmes when he sat on the Supreme Judicial Court of Massachusetts. In a case involving a police officer, Holmes famously wrote, "Petitioner may have a constitutional right to talk politics, but he does not have a constitutional right to be a policeman."

Pickering provides a useful starting point in explaining the Court's doctrine. There the relevant speech was a teacher's letter to a local newspaper addressing issues including the funding policies of his school board. "The problem in any case," the Court stated, "is to arrive at a balance[11] between the interests of the teacher, as a citizen, in commenting upon matters of public concern and the interest of the State, as an employer, in promoting the efficiency of the public services it performs through its employees." The Court found the teacher's speech "neither [was] shown nor can be presumed to have in any way either impeded the teacher's proper performance of his daily duties in the classroom or to have interfered with the regular operation of the schools generally." Thus, the Court concluded that "the interest of the school administration in limiting teachers' opportunities to contribute to public debate is not significantly greater than its interest in limiting a similar contribution by any member of the general public."

[11] The *Pickering* case established what has become known as the "Pickering balancing test" or the Pickering-Connick balancing test, after a later decision known as *Connick v. Myers* (1983). Under this test, the first inquiry is whether the employee spoke on a matter of public concern. If the employee spoke on a matter of public concern, then the court must balance the employee's right to free speech against the employer's efficiency interests.

Pickering and the cases decided in its wake identify two inquiries to guide interpretation of the constitutional protections accorded to public employee speech. The first requires determining whether the employee spoke as a citizen on a matter of public concern. If the answer is no, the employee has no First Amendment cause of action based on his or her employer's reaction to the speech. If the answer is yes, then the possibility of a First Amendment claim arises. The question becomes whether the relevant government entity had an adequate justification for treating the employee differently from any other member of the general public. This consideration reflects the importance of the relationship between the speaker's expressions and employment. A government entity has broader discretion to restrict speech when it acts in its role as employer, but the restrictions it imposes must be directed at speech that has some potential to affect the entity's operations.

. . .

When a citizen enters government service, the citizen by necessity must accept certain limitations on his or her freedom. See, e.g., *Waters v. Churchill*, 511 U.S. 661, 671 (1994) (plurality opinion) ("[T]he government as employer indeed has far broader powers than does the government as sovereign"). Government employers, like private employers, need a significant degree of control over their employees' words and actions; without it, there would be little chance for the efficient provision of public services. Cf. *Connick*, *supra*, at 143 ("[G]overnment offices could not function if every employment decision became a constitutional matter"). Public employees, moreover, often occupy trusted positions in society. When they speak out, they can express views that contravene governmental policies or impair the proper performance of governmental functions.

At the same time, the Court has recognized that a citizen who works for the government is nonetheless a citizen.[12] The First Amendment limits the ability of a public employer to leverage the employment relationship to restrict, incidentally or intentionally, the liberties employees enjoy in their capacities as private citizens. So long as employees are speaking as citizens about matters of public concern, they must face only those speech restrictions that are necessary for their employers to operate efficiently and effectively. . . .

[12] The Court in *Garcetti* emphasizes the distinction between an employee speaking as an employee and an employee speaking as a citizen. The Court majority recognizes that employees are still citizens and retain at least some free-speech rights.

The Court's employee-speech jurisprudence protects, of course, the constitutional rights of public employees. Yet the First Amendment interests at stake extend beyond the individual speaker. The Court has acknowledged the importance of promoting the public's interest in receiving the well-informed views of government employees engaging in civic discussion.

. . .

With these principles in mind we turn to the instant case. Respondent Ceballos believed the affidavit used to obtain a search warrant contained serious misrepresentations. He conveyed his opinion and recommendation in a memo to his supervisor. That Ceballos expressed his views inside his office, rather than publicly, is not dispositive. Employees in some cases may receive First Amendment protection for expressions made at work.[13] Many citizens do much of their talking inside their respective workplaces, and it would not serve the goal of treating public employees like "any member of the general public," *Pickering*, to hold that all speech within the office is automatically exposed to restriction.

The memo concerned the subject matter of Ceballos' employment, but this, too, is nondispositive. The First Amendment protects some expressions related to the speaker's job. As the Court noted in *Pickering:* "Teachers are, as a class, the members of a community most likely to have informed and definite opinions as to how funds allotted to the operation of the schools should be spent. Accordingly, it is essential that they be able to speak out freely on such questions without fear of retaliatory dismissal." The same is true of many other categories of public employees.

The controlling factor in Ceballos' case is that his expressions were made pursuant to his duties as a calendar deputy. That consideration—the fact that Ceballos spoke as a prosecutor fulfilling a responsibility to advise his supervisor about how best to proceed with a pending case—distinguishes Ceballos' case from those in which the First Amendment provides protection against discipline. We hold that when public employees make statements pursuant to their official duties, the employees are not speaking as citizens for First Amendment purposes,[14] and the Constitution does not insulate their communications from employer discipline.

[13] Mr. Ceballos wrote his memo at work. The Court emphasizes that a public employee may retain free-speech protection even for speech that takes place at work. The Court cites the example of Bessie Givhan, a public-school teacher who was dismissed after speaking out against racial discrimination in her principal's office. The Supreme Court ruled in *Givhan v. Western Line Consol. School Dist.* (1979) that her speech to her principal in his office was a form of protected speech.

[14] The Court majority creates a categorical rule in *Garcetti*—that when public employees make statements pursuant to their official job duties, they have no free-speech protection. This is a breathtakingly broad rule that has harmed many public employees. But this is the key holding of the *Garcetti* case. It also is why the case is considered controversial.

Ceballos wrote his disposition memo because that is part of what he, as a calendar deputy, was employed to do. It is immaterial whether he experienced some personal gratification from writing the memo; his First Amendment rights do not depend on his job satisfaction. The significant point is that the memo was written pursuant to Ceballos' official duties.[15] Restricting speech that owes its existence to a public employee's professional responsibilities does not infringe any liberties the employee might have enjoyed as a private citizen. It simply reflects the exercise of employer control over what the employer itself has commissioned or created.

[15] Writing such memos was a form of official job duty speech, and as such, Garcetti had no free-speech protection for writing it.

. . .

This result is consistent with our precedents' attention to the potential societal value of employee speech. Refusing to recognize First Amendment claims based on government employees' work product does not prevent them from participating in public debate. The employees retain the prospect of constitutional protection for their contributions to the civic discourse. This prospect of protection, however, does not invest them with a right to perform their jobs however they see fit.

Our holding likewise is supported by the emphasis of our precedents on affording government employers sufficient discretion to manage their operations. Employers have heightened interests in controlling speech made by an employee in his or her professional capacity. Official communications have official consequences, creating a need for substantive consistency and clarity.[16] Supervisors must ensure that their employees' official communications are accurate, demonstrate sound judgment, and promote the employer's mission. Ceballos' memo is illustrative. It demanded the attention of his supervisors and led to a heated meeting with employees from the sheriff's department. If Ceballos' superiors thought his memo was inflammatory or misguided, they had the authority to take proper corrective action.

[16] The Court explains that public employers have an interest in ensuring that official communications from a government office are done in a professional manner. The Court reasons that Ceballos's superiors have the ability to take corrective action if they did not think his memo was proper.

Ceballos' proposed contrary rule, adopted by the Court of Appeals, would commit state and federal courts to a new, permanent, and intrusive role, mandating judicial oversight of communications between and among government employees and their superiors in the course of official business. This displacement of managerial discretion by judicial supervision finds no support in our precedents. When an employee speaks as a citizen addressing a matter of public concern, the First Amendment requires a delicate balancing of the competing interests surrounding the speech and its consequences. When, however, the employee is simply performing his or her job duties, there is no warrant for a similar degree of scrutiny. To hold otherwise would be to demand permanent judicial intervention[17] in the conduct of governmental operations to a degree inconsistent with sound principles of federalism and the separation of powers.

[17] Here, the Court explains that the judiciary should not interfere too much with the internal operation of public employers. These employers must have the ability to run their offices generally as they see fit. The Court invokes the concepts of federalism and the separation of powers to emphasize its point. In other words, the Court is saying that it does not serve as a super-personnel review department.

The Court of Appeals based its holding in part on what it perceived as a doctrinal anomaly. The court suggested it would be inconsistent to compel public employers to tolerate certain employee speech made publicly but not speech made pursuant to an employee's assigned duties. This objection misconceives the theoretical underpinnings of our decisions. Employees who make public statements outside the course of performing their official duties retain some possibility of First Amendment protection because that is the kind of activity engaged in by citizens who do not work for the government. The same goes for writing a letter to a local newspaper, or discussing politics with a co-worker. When a public employee speaks pursuant to employment responsibilities, however, there is no relevant analogue[18] to speech by citizens who are not government employees.

[18] Many lower courts have seized upon this language of "no relevant analogue." In other words, when there is a citizen analogue to public employee speech, then the employee has a better chance of claiming that she or he is speaking as a citizen. When there is no relevant citizen analogue, then the employee is speaking only as an employee, not as a citizen.

. . .

Proper application of our precedents thus leads to the conclusion that the First Amendment does not prohibit managerial discipline based on an employee's expressions made pursuant to official responsibilities. Because Ceballos' memo falls into this category, his allegation of unconstitutional retaliation must fail.

Two final points warrant mentioning. First, as indicated above, the parties in this case do not dispute that Ceballos wrote his disposition memo pursuant to his employment duties. We thus have no occasion to articulate a comprehensive framework for defining the scope of an employee's duties in cases where there is room for serious debate. We reject, however, the suggestion that employers can restrict employees' rights by creating excessively broad job descriptions.[19] The proper inquiry is a practical one. Formal job descriptions often bear little resemblance to the duties an employee actually is

[19] The Court warns that public employers cannot expand on employees' official job duties by creating "excessively broad job descriptions." This is an important point that prohibits public employers from trying to fall within the *Garcetti* rule by claiming that nearly all employee speech is official job-duty speech.

expected to perform, and the listing of a given task in an employee's written job description is neither necessary nor sufficient to demonstrate that conducting the task is within the scope of the employee's professional duties for First Amendment purposes.

Second, Justice Souter suggests today's decision may have important ramifications for academic freedom,[20] at least as a constitutional value. There is some argument that expression related to academic scholarship or classroom instruction implicates additional constitutional interests that are not fully accounted for by this Court's customary employee-speech jurisprudence. We need not, and for that reason do not, decide whether the analysis we conduct today would apply in the same manner to a case involving speech related to scholarship or teaching.

[20] In his dissenting opinion, Justice David Souter warned that the Court's rule in *Garcetti* could threaten academic freedom. Souter had pointed out that official job-duty speech of a professor includes scholarship and teaching. Justice Anthony Kennedy responds in his majority opinion that the *Garcetti* opinion does not deal with academic freedom and may not apply with full force to that type of environment. This remains an open question in the law—whether *Garcetti* applies on college and university campuses.

Exposing governmental inefficiency and misconduct is a matter of considerable significance. As the Court noted in *Connick*, public employers should, "as a matter of good judgment," be "receptive to constructive criticism offered by their employees." These imperatives, as well as obligations arising from any other applicable constitutional provisions and mandates of the criminal and civil laws, protect employees and provide checks on supervisors[21] who would order unlawful or otherwise inappropriate actions.

[21] A terrible impact of *Garcetti* is that whistleblowing employees may not have any free-speech protection. Justice Kennedy tries to soften that blow by saying that there are laws that may provide protection to many of these whistleblowers.

We reject, however, the notion that the First Amendment shields from discipline the expressions employees make pursuant to their professional duties. Our precedents do not support the existence of a constitutional cause of action behind every statement a public employee makes in the course of doing his or her job.

The judgment of the Court of Appeals is reversed, and the case is remanded for proceedings consistent with this opinion.

Source: *Garcetti v. Ceballos*, 547 U.S. 410 (2006).

Brown v. Entertainment Merchants Association

June 27, 2011

INTRODUCTION

In First Amendment law, there are a few unprotected categories of expression. These include fighting words, true threats, incitement to imminent lawless action, obscenity, child pornography, and defamation.

In recent years, government officials have tried to expand the list of unprotected categories for expressive materials, such as depictions of animal cruelty, protests at funerals, and violent video games. In *Brown v. Entertainment Merchants Association* (2011), the Supreme Court examined a California law that imposed restrictions on the sale or rental of violent video games to minors.

The California law treated violent video games as a form of obscenity. This was controversial, because obscenity had been associated with sexual materials, not violence. In this case, Justice Antonin Scalia explains that the concept of violence as obscenity is foreign to First Amendment jurisprudence.

Scalia, who passed away in 2016, was one of the more creative wordsmiths on the U.S. Supreme Court. In examining this opinion, readers will be able to appreciate some of his humor and sarcasm.

Justice Scalia delivered the opinion of the Court.

We consider whether a California law imposing restrictions on violent video games comports with the First Amendment.

California Assembly Bill 1179 (2005), Cal. Civ. Code Ann. §§1746–1746.5 (West 2009) (Act), prohibits the sale or rental of "violent video games"[1] to minors, and requires their packaging to be labeled "18." The Act covers games "in which the range of options available to a player includes killing, maiming, dismembering, or sexually assaulting an image of a human being, if those acts are depicted" in a manner that "[a] reasonable person, considering the game as a whole, would find appeals to a deviant or morbid interest of minors," that is "patently offensive to prevailing standards in the community as to what is suitable for minors," and that "causes the

[1] The idea behind the legislation is that these violent video games desensitize young people to violence and may make them more likely to engage in violent action. A group representing the video-game and software industries challenged the law on First Amendment grounds.

game, as a whole, to lack serious literary, artistic, political, or scientific value for minors."

. . .

California correctly acknowledges that video games qualify for First Amendment protection. The Free Speech Clause exists principally to protect discourse on public matters, but we have long recognized that it is difficult to distinguish politics from entertainment, and dangerous to try. "Everyone is familiar with instances of propaganda through fiction. What is one man's amusement, teaches another's doctrine." Like the protected books, plays, and movies that preceded them, video games communicate ideas[2]—and even social messages—through many familiar literary devices (such as characters, dialogue, plot, and music) and through features distinctive to the medium (such as the player's interaction with the virtual world). That suffices to confer First Amendment protection. Under our Constitution, "esthetic and moral judgments about art and literature . . . are for the individual to make, not for the Government to decree, even with the mandate or approval of a majority." . . .

The most basic of those principles is this: "[A]s a general matter, . . . government has no power to restrict expression because of its message, its ideas, its subject matter, or its content."[3] There are of course exceptions. "'From 1791 to the present,' . . . the First Amendment has 'permitted restrictions upon the content of speech in a few limited areas,' and has never 'include[d] a freedom to disregard these traditional limitations.'" These limited areas—such as obscenity, incitement, and fighting words . . . represent "well-defined and narrowly limited classes of speech, the prevention and punishment of which have never been thought to raise any Constitutional problem."

. . .

As in *Stevens*, California has tried to make violent-speech regulation look like obscenity[4] regulation by appending a saving clause required for the latter. That does not suffice. Our cases have been clear that the obscenity exception to the First Amendment does not cover whatever a legislature finds shocking, but only depictions of "sexual conduct."

. . .

[2] An initial question is whether video games qualify as expression within the meaning of the First Amendment. Justice Scalia explains that video games are a form of expression, in part because they express ideas and have themes, plots, dialogues, music, and other forms of interactive device. Some courts 30 years before had contended that video games were not protected by the First Amendment. Those types of game, however, were not nearly as expressive as current video games.

[3] The content discrimination principle is a chief methodology tool in First Amendment cases. Reviewing courts apply a different level of review depending on whether law is content-based or content-neutral. A content-based law is one that distinguishes or discriminates against speech based on content. A content-neutral law is one that applies across the board to all forms of speech and does not treat some speech better than other forms of speech.

[4] *United States v. Stevens* (2010) was a case involving a federal law that criminalized the making of images of animal cruelty. The Court in *Stevens* rejected the idea that Congress could easily create new unprotected categories of speech, like incitement to imminent lawless action, fighting words, or obscenity. The Court in *Stevens* also rejected the idea that violent expression qualifies as obscenity, which normally applies to sexually explicit material that has no serious value.

Because speech about violence is not obscene,[5] it is of no consequence that California's statute mimics the New York statute regulating obscenity-for-minors that we upheld in *Ginsberg* v. *New York*. That case approved a prohibition on the sale to minors of *sexual* material that would be obscene from the perspective of a child. We held that the legislature could "adjus[t] the definition of obscenity 'to social realities by permitting the appeal of this type of material to be assessed in terms of the sexual interests . . .' of . . . minors." And because "obscenity is not protected expression," the New York statute could be sustained so long as the legislature's judgment that the proscribed materials were harmful to children "was not irrational."

[5] "Obscenity" refers to a narrow category of hardcore sexual conduct, not hardcore violence without an erotic or sexual element. Thus, the Court rejects the concept of violence as obscenity.

. . .

California's argument would fare better if there were a longstanding tradition in this country of specially restricting children's access to depictions of violence,[6] but there is none. Certainly the *books* we give children to read—or read to them when they are younger—contain no shortage of gore. Grimm's Fairy Tales, for example, are grim indeed. As her just deserts for trying to poison Snow White, the wicked queen is made to dance in red hot slippers "till she fell dead on the floor, a sad example of envy and jealousy."

[6] Justice Scalia writes that there is not a tradition of protecting children from violent content in books or other forms of expression. He wrote a line that received a significant amount of attention from the press: "Grimm's Fairy Tales, for example, are grim indeed." He later explains that there are numerous literary examples of violence in literature.

. . .

California claims that video games present special problems because they are "interactive,"[7] in that the player participates in the violent action on screen and determines its outcome. The latter feature is nothing new: Since at least the publication of The Adventures of You: Sugarcane Island in 1969, young readers of choose-your-own-adventure stories have been able to make decisions that determine the plot by following instructions about which page to turn to. As for the argument that video games enable participation in the violent action, that seems to us more a matter of degree than of kind. As Judge Posner has observed, all literature is interactive.

[7] California argued that violent video games present a special form of violence because they are very interactive. In this passage, Justice Scalia refutes that argument by noting that much literature is interactive.

. . .

Because the Act imposes a restriction on the content of protected speech, it is invalid unless California can demonstrate that it passes strict scrutiny[8]—that is, unless it is justified by a compelling

[8] "Strict scrutiny" is the legal term given to the highest form of judicial review. In First Amendment law, most content-based laws are subject to strict scrutiny. The government can meet this standard only if it has a compelling, or very important, interest that is advanced in the least speech-restrictive means. Often, laws evaluated under strict scrutiny are ruled unconstitutional.

government interest and is narrowly drawn to serve that interest. The State must specifically identify an "actual problem" in need of solving, and the curtailment of free speech must be actually necessary to the solution. That is a demanding standard. "It is rare that a regulation restricting speech because of its content will ever be permissible."

. . .

The State's evidence is not compelling. California relies primarily on the research of Dr. Craig Anderson and a few other research psychologists whose studies purport to show a connection between exposure to violent video games and harmful effects on children. These studies have been rejected by every court to consider them, and with good reason: They do not prove that violent video games *cause* minors to *act* aggressively (which would at least be a beginning). Instead, "[n]early all of the research is based on correlation, not evidence of causation, and most of the studies suffer from significant, admitted flaws in methodology." They show at best some correlation between exposure to violent entertainment and minuscule real-world effects,[9] such as children's feeling more aggressive or making louder noises in the few minutes after playing a violent game than after playing a nonviolent game.

[9] The state contended that it had social science studies showing a close connection between exposure to violent video games and aggressive acts committed by children. The Supreme Court majority disagreed, finding that the state's evidence showed, at best, "some correlation." The Court also noted that several lower courts had rejected such findings.

Of course, California has (wisely) declined to restrict Saturday morning cartoons, the sale of games rated for young children, or the distribution of pictures of guns. The consequence is that its regulation is wildly underinclusive when judged against its asserted justification, which in our view is alone enough to defeat it. Underinclusiveness raises serious doubts about whether the government is in fact pursuing the interest it invokes, rather than disfavoring a particular speaker or viewpoint. Here, California has singled out the purveyors of video games[10] for disfavored treatment—at least when compared to booksellers, cartoonists, and movie producers—and has given no persuasive reason why.

[10] Justice Scalia writes that California has "singled out the purveyors of video game" while not addressing violent content for minors in the form of books, cartoons, and movies. According to Justice Scalia, this law is too underinclusive and shows that the state has selectively targeted video games.

. . .

But leaving that aside, California cannot show that the Act's restrictions meet a substantial need of parents who wish to restrict their children's access to violent video games but cannot do so. The video-game industry has in place a voluntary rating system[11] designed to inform consumers about the content of games. The system, implemented by the Entertainment Software Rating Board (ESRB), assigns age-specific ratings to each video game submitted: EC (Early Childhood); E (Everyone); E10+ (Everyone 10 and older); T (Teens); M (17 and older); and AO (Adults Only—18 and older).... This system does much to ensure that minors cannot purchase seriously violent games on their own, and that parents who care about the matter can readily evaluate the games their children bring home. Filling the remaining modest gap in concerned-parents' control can hardly be a compelling state interest.

[11] The video software industry aids parents by placing ratings on games. This rating system can help parents or guardians determine what video games are suitable for their children. The state of California claimed that its violent-video-game law aided parents in dealing with harmful content. The Court seems to suggest that this issue should be handled by parents without governmental intervention.

...

California's legislation straddles the fence between (1) addressing a serious social problem and (2) helping concerned parents control their children.... And as a means of assisting concerned parents it is seriously overinclusive because it abridges the First Amendment rights of young people[12] whose parents (and aunts and uncles) think violent video games are a harmless pastime. And the overbreadth in achieving one goal is not cured by the underbreadth in achieving the other. Legislation such as this, which is neither fish nor fowl, cannot survive strict scrutiny.

[12] Justice Scalia emphasizes a point he made earlier in the opinion—that minors retain a significant degree of First Amendment rights. He emphasizes the point again in concluding that the well-intentioned California law does not pass strict scrutiny and thus violates the First Amendment.

We affirm the judgment below.

Source: *Brown v. Entertainment Merchants Association*, 564 U.S. 08-1448 (2011).

Barack Obama's Statement after the *Charlie Hebdo* Attack

January 7, 2015

INTRODUCTION

On January 7, 2015, two members of al-Qaeda invaded the offices of the French weekly magazine *Charlie Hebdo* and opened fire. They killed 11 people and injured 11 others in the building. The gunmen engaged in their murderous rampage after the magazine had published a satirical photo and cartoon of the prophet Muhammad, the leading religious figure in Islam.

While many may not have liked the satire of Muhammad, nearly everyone condemned the actions of the gunmen and deplored the attack on freedom of expression. Satire is a recognized form of free expression.

President Barack Obama, who used to teach constitutional law at the University of Chicago, delivered a statement deploring the attack and defending the right of freedom of expression.

THE PRESIDENT: I've reached out to President Hollande of France and hope to have the opportunity to talk to him today. But I thought it was appropriate for me to express my deepest sympathies to the people of Paris and the people of France for the terrible terrorist attack that took place earlier today.

I think that all of us recognize that France is one of our oldest allies,[1] our strongest allies. They have been with us at every moment when we've—from 9/11 on, in dealing with some of the terrorist organizations around the world that threaten us. For us to see the kind of cowardly evil attacks that took place today I think reinforces once again why it's so important for us to stand in solidarity with them, just as they stand in solidarity with us.

[1] France was our original ally during the Revolutionary War that the American colonists fought against Great Britain. France sent army and naval forces to help the colonists fight the British. France also loaned the fledging American leaders much-needed monies to help finance the war effort.

The fact that this was an attack on journalists, attack on our free press, also underscores the degree to which these terrorists fear freedom—of speech and freedom of the press. But the one thing that I'm very confident about is that the values that we share with the French people, a belief—a universal belief in the freedom of expression,[2] is something that can't be silenced because of the senseless violence[3] of the few.

And so our counterterrorism cooperation with France is excellent. We will provide them with every bit of assistance that we can going forward. I think it's going to be important for us to make sure that we recognize these kinds of attacks can happen anywhere in the world. And one of the things I'll be discussing with Secretary Kerry today is to make sure that we remain vigilant not just with respect to Americans living in Paris, but Americans living in Europe and in the Middle East and other parts of the world, and making sure that we stay vigilant in trying to protect them—and to hunt down and bring the perpetrators of this specific act to justice, and to roll up the networks that help to advance these kinds of plots.

In the end, though, the most important thing I want to say is that our thoughts and prayers are with the families of those who've been lost in France, and with the people of Paris and the people of France. What that beautiful city represents—the culture and the civilization that is so central to our imaginations—that's going to endure. And those who carry out senseless attacks against innocent civilians, ultimately they'll be forgotten. And we will stand with the people of France through this very, very difficult time.

Thank you very much, everybody.

[2] President Obama condemned the terrorists' attack on the offices of the French magazine as a flagrant attack on freedom of the press. The president explained that the freedoms of speech and press represent a "universal belief in the freedom of expression." Unfortunately, some people react violently when faced with expression that they do not like.

[3] President Obama also explains that support for freedom of expression must remain strong even when facing "senseless violence."

Source: "Remarks by the President on the Terrorist Attack in Paris." January 7, 2015. Office of the Press Secretary, the White House.

House Joint Resolution No. 48

April 28, 2015

INTRODUCTION

One of the more controversial areas of free-speech law is how the First Amendment intersects with campaign finance reform. The U.S. Supreme Court first examined this area in depth in *Buckley v. Valeo* (1976). In that decision, the Court ruled that contributions and expenditures to political candidates were a form of expression. The Court upheld the contribution limits but struck down the expenditure limits.

In its decision, the Court essentially held that money is more speech than property. In other words, when a person contributes to or spends money on a candidate, the person is, in effect, saying "I support that candidate."

Many disagree with this basic proposition and believe that money is more property than speech. They also point out that the influx of large amounts of money, particularly corporate money, corrupts the political process. At the very least, they say it creates an appearance of impropriety.

Perhaps the most talked-about decision in this area was the Supreme Court's decision in *Citizens United v. Federal Election Commission* (2010). The Court, by a single vote (5–4), invalidated provisions of the Bipartisan Campaign Reform Act and invalidated restrictions on spending by a nonprofit corporation.

There are many aspects worth examining about *Citizens United*. One of the most pressing is whether a corporation should be treated like an individual for purposes of the First Amendment. In his opinion, Justice Anthony Kennedy wrote, "The First Amendment does not allow political speech restrictions based on a speaker's corporate identity." In other words, a corporation is treated like an individual for free-speech purposes.

There have been numerous attempts to undo *Citizens United*. The one way to undo a U.S. Supreme Court decision is to amend the Constitution. Below, readers will find the text of a proposed constitutional amendment that would overrule *Citizens United*.

Proposing an amendment to the Constitution[1] of the United States providing that the rights extended by the Constitution are the rights of natural persons only.

[1] There have been tens of thousands of proposed amendments to the U.S. Constitution. However, only 27 amendments to the U.S. Constitution have been ratified. The last one—the 27th—was ratified in 1992.

In the House of Representatives

APRIL 28, 2015

Mr. Nolan[2] (for himself, Mr. POCAN, Mr. CARTWRIGHT, Mr. HUFFMAN, Mr. ELLISON, and Mr. GRIJALVA) introduced the following joint resolution; which was referred to the Committee on the Judiciary

[2] Mr. Nolan is Rep. Rick Nolan, a Democratic congressman from Minnesota. He is the chief sponsor of this measure to try to overturn the U.S. Supreme Court's decision in *Citizens United v. Federal Elections Commission* (2010).

Joint Resolution

Proposing an amendment to the Constitution of the United States providing that the rights extended by the Constitution are the rights of natural persons only.

Resolved by the Senate and House of Representatives of the United States of America in Congress assembled (two-thirds of each House concurring therein), That the following article is proposed as an amendment to the Constitution of the United States, which shall be valid to all intents and purposes as part of the Constitution when ratified by the legislatures of three-fourths of the several States:

"Article—

"section I. The rights protected by the Constitution of the United States are the rights of natural persons only.[3] Artificial entities, such as corporations, limited liability companies, and other entities, established by the laws of any State, the United States, or any foreign state shall have no rights under this Constitution and are subject to regulation by the People, through Federal, State, or local law. The privileges of artificial entities shall be determined by the People, through Federal, State, or local law, and shall not be construed to be inherent or inalienable.

[3] A key holding of the Supreme Court's *Citizens United* decision was that corporations, as persons, are entitled to First Amendment rights. Section 1 of this proposed amendment clarifies that corporations are not "natural persons" and thus do not possess First Amendment rights.

"SECTION 2. Federal, State and local government shall regulate, limit, or prohibit contributions and expenditures, including a candidate's own contributions and expenditures, to ensure that all citizens, regardless of their economic status, have access to the political process, and that no person gains, as a result of that person's money, substantially more access or ability to influence in any way the election of any candidate for public office or any ballot measure. Federal, State, and local governments shall require that any permissible contributions and expenditures be publicly disclosed. The judiciary shall not construe the spending of money to influence elections to be speech under the First Amendment."[4]

[4] In *Buckley v. Valeo* (1976), the U.S. Supreme Court ruled that contributing money and spending money on a candidate (called "expenditures") were forms of speech that triggered First Amendment review. In *Buckley*, the Court upheld some limits on campaign contributions but struck down some limits on expenditures. But a key element of the holding in *Buckley* was that money was more speech than property. Section 2 of this proposed amendment would change that.

CONCLUSION

Many attempts have been made to nullify *Citizens United*, but the amendment failed to move out of committee. If such a provision were enacted, it would become the 28th Amendment to the U.S. Constitution.

Source: H.J. Res. 48, 114th Congress, April 28, 2015.

Reed v. Town of Gilbert

June 18, 2015

INTRODUCTION

A key methodological tool in First Amendment law is determining whether a law is content-based or content-neutral. This distinction is very important, because courts view content-based laws with much more rigor and vigor than content-neutral laws.

Some argue that a law should not be considered content-based if the government did not intend to restrict or discriminate against speech and there is no silencing of particular viewpoints. Others believe that if a law draws distinctions based on speech, it clearly is content-based even if there is no real intent to censor or punish certain speakers.

In *Reed v. Town of Gilbert* (2015), Justice Clarence Thomas explains that a law is content-based if it makes any facial distinctions based on content. This is a strong opinion for those who believe that content discrimination should be a guiding free-speech principle.

Justice Thomas[1] delivered the opinion of the Court.

The town of Gilbert, Arizona (or Town), has adopted a comprehensive code governing the manner in which people may display outdoor signs. The Sign Code identifies various categories of signs[2] based on the type of information they convey, then subjects each category to different restrictions. One of the categories is "Temporary Directional Signs Relating to a Qualifying Event," loosely defined as signs directing the public to a meeting of a nonprofit group. §4.402(P). The Code imposes more stringent restrictions on these signs than it does on signs conveying other messages. We hold that these provisions are content-based regulations of speech that cannot survive strict scrutiny.

The Sign Code prohibits the display of outdoor signs anywhere within the Town without a permit, but it then exempts 23 categories of signs from that requirement. These exemptions include everything from bazaar signs to flying banners. Three categories of exempt signs are particularly relevant here.

[1] Justice Clarence Thomas joined the Court in 1991 and is considered the Court's most staunch conservative. Sometimes his positions seem to restrict constitutional rights. For example, Thomas has called for the Court to overrule *Tinker v. Des Moines Independent Community School District* (1969) and find that students do not have free-speech rights. However, in other areas—such as commercial speech—Thomas has been very protective of speakers. In this case, Thomas writes an opinion that is very protective of free speech.

[2] The town of Gilbert, Arizona, had a sign ordinance that treated different types of signs very differently. This implicates the First Amendment, because signs are a recognized medium of communication. The U.S. Supreme Court found that the town's sign ordinance was a content-based restriction on speech, precisely *because* it treated different types of sign differently.

The first is "Ideological Sign[s]."[3] This category includes any "sign communicating a message or ideas for noncommercial purposes that is not a Construction Sign, Directional Sign, Temporary Directional Sign Relating to a Qualifying Event, Political Sign, Garage Sale Sign, or a sign owned or required by a governmental agency." Of the three categories discussed here, the Code treats ideological signs most favorably, allowing them to be up to 20 square feet in area and to be placed in all "zoning districts" without time limits.

[3] Under the sign ordinance, "ideological signs" were treated the most favorably. There were no time limits placed on this type of sign. "Ideological signs" would refer to signs containing statements about certain issues—such as abortion, affirmative action, or the death penalty—but not in connection with a specific candidate or campaign.

The second category is "Political Sign[s]."[4] This includes any "temporary sign designed to influence the outcome of an election called by a public body." The Code treats these signs less favorably than ideological signs. The Code allows the placement of political signs up to 16 square feet on residential property and up to 32 square feet on nonresidential property, undeveloped municipal property, and "rights-of-way." These signs may be displayed up to 60 days before a primary election and up to 15 days following a general election.

[4] The second category of signs is "political signs." They are subject to more regulation than the ideological signs but not nearly as much regulation as the temporary directional signs.

The third category is "Temporary Directional Signs Relating to a Qualifying Event."[5] This includes any "Temporary Sign intended to direct pedestrians, motorists, and other passersby to a 'qualifying event.'" A "qualifying event" is defined as any "assembly, gathering, activity, or meeting sponsored, arranged, or promoted by a religious, charitable, community service, educational, or other similar non-profit organization." The Code treats temporary directional signs even less favorably than political signs. Temporary directional signs may be no larger than six square feet. They may be placed on private property or on a public right-of-way, but no more than four signs may be placed on a single property at any time. And, they may be displayed no more than 12 hours before the "qualifying event" and no more than 1 hour afterward.

[5] The third category of signs under the ordinance is called "temporary directional signs." Pastor Clyde Reed and his church posted several of these signs around town. The problem for Mr. Reed was that there were many limits placed on these signs. They couldn't be larger than six square feet, and they could be displayed twelve hours before and one hour after the event.

Petitioners Good News Community Church (Church) and its pastor, Clyde Reed, wish to advertise the time and location of their Sunday church services. The Church is a small, cash-strapped entity that owns no building, so it holds its services at elementary schools or other locations in or near the Town. In order to inform the public about its services, which are held in a variety of different locations, the Church began placing 15 to 20 temporary signs around the Town, frequently in the public right-of-way abutting the street. The signs typically displayed the Church's name, along with the time and location of the upcoming service. Church members would post the signs early in the day on Saturday and then remove them around midday on Sunday. The display of these signs requires little money and manpower, and thus has proved to be an economical and effective way for the Church to let the community know where its services are being held each week.

This practice caught the attention of the Town's Sign Code compliance manager, who twice cited the Church for violating the Code. The first citation noted that the Church exceeded the time limits[6] for displaying its temporary directional signs. The second citation referred to the same problem, along with the Church's failure to include the date of the event on the signs. Town officials even confiscated one of the Church's signs, which Reed had to retrieve from the municipal offices.

[6] Town officials cited the church for violating the sign ordinance by displaying its signs more than 12 hours before church service.

Reed contacted the Sign Code Compliance Department in an attempt to reach an accommodation. His efforts proved unsuccessful. The Town's Code compliance manager informed the Church that there would be "no leniency under the Code" and promised to punish any future violations.

Shortly thereafter, petitioners filed a complaint in the United States District Court for the District of Arizona, arguing that the Sign Code abridged their freedom of speech in violation of the First and Fourteenth Amendments. The District Court denied the petitioners' motion for a preliminary injunction. The Court of Appeals for the Ninth Circuit affirmed, holding that the Sign Code's provision regulating temporary directional signs did not regulate speech on the basis of content.[7] It reasoned that, even though an enforcement officer would have to read the sign to determine what provisions of the Sign Code applied to it, the "kind of cursory examination" that would be necessary for an officer to classify it as a temporary directional sign was "not akin to an officer synthesizing the expressive content of the sign." It then remanded for the District Court to determine in the first instance whether the Sign Code's distinctions among temporary directional signs, political signs, and ideological signs nevertheless constituted a content-based regulation of speech.

[7] The lower courts believed that the sign ordinance did not regulate speech based on content. In other words, the lower courts determined that the sign ordinance was content-neutral. This was not the position taken by the U.S. Supreme Court.

. . .

We granted certiorari, 573 U.S. ___ (2014), and now reverse.

The First Amendment, applicable to the States through the Fourteenth Amendment, prohibits the enactment of laws "abridging the freedom of speech." U.S. Const., Amdt. 1. Under that Clause, a government, including a municipal government vested with state authority, "has no power to restrict expression because of its message, its ideas, its subject matter, or its content."[8] *Police Dept. of Chicago* v. *Mosley* (1972). Content-based laws—those that target speech based on its communicative content—are presumptively unconstitutional and may be justified only if the government proves that they are narrowly tailored to serve compelling state interests.

[8] Recall Justice Thurgood Marshall's ringing passage about content discrimination in *Chicago Police Dept. v. Mosley* (1972). That case involved the punishment of a man who picketed about racial discrimination. The Court explained that the First Amendment generally prohibits discriminating against speech based on "its message, its ideas, its subject matter, or its content."

Government regulation of speech is content based if a law applies to particular speech because of the topic discussed or the idea or message expressed. This commonsense meaning of the phrase "content based" requires a court to consider whether a regulation of speech "on its face" draws distinctions based on the message a speaker conveys. Some facial distinctions[9] based on a message are obvious, defining regulated speech by particular subject matter, and others are more subtle, defining regulated speech by its function or purpose. Both are distinctions drawn based on the message a speaker conveys, and, therefore, are subject to strict scrutiny.

[9] A law makes facial distinctions on speech when it treats signs differently based on their content or subject matter. The town of Gilbert's sign ordinance clearly made facial distinctions based on grouping signs into ideological signs, political signs, and temporary directional signs.

Our precedents have also recognized a separate and additional category of laws that, though facially content neutral, will be considered content-based regulations of speech: laws that cannot be "justified without reference to the content of the regulated speech," or that were adopted by the government "because of disagreement with the message[10] [the speech] conveys." Those laws, like those that are content based on their face, must also satisfy strict scrutiny.

[10] The Court explains that a law can be content-based even if it does make facial distinctions among different speakers. In other words, a law can seem to be content-neutral but actually be content-based if the government passed the law because it disagreed with the speaker's message or content.

The Town's Sign Code is content based on its face.[11] It defines "Temporary Directional Signs" on the basis of whether a sign conveys the message of directing the public to church or some other "qualifying event." It defines "Political Signs" on the basis of whether a sign's message is "designed to influence the outcome of an election." And it defines "Ideological Signs" on the basis of whether a sign "communicat[es] a message or ideas" that do not fit within the Code's other categories. It then subjects each of these categories to different restrictions.

[11] This case was straightforward, according to Justice Thomas. The sign ordinance was content-based on its face, because it clearly applied different rules to different types of signs.

The restrictions in the Sign Code that apply to any given sign thus depend entirely on the communicative content of the sign. If a sign informs its reader of the time and place a book club will discuss John Locke's Two Treatises of Government, that sign will be treated differently from a sign expressing the view that one should vote for one of Locke's followers in an upcoming election, and both signs will be treated differently from a sign expressing an ideological view rooted in Locke's theory of government. More to the point, the Church's signs inviting people to attend its worship services are treated differently from signs conveying other types of ideas. On its face, the Sign Code is a content-based regulation of speech. We thus have no need to consider the government's justifications or purposes for enacting the Code to determine whether it is subject to strict scrutiny.

In reaching the contrary conclusion, the Court of Appeals offered several theories to explain why the Town's Sign Code should be deemed content neutral. None is persuasive.

The Court of Appeals first determined that the Sign Code was content neutral because the Town "did not adopt its regulation of speech [based on] disagree[ment] with the message conveyed," and its justifications for regulating temporary directional signs were "unrelated to the content of the sign." In its brief to this Court, the United States similarly contends that a sign regulation is content neutral—even if it expressly draws distinctions based on the sign's communicative content—if those distinctions can be "justified without reference to the content of the regulated speech."

But this analysis skips the crucial first step[12] in the content-neutrality analysis: determining whether the law is content neutral on its face. A law that is content based on its face is subject to strict scrutiny regardless of the government's benign motive, content-neutral justification, or lack of "animus toward the ideas contained" in the regulated speech. We have thus made clear that "[i]llicit legislative intent is not the *sine qua non* of a violation of the First Amendment," and a party opposing the government "need adduce 'no evidence of an improper censorial motive.'" Although "a content-based purpose may be sufficient in certain circumstances to show that a regulation is content based, it is not necessary." In other words, an innocuous justification cannot transform a facially content-based law into one that is content neutral.

[12] The town argued that its sign ordinance was content-neutral because the town did not adopt the sign ordinance to disagree with any particular messages. Justice Thomas explains that this doesn't matter, because the law is content-based on its face. He calls this "the crucial first step" in the analysis. Because the law distinguishes between different types of signs, it is content-based.

. . .

[13] In constitutional law, there are different standards of review. The highest form of judicial review is strict scrutiny. This means that a reviewing court will scrutinize the law carefully. For a law to pass strict scrutiny analysis in a First Amendment case, the law must advance a compelling, or very strong, interest, and it must be very narrowly tailored.

Because strict scrutiny[13] applies either when a law is content based on its face or when the purpose and justification for the law are content based, a court must evaluate each question before it concludes that the law is content neutral and thus subject to a lower level of scrutiny.

The Court of Appeals and the United States misunderstand our decision in *Ward* as suggesting that a government's purpose is relevant even when a law is content based on its face. That is incorrect. *Ward* had nothing to say about facially content-based restrictions because it involved a facially content-*neutral* ban on the use, in a city-owned music venue, of sound amplification systems not provided by the city. In that context, we looked to governmental motive, including whether the government had regulated speech "because of disagreement" with its message, and whether the regulation was "justified without reference to the content of the speech." But *Ward*'s framework "applies only if a statute is content neutral." Its rules thus operate "to protect speech," not "to restrict it."

[14] The town argued that the law should not be considered content-based, because the town did not have any bad motive for censorship. Justice Thomas responds, "Innocent motives do not eliminate the danger of censorship." The government could pass a law that censors speech, and the government could have a laudable purpose for such a law.

The First Amendment requires no less. Innocent motives do not eliminate the danger of censorship[14] presented by a facially content-based statute, as future government officials may one day wield such statutes to suppress disfavored speech. That is why the First Amendment expressly targets the operation of the laws—*i.e.,* the "abridg[ement] of speech"—rather than merely the motives of those who enacted them. "The vice of content-based legislation . . . is not that it is always used for invidious, thought-control purposes, but that it lends itself to use for those purposes."

[15] The town also argued that its law was constitutional because it did not discriminate on the basis of viewpoint. There is a difference between a law that distinguishes among speakers based on topic and a law that discriminates against speakers based on viewpoint. For example, a city passes a law that says no political speeches are allowed in the public park. That is a content-based law that discriminates against speech that is political. However, let's say that the city passes a law that says no Green Party political speeches are allowed in the park. That would be a viewpoint-based law, because the government is selectively targeting speakers affiliated with a particular political party.

. . .

The Court of Appeals next reasoned that the Sign Code was content neutral because it "does not mention any idea or viewpoint,[15] let alone single one out for differential treatment." It reasoned that, for the purpose of the Code provisions, "[i]t makes no difference which candidate is supported, who sponsors the event, or what ideological perspective is asserted."

The Town seizes on this reasoning, insisting that "content based" is a term of art that "should be applied flexibly" with the goal of protecting "viewpoints and ideas from government censorship or favoritism." In the Town's view, a sign regulation that "does not censor or favor particular viewpoints or ideas" cannot be content based. The Sign Code allegedly passes this test because its treatment of temporary directional signs does not raise any concerns that the government is "endorsing or suppressing 'ideas or viewpoints," and the provisions for political signs and ideological signs "are neutral as to particular ideas or viewpoints" within those categories.

This analysis conflates two distinct but related limitations that the First Amendment places on government regulation of speech. Government discrimination among viewpoints—or the regulation of speech based on "the specific motivating ideology or the opinion or perspective of the speaker"—is a "more blatant" and "egregious form of content discrimination."[16] But it is well established that "[t]he First Amendment's hostility to content-based regulation extends not only to restrictions on particular viewpoints, but also to prohibition of public discussion of an entire topic."

[16] Justice Thomas quotes his colleague Justice Anthony Kennedy, who wrote in a 1995 case that viewpoint discrimination is an "egregious form of content discrimination." This phrase is commonly cited when a court is examining a law that it feels is viewpoint discriminatory. To reiterate, viewpoint discriminatory laws are considered the worst, because the government is silencing a particular point of view.

Thus, a speech regulation targeted at specific subject matter is content based even if it does not discriminate among viewpoints within that subject matter. For example, a law banning the use of sound trucks for political speech—and only political speech—would be a content-based regulation, even if it imposed no limits on the political viewpoints that could be expressed. The Town's Sign Code likewise singles out specific subject matter for differential treatment, even if it does not target viewpoints within that subject matter. Ideological messages are given more favorable treatment than messages concerning a political candidate, which are themselves given more favorable treatment than messages announcing an assembly of like-minded individuals. That is a paradigmatic example of content-based discrimination.

Finally, the Court of Appeals characterized the Sign Code's distinctions as turning on "the content-neutral elements of who is speaking through the sign and whether and when an event is occurring." That analysis is mistaken on both factual and legal grounds.

. . .

And, just as with speaker-based laws, the fact that a distinction is event based does not render it content neutral. The Court of Appeals cited no precedent from this Court supporting its novel theory of an exception from the content-neutrality requirement for event-based laws. As we have explained, a speech regulation is content based if the law applies to particular speech because of the topic discussed or the idea or message expressed. A regulation that targets a sign because it conveys an idea about a specific event is no less content based than a regulation that targets a sign because it conveys some other idea. Here, the Code singles out signs bearing a particular message: the time and location of a specific event. This type of ordinance may seem like a perfectly rational way to regulate signs, but a clear and firm rule governing content neutrality is an essential means of protecting the freedom of speech, even if laws that might seem "entirely reasonable" will sometimes be "struck down because of their content-based nature."

Because the Town's Sign Code imposes content-based restrictions on speech, those provisions can stand only if they survive strict scrutiny, "which requires the Government to prove that the restriction furthers a compelling interest and is narrowly tailored to achieve that interest."...

The Town cannot do so. It has offered only two governmental interests in support of the distinctions the Sign Code draws: preserving the Town's aesthetic appeal and traffic safety.[17] Assuming for the sake of argument that those are compelling governmental interests, the Code's distinctions fail as hopelessly underinclusive.

[17] The town argued that its sign law served two interests: (1) preserving the town's beauty and (2) improving traffic safety. The first question under the analysis is whether the town's ordinance really serves those interests.

Starting with the preservation of aesthetics, temporary directional signs are "no greater an eyesore" than ideological or political ones.[18] Yet the Code allows unlimited proliferation of larger ideological signs while strictly limiting the number, size, and duration of smaller directional ones. The Town cannot claim that placing strict limits on temporary directional signs is necessary to beautify the Town while at the same time allowing unlimited numbers of other types of signs that create the same problem.

[18] The problem for the town is that ideological and political signs create just as much an eyesore as temporary directional signs. This shows that the law is not drafted properly to fit the governmental interest.

The Town similarly has not shown that limiting temporary directional signs is necessary to eliminate threats to traffic safety, but that limiting other types of signs is not. The Town has offered no reason to believe that directional signs pose a greater threat to safety than do ideological or political signs. If anything, a sharply worded ideological sign[19] seems more likely to distract a driver than a sign directing the public to a nearby church meeting.

[19] Justice Thomas explains that a "sharply worded ideological sign" can be more distracting to motorists than a temporary directional sign. Again, this shows that the law does not really serve the governmental interests.

In light of this underinclusiveness, the Town has not met its burden to prove that its Sign Code is narrowly tailored to further a compelling government interest. Because a "law cannot be regarded as protecting an interest of the highest order, and thus as justifying a restriction on truthful speech, when it leaves appreciable damage to that supposedly vital interest unprohibited," the Sign Code fails strict scrutiny.

Our decision today will not prevent governments from enacting effective sign laws. The Town asserts that an "absolutist" content-neutrality rule would render "virtually all distinctions in sign laws . . . subject to strict scrutiny," but that is not the case. Not "all distinctions" are subject to strict scrutiny, only *content-based* ones are. Laws that are *content neutral* are instead subject to lesser scrutiny.

The Town has ample content-neutral options[20] available to resolve problems with safety and aesthetics. For example, its current Code regulates many aspects of signs that have nothing to do with a sign's message: size, building materials, lighting, moving parts, and portability. And on public property, the Town may go a long way toward entirely forbidding the posting of signs, so long as it does so in an evenhanded, content-neutral manner. Indeed, some lower courts have long held that similar content-based sign laws receive strict scrutiny, but there is no evidence that towns in those jurisdictions have suffered catastrophic effects. . . .

[20] Here, Justice Thomas explains that cities can regulate signs in many ways that are content-neutral. For example, a city could limit the size of all signs or prohibit any signs that have certain types of lighting.

We acknowledge that a city might reasonably view the general regulation of signs as necessary because signs "take up space and may obstruct views, distract motorists, displace alternative uses for land, and pose other problems that legitimately call for regulation." At the same time, the presence of certain signs may be essential, both for vehicles and pedestrians, to guide traffic or to identify hazards and ensure safety. A sign ordinance narrowly tailored to the challenges of protecting the safety of pedestrians, drivers, and passengers—such as warning signs marking hazards on private property, signs directing traffic, or street numbers associated with private houses—well might survive strict scrutiny. The signs at issue in this case, including political and ideological signs and signs for events, are far removed from those purposes. As discussed above, they are facially content based and are neither justified by traditional safety concerns nor narrowly tailored.

. . .

We reverse the judgment of the Court of Appeals and remand the case for proceedings consistent with this opinion.

Source: *Reed v. Town of Gilbert*, 576 U.S. ___ (2015).

Timeline of Events

1787
On September 17, the Constitutional Convention approves of a constitution for the United States of America. There is no Bill of Rights in the Constitution.

1791
On December 15, Virginia becomes the 10th state to approve of the first amendments to the Constitution. This ensures the ratification of the Bill of Rights.

1798
President John Adams oversees the passage of the dreaded Alien and Sedition Acts, including the Sedition Act of 1798. In response, James Madison issues the "Virginia Resolution" and Thomas Jefferson introduces the "Kentucky Resolution" to give states the power to declare the Alien and Sedition Acts null and void.

1836
The House imposes a "gag rule" on petitions to abolish slavery.

1844
Representative John Quincy Adams, the former president, finally leads enough of his colleagues in the House to inter the "gag rule" on abolitionist petitions.

1917
Congress passes the Espionage Act, which imposes heavy penalties for anyone causing or attempting to cause "insubordination, disloyalty, mutiny, or refusal of duty" in the United States military.

1918
Congress passes the Sedition Act, which prohibits Americans from using "disloyal, profane, scurrilous, or abusive language" about the United States government, flag, or military. (Congress repeals the Sedition Act in 1920.)

Union leader and Socialist presidential candidate Eugene Debs delivers an antiwar speech in Canton, Ohio. He later is charged and convicted for violating the Espionage Act for comments made during this speech.

1919
In *Schenck v. United States*, the U.S. Supreme Court upholds the convictions of Socialists Charles Schenck and Elizabeth Baer for violating the Espionage Act. Writing for the Court, Justice Oliver Wendell Holmes Jr. introduces the "clear and present danger" test.

In *Abrams v. United States*, the U.S. Supreme Court upholds the convictions of several Russian immigrants for circulating antiwar documents. However, Justice Holmes writes a dissenting opinion that provides the blueprint for more speech protection in later cases.

1927
In *Whitney v. California*, the U.S. Supreme Court upholds the criminal syndicalism conviction of Charlotte Anita Whitney. Justice Louis Brandeis writes an influential concurring opinion that is the source of much First Amendment law.

1940
In *Minersville School District v. Gobitis*, the U.S. Supreme Court rules 8–1 that school officials did

not violate First Amendment freedom of religion rights. The case will be overruled a mere three years later in *West Virginia v. Barnette*.

1942

In *Chaplinsky v. New Hampshire*, the U.S. Supreme Court creates the fighting-words exception to the First Amendment. It defines "fighting words" as those words "which by their very utterance inflict injury or tend to incite an immediate breach of the peace."

1943

In *West Virginia Bd. of Educ. v. Barnette*, the U.S. Supreme Court invalidates a West Virginia flag salute law. The Barnette sisters were expelled from their elementary school for refusing to salute the flag for religious reasons.

1950

Senator Margaret Chase Smith delivers her famous "Declaration of Conscience" speech objecting to the excesses during the McCarthy era.

1952

Justice William O. Douglas warns of the "Black Silence of Fear" permeating American society in the McCarthy era. Douglas pens his piece for the *New York Times Magazine.*

1963

In *Edwards v. South Carolina*, the U.S. Supreme Court invalidated the breach-of-the-peace convictions of 187 students who marched to the Columbia statehouse to protest segregation.

1964

In *New York Times Co. v. Sullivan*, the U.S. Supreme Court rules that public officials cannot recover damages for libel unless they show, by clear and convincing evidence, that the speaker acted with "actual malice," defined as acting with knowing falsity or reckless disregard for the truth or falsity of a statement.

1968

In *United States v. O'Brien*, the U.S. Supreme Court upholds a criminal law prohibiting the knowing mutilation or destruction of draft cards. The Court establishes a test for evaluating restrictions on communication that contains both speech and non-speech elements.

In *Pickering v. Board of Education*, the U.S. Supreme Court rules that a public school teacher has a First Amendment right to speak as a citizen on a matter of public concern. The teacher had written a letter to the editor criticizing how the school board allocated monies.

1969

In *Watts v. United States*, the U.S. Supreme Court explains that true threats are not protected speech but rules that a young war protester did not utter such a true threat at a demonstration in Washington, D.C.

In *Tinker v. Des Moines Indep. Comm. Sch. Dist.*, the U.S. Supreme Court rules that Iowa public school officials violated the First Amendment rights of several students by suspending them for wearing black armbands to protest U.S. involvement in Vietnam. The Court determines that school officials may not censor student expression unless they can reasonably forecast that the expression will cause a substantial disruption of school activities.

In *Brandenburg v. Ohio*, the U.S. Supreme Court reverses the conviction of a Ku Klux Klan leader for a speech he made at a Klan rally, but also it states that speech advocating the use of force or crime is not protected if it is directed at producing "imminent" action and is "likely" to cause such action. This decision creates a free-speech exception known as "incitement to imminent lawless action."

1971

In *Cohen v. California*, the U.S. Supreme Court reverses the breach-of-the-peace conviction of a young man who wore a jacket with a profane word on it in a Los Angeles County courthouse. The Court explains that "one man's vulgarity is another's lyric" and emphasizes that government officials cannot camouflage their distaste for certain viewpoints by trying to cleanse the nation's vocabulary.

1973
In *Miller v. California*, the U.S. Supreme Court reaffirms that obscenity is not protected speech. The Court also creates a three-part test, known as the Miller test, to guide jurors in obscenity cases.

1977
In *Bates v. State Bar of Arizona*, the U.S. Supreme Court rules that truthful attorney advertising is a form of commercial speech deserving of First Amendment protection.

1988
In *Hazelwood School District v. Kuhlmeier*, the U.S. Supreme Court rules that schools may regulate school-sponsored student publications if such regulation is "reasonably related to a legitimate pedagogical" purpose. The Court sanctions the actions of a high school principal who censored two articles in the school newspaper.

In *Hustler Magazine v. Falwell*, the U.S. Supreme Court unanimously rules that evangelist Jerry Falwell cannot recover for intentional infliction of emotional distress from pornography publisher Larry Flynt for a parody.

1989
In *Texas v. Johnson*, the U.S. Supreme Court strikes down a Texas flag desecration law on First Amendment grounds.

The U.S. Congress passes the Flag Protection Act. The act punishes anyone who "knowingly mutilates, defaces, physically defiles, burns, maintains on the floor or ground, or tramples upon any U.S. flag."

1990
A flag desecration constitutional amendment is introduced in the U.S. Congress. It provides, "The Congress and the States have the power to prohibit the physical desecration of the flag of the United States." The measure fails.

1995
After the House votes 312–120 for a flag desecration amendment, the measure fails in the Senate by only three votes.

1997
In *Reno v. ACLU*, the U.S. Supreme Court strikes down two provisions of the Communications Decency Act, which criminalized the online transmission of patently offensive and indecent speech.

2011
In *Snyder v. Phelps*, the U.S. Supreme Court rules that the Westboro Baptist Church is not liable for intentional infliction of emotional distress for its offensive picketing at a slain marine's funeral.

In *Brown v. Entertainment Merchants Assn.*, the U.S. Supreme Court invalidates a California law restricting the sale or rental of violent video games to minors.

Further Reading

Abrams, Floyd. *Speaking Freely: Trials of the First Amendment.* New York: Viking Press, 2005.

Baker, Edwin C. *Human Liberty and Freedom of Speech.* New York: Oxford University Press, 1989.

Chafee, Zechariah, Jr. *Free Speech in the United States.* Cambridge: Harvard University Press, 1941.

Collins, Ronald K. L., and Sam Chaltain. *We Must Not Be Afraid to Be Free: Stories of Free Expression in America.* New York: Oxford University Press, 2011.

Cox, Archibald. *Freedom of Expression.* Cambridge: Harvard University Press, 1981.

Curtis, Michael Kent. *Free Speech: The People's Darling Privilege: Struggles for Freedom of Expression in American History.* Durham: Duke University Press, 2000.

Emerson, Thomas I. *The System of Free Expression.* New York: Random House, 1970.

Finan, Christopher M. *From the Palmer Raids to the Patriot Act: A History of the Fight for Free Speech in America.* Boston: Beacon Press, 2007.

Goines, David Lance. *The Free Speech Movement: Coming of Age in the 1960s.* Berkeley, CA: Ten Speed Press, 1993.

Healy, Thomas. *The Great Dissent: How Oliver Wendell Holmes Changed His Mind—and Changed the History of Free Speech in America.* New York: Macmillan Publishers, 2013.

Hentoff, Nat. *The First Freedom: The Tumultuous History of Free Speech in America.* New York: Delacorte Press, 1980.

Hudson, David L., Jr. *Let the Students Speak: A History of the Fight for Freedom of Expression in American Schools.* Boston: Beacon Press, 2011.

Hudson, David L., Jr. *The First Amendment: Freedom of Speech.* St. Paul: Thomson Reuters, 2012.

Kalven, Harry, Jr. *The Negro and the First Amendment.* Columbus: Ohio State University Press, 1965.

Kalven, Harry, Jr. *A Worthy Tradition: Freedom of Speech in America.* New York: Harper and Row, 1988.

Lewis, Anthony. *Freedom for the Thought That We Hate: A Biography of the First Amendment.* New York: Basic Books, 2007.

Murphy, Paul. *World War I and the Origin of Civil Liberties.* New York: W. W. Norton and Co., 1979.

Nelson, Jack. *Captive Voices: High School Journalism in America.* New York: Schocken Books, 1974.

O'Neil, Robert M. *The First Amendment and Civil Liability.* Bloomington: Indiana University Press, 2001.

Peters, Shawn Francis. *Judging Jehovah's Witnesses: Religious Persecution and the Dawn of the Rights Revolution.* Lawrence: University Press of Kansas, 2000.

Rabban, David M. *Free Speech in Its Forgotten Years.* New York: Cambridge University Press, 1997.

Rembar, Charles. *The End of Obscenity: The Trials of Lady Chatterley, Tropic of Cancer, and Fanny Hill.* New York: Random House, 1968.

Richards, Robert D. *Freedom's Voice: The Perilous Present and Uncertain Future of the First Amendment.* Washington, D.C: Brassey's, 1998.

Ross, Catherine J. *Lessons in Censorship: How Schools and Courts Subvert Students' First Amendment Rights.* Cambridge: Harvard University Press, 2015.

Smith, James Morton. *Freedom's Fetters: Alien and Sedition Laws and American Civil Liberties.* Ithaca, NY: Cornell University Press, 1956.

Smolla, Rodney M. *Free Speech in an Open Society.* New York: Alfred A. Knopf, 1992.

Smolla, Rodney M. *Jerry Falwell v. Larry Flynt: The First Amendment on Trial.* Urbana: University of Illinois Press, 1990.

Stone, Geoffrey. *Perilous Times: Free Speech in Wartime: From the Sedition Act of 1798 to the War on Terrorism.* New York: W. W. Norton, 2005.

Strossen, Nadine. *Defending Pornography: Free Speech, Sex, and the Fight for Women's Rights.* New York: Scribner, 1995.

Turner, William Bennett. *Figures of Speech: First Amendment Heroes and Villains.* Oakland: Berrett Koehler Publishers, 2011.

Vile, John R., David L. Hudson Jr., and David Schultz (eds.). *The Encyclopedia of the First Amendment* (2 volumes). Washington, D.C.: CQ Press, 2011.

Index

About the Author

David L. Hudson Jr. is an attorney, author, and educator from Nashville, Tennessee. He is the Ombudsman for the Newseum Institute First Amendment Center and the Director of Academic Affairs at the Nashville School of Law. He also teaches classes at the Nashville School of Law and Vanderbilt Law School. He is the author, coauthor, or coeditor of 40 books, including many on the First Amendment. He is a coeditor of *The Encyclopedia of the First Amendment* (2008), the author of *First Amendment: Freedom of Speech* (2012), and the author of *Let the Students Speak: A History of the Fight for Freedom of Expression in American Schools* (2008). He frequently speaks across the country on school law issues, civic education, and other First Amendment topics.